IF NO NEWS, SEND RUMORS

IF NO NEWS, SEND RUMORS

Anecdotes of American Journalism

....

Stephen Bates

An Owl Book · Henry Holt and Company · New York

To Polly

Published by Henry Holt and Company, Inc.,
115 West 18th Street, New York, New York 10011.

Library of Congress Cataloging-in-Publication Data
Bates, Stephen
If no news, send rumors : anecdotes of American journalism /
Stephen Bates. — 1st Owl book ed.
p. cm.
Includes bibliographical references and index.
ISBN 0-8050-1610-4
1. Journalism—United States—Anecdotes. I. Title.
[PN4847.B38 1991]
070.4′0207—dc20 90-25500
CIP

Henry Holt books are available at special discounts
for bulk purchases for sales promotions, premiums,
fund-raising, or educational use. Special editions
or book excerpts can also be created to specification.
For details contact:
Special Sales Director, Henry Holt and Company, Inc.,
115 West 18th Street, New York, New York 10011.

First published in hardcover by
St. Martin's Press in 1985.

First Owl Book Edition—1991

Printed in the United States of America
Recognizing the importance of preserving the written word,
Henry Holt and Company, Inc., by policy, prints all of its
first editions on acid-free paper. ∞

1 3 5 7 9 10 8 6 4 2

CONTENTS

INTRODUCTION

On September 25, 1690, the first newspaper in the American colonies appeared on the streets of Boston. In the inaugural issue of *Publick Occurrences Both Forreign and Domestick,* Indians were much in the news: a Captain Mason had "cut the faces and ripped the bellies" of two Indians, "Christianized Indians" had declared a day of thanks for the harvest, and Britain's Mohawk allies had treated French prisoners "in a manner too barbarous for any English to approve." The newspaper also reported that a Watertown man had hanged himself, an epidemic of "Fevers and Agues" had left many people unable to work, and the son of the king of France had "revolted against him lately, and has great reason if reports be true, that the Father used to lie with the Son's Wife."

Publick Occurrences was scheduled to appear "once a month (or if any Glut of Occurrences happen, oftener)." As it happened, though, the first issue was also the last. The royal governor and his council ordered the newspaper permanently suppressed because of its "Reflections of a very high nature"—especially those concerning the Indian allies and the king of France—and because the newspaper's publisher, Benjamin Harris, had neglected to get the required printing license.[1]

If No News, Send Rumors sketches the development of American journalism in the three centuries since *Publick Occurrences.* The book is not a comprehensive history. It is more like, as Walter Lippmann once deprecatingly described the press, "a searchlight that moves restlessly about, bringing one episode and then another out of darkness into vision."

The sources of illumination here are anecdotes and quotations. They feature such figures as Benjamin Franklin, Horace Greeley, Joseph Pulitzer, Walter Winchell, Ben Bradlee, Rupert Murdoch, Dan Rather, Barbara Walters, Garry Trudeau, and J. Fred Muggs. Most of the stories are light; some are pointed. Many of them touch on themes first raised by *Publick Occurrences* three hundred years ago: the proper mix of good news and bad news, the relevance of public figures' private lives, and the inexorable frictions between government and press.

The vast majority of the stories deal with the American news media. Throughout, I have generally identified people by the position they held at the time the described event occurred, and not indicated subsequent job changes, retirements, and deaths.

In researching the book, I relied on a variety of sources, including scholarly studies of the press, biographies and autobiographies of journalists and of the public figures who dealt with them, journalism reviews, newspaper and magazine articles by and about journalists, university case studies, speeches, judicial opinions, and interviews. The sources are listed in endnotes.

I gratefully acknowledge the assistance of Peter Ginna, my editor at St. Martin's Press, whose suggestions greatly improved the manuscript; Susan Rabiner, who got the project started at St. Martin's; Laura Hamilton, Martin Linsky, and Abigail Thernstrom, who read drafts closely and critically; Inigo Garcia-Bryce, who helped with library research; the Kaltenborn Foundation, which partially underwrote research costs; as well as David Stephens, Brian Gross, my parents, and my wife Polly.

I

......

INSIDE THE PRESS

convicted on
he had been impli-
Jefferies, the for-
rokerage firm that
Mr. Jefferies agreed
securities law viola-
rate with the Govern-
gation of crime on Wall
was implicated by Mr.

nment charged that Mr.
ade millions of dollars by
ng stock in takeover tar-
ng his ownership in those
s by using secret accounts
ies & Company, a West Coast
ge, and later selling his holder the stock price had risen.

Tax Losses

Bilzerian is also c
fraud for engagi
des in two securities
losses. The charg
olve Mr. Bilzerian
nger.
The charges in
Cluett, Peabody &
Robertson & Comp
mermill Paper Co
ce stock transaction
ol of Armco Inc

ersey City became a Superior Court
en Auto Body's lawyer a request from
ue a restraining order to have the
rom entering into an agreement preventing
en Towing. Judge James Dow-
he request, but scheduled
ve the matter
ASHINGT
Federal
approv
ver Tr
New Y
acc
ne of

The city's specifications. could comply
that when it rejected Hoboken the city's response to the alle
sole bid on the contract
because it thought
favorable offe
tised, an
bid

The Goldome offices that Mar
turers Hanover is acquiring in
York, Nassau, Orange and
counties hold total deposits o
billion.
In approving the purchase,
rejected arguments that Man
ers Hanover had failed to r
credit needs of low- and mod
come communities, prim
oklyn. The complaint wa
Mine Workers o
Association of C
tions for Reform

The Fed s
reed
ent of drug profit
zations."
k of detection i
the enormou
s the generall

ort
cials of the
hoped to
long
and

Continued

form the basis
regulatory recommen
ted States, banks
currency transac
than $10,000
such law.
st year Car
it permit
assets
or conv
The new law
ering a crime
Canada, though
ies believe the
but as effective as those in
United States.

banks, came to light at
traffickers to use
further
the Senate Foreign Rel
mittee's subcommittee o
narcotics and internat
tions. John F. Kerry, a M
Democrat who is chai
committee, obtained a c
port and cited it as
friendly country whose
thumbing their noses a
banki

s in prison and $2.25 mil-
The case was the first
ial of illegal stock parking,
ownership of securities is
d to avoid disclosure or other

Bilzerian was charged with two
al laws.
nts of securities fraud, five counts
filing false statements with the
overnment and two counts of con-
spiracy.

Net Worth Put at $81 Million

Yesterday's sentence capped the
undoing of the career of a man who
appeared seemingly from nowhere to
some of the most lucrative
engineer
that should
or failing to cooperate.

xt Week

fficials are scheduled to
week and are expected to
ed by the subcommittee
h Administration's views
rowing Canadian problem.
ce of National Drug Control
hich is directed by William
is expected to announce the
of a committee next month
tional and domestic
lems. The

Several recent investigations have
disclosed significant ties between
money laundering operations by drug
dealers in the United States and Latin
America who have made use of Cana
dian banks, many of which ha
branches throughout Latin Amer
Federal authorities say that C
tion Polar Cap, the largest
laundering investigation in A
history, uncovered more th
lion that was laundered
month period, some of
through banks in Toron

Panama Bank Conv

In that case, Ca
authorities

he wrote. "I wish
the clock of time a
ever mistakes I may
a statement to the
rian said his letter was
declined to say anything
However, Judge Ward
lieved Mr. Bilzerian ha
guided by the desire for
had begun to misrepresent
to obtain it.

'In Short, He Lies'

"I have no doubt that in
years, he has done good thin
other people, but there is anothe
to the defendant," Judge Ward
"The allure of money has caused
to lose what I believe to be prop
perspective. In short, he lies."
Judge Ward added that the cas
was "replete with false documents"
that supported his opinion.
While Mr. Bilzerian was no
charged with perjury, a Federal
judge can be permitted to consider
such a possibility when announcing
sentence.
During his testimony, M
spoke as though he
about many
financial

1

REPORTERS AT WORK

MURDER OF A PROSTITUTE

In 1836 James Gordon Bennett of the *New York Herald* wrote a series of articles about, as he put it, "one of the most foul and premeditated murders that ever fell to our lot to record," the slaying of a prostitute named Ellen Jewett. According to Bennett, the murder occurred when one of Jewett's "admirers," Richard Robinson, grew enraged over her infidelities. He "drew from beneath his cloak the hatchet," Bennett reported, "and inflicted upon her head three blows, either of which must have proved fatal, as the bone was cleft to the extent of three inches in each place." After that, "the cold blooded villain" proceeded to "cast the lifeless body upon the bed and set fire to that."

A few days later Bennett reversed course, arguing that Robinson was not the villain after all. "Is it possible," he asked readers, "for a youth, hitherto unimpeached and unimpeachable in his character, to have engendered and perpetrated so diabolical an act as the death of Ellen Jewett was?" At trial Robinson was acquitted.

Throughout, the *Herald*'s coverage was supported by Bennett's painstaking investigation. He repeatedly searched the crime scene for clues. He convinced the police to let him examine Jewett's body (her skin, Bennett reported, was "as polished as the purest Parisian marble"). He conducted what scholars believe to have been the first newspaper interview in the United States, closely questioning Jewett's madam. The frenetic coverage tripled the *Herald*'s circulation.[1]

PULITZER'S PISTOL

In 1870 Joseph Pulitzer, at the time a Missouri state legislator and a reporter for a German-language newspaper, got into an argument with a political opponent named Edward Augustine. After Augustine called Pulitzer a "damn liar," Pulitzer went home, got his pistol, and confronted Augustine again. Augustine called him a "puppy." Infuriated, Pulitzer yanked out his gun and aimed at Augustine's torso. Augustine tackled Pulitzer, and the gun discharged, wounding Augustine in the lower leg. Although Pulitzer later insisted that Augustine had been brandishing a gun too, most witnesses didn't mention one. Pulitzer paid a $400 fine and, a short time later, left town.[2]

CIRCLING THE WORLD

In 1889 the *New York World* announced that its reporter Nellie Bly (her real name was Elizabeth Cochran) would voyage around the world. In the early 1870s Jules Verne's book *Around the World in Eighty Days* had been sheer fantasy, but transportation had improved in the years since. "Can Jules Verne's Great Dream Be Reduced to Actual Fact?" the *World* asked in a headline. Carrying only a small satchel, Bly was about to find out.

The *World* shamelessly publicized the stunt. It printed her dispatches as well as charts and maps showing her progress. It published a " 'Round the World With Nellie Bly" game (a typical square read, "Iceberg: Go back to port"). It announced a contest: Whoever came closest to guessing Bly's time of return would win a free trip to Europe. When a savvy manufacturer started marketing the Nellie Bly dressing gown, a *World* cartoon showed Bly getting off the ship and confronting Nellie Bly Tooth Powder, Nellie Bly Hay Fever Cure, Nellie Bly Snuff, and various other products. "The whole civilized world," the newspaper boasted, "is watching Nellie Bly."

When Bly made it back to New York in 72 days, 6 hours, and 11 minutes, the *World* published the triumphant headline "FATHER TIME OUTDONE!" "The stage-coach days are ended," the article said, "and the new age of lightning travel begun."[3]

TURNABOUT

At the turn of the century, a woman who ran a boardinghouse in Chicago was accused of killing one of her tenants with arsenic. The police could find no sign of the poison in the woman's house, though, and it looked as if the prosecution would have no case. But the *Chicago American*'s Arthur Pegler (father of columnist Westbrook Pegler) conducted a thorough search, and he discovered a container of arsenic in the salt cellar. That was enough for a jury. The woman was convicted and sentenced to death.

Pegler had actually gotten the arsenic from a photographer and planted it in the cellar, because he was convinced of the woman's guilt. As the execution date drew near, the photographer-accomplice started fretting, and Pegler had to reveal his deed to his managing editor. Rather than disclosing that the key evidence was fraudulent, the managing editor energetically started a new crusade, calling on the state to show compassion to the poor, misguided killer. The crusade succeeded, but only to a degree: The governor commuted the woman's sentence to life in prison.[4]

THE REAL FRONT PAGE

When Ben Hecht and Charles MacArthur wrote the play *The Front Page,* they based the two main characters on actual newspapermen. MacArthur had worked with the role models at the *Chicago Herald & Examiner,* and Hecht had heard stories about them when he worked at the rival *Chicago Journal* and later the *Chicago Daily News.*

The character Hildy Johnson came in large part from a genuine Hildy Johnson, a reporter for the *Herald & Examiner.* The real Johnson, like the fictional one, once locked a witness in a rolltop desk. On another occasion Johnson broke into an empty jury room, figured out the verdict by going through the ballots in the trash, and left behind phony ballots for his competitors to find. Another time Johnson paid two hundred dollars to a murderer on death row for the exclusive rights to his story, and then won the money back from him in a card game. "Don't play rummy with Hildy Johnson," the prisoner later told a priest. "I think he cheats."

The other principal *Front Page* character, editor Walter Burns, was based on the *Herald*'s managing editor, Walter C. Howey. Howey confronted several Chicago officials with evidence of their corruption and threatened to go public with the information unless they signed undated letters of resignation. Most of them signed the letters, which Howey used to guarantee the officials' cooperation with the *Herald.* Howey also commanded a small police force all his own. Chicago Mayor William Hale Thompson was so grateful for the *Herald*'s 1919 endorsement, when all other Chicago newspapers had endorsed another candidate, that he assigned three policemen to Howey. The officers would arrest anyone Howey told them to, and they would bar competing reporters and photographers from crime scenes while the *Herald* racked up exclusives.[5]

CAVE CAPTIVE

For eighteen days in 1925 the press feverishly covered a rescue effort in Kentucky. Reporters from across the country appeared, and thousands of tourists came to see for themselves. Floyd Collins, a young amateur spelunker, had been exploring a cave when a boulder had dislodged and pinned him in a small chamber. He was sixty feet underground and could be reached only by a narrow, hundred-foot-long passageway.

William "Skeets" Miller, a small-framed, twenty-one-year-old reporter for the *Louisville Courier-Journal,* decided to try to get to Collins. As he later described the task: "I had to squirm like a snake. Water covers almost every inch of the ground, and after the first few feet I was wet through and through. Every moment it got colder. It seemed that I would crawl forever. . . ." Finally he reached the end. He found Collins lying on his back. "His two arms are held fast in the crevice beside his body, so that he really is in a natural strait-jacket." Water had dripped torturously on Collins's face until an earlier rescuer had draped an oilcloth over his head. "You're small," Collins told Miller, "and I believe you're going to get me out."

Miller tried. Rescuers managed to get a body harness around Collins, and Miller and three other men heaved on a rope in the narrow passage. By the time exhaustion and numbness set in, they had moved Collins five inches. Later Miller tried to enlarge the compartment with a small hammer. He passed each piece of rock to another man, who relayed it through the passageway. Progress was immeasurably slow. A crew briefly tried to drill a new hole from the surface to Collins, but the vibrations threatened to shake boulders loose, which might have closed the passage or crushed him.

On the eighteenth day, as rescue efforts were continuing, Collins died. "In death, as in the last week or more of his life," Miller wrote, "Floyd Collins must remain entrapped in Sand Cave."

For his reporting, Miller won a Pulitzer Prize and immortality of sorts—the episode reappeared, in altered form, in Robert Penn Warren's novel *The Cave* and in the Kirk Douglas film *Ace in the Hole.*[6]

INQUIRING FOTOGRAPHER

In the '20s New York's newest paper, the *Daily News,* started a regular feature called "Inquiring Fotographer," which gave everyday people a chance to respond to various questions. "Fotographer" Jimmy Jemail spent one day in Jersey City, where few people read the *News,* asking the question "Do you remember your first kiss and did you enjoy it?" Someone told the police that a lunatic was wandering the streets harassing people, and Jemail was picked up for psychiatric evaluation. At the hospital Jemail insisted that he was a newspaper photographer and finally convinced a doctor to call the *News* office. Jemail's editor, Harry Nichols, said: "Doctor, we never heard of the guy." A few hours later the *News* liberated him.[7]

HIDDEN CAMERA

In 1928 Tom Howard, also a *New York Daily News* photographer, arranged to be an official witness at the execution of Ruth Snyder, who had been convicted of murdering her husband. As he waited, Howard lifted his trouser leg slightly. When the electric-chair switch was thrown, Howard threw a switch of his own, activating a small camera strapped to his ankle. The *Daily News* published Howard's grisly moment-of-death photo, pointing out proudly in a cutline that it was "the first Sing Sing execution picture and the first of a woman's execution." *Daily News* presses had to run overtime: The issue sold 250,000 extra copies that day, and the *News* later printed and sold another 750,000.[8]

SIREN

The police department let columnist Walter Winchell mount a siren on his car, and Winchell often blasted it as he drove around New York City. He always turned it off as he approached his own house because, he explained, he didn't want to wake his children.[9]

ROUTINE

Cissy Patterson, owner of the *Washington Times-Herald,* once described her daily routine: "I get up in the morning and look in the mirror and see that I'm never going to be young and pretty again, then I go down to the office and give Roosevelt hell."[10]

BEST-KNOWN LEAD

One of the most famous leads (which is probably apocryphal) concerned the death of Richard Loeb. In 1924 Loeb and Nathan Leopold, both graduate students at the University of Chicago, had murdered a fourteen-year-old boy. Leopold and Loeb were convicted and sentenced to life-plus-prison terms.

In 1936 Loeb apparently made advances to a fellow inmate, who turned on Loeb and killed him. For Loeb's obituary, according to legend, Edwin Lahey of the *Chicago Daily News* wrote this lead: "Richard Loeb, the well-known student of English, yesterday ended a sentence with a proposition."[11]

RESTON'S FIRST SCOOPS

James Reston of *The New York Times* got his first major scoops during the Dumbarton Oaks meetings that produced the United Nations Charter. Reston's articles revealed, in unmatched detail, what was happening in the secret sessions. Some reporters believed Reston's source must be with the British delegation. Others thought the State Department was responsible. Forty years later Reston revealed that both theories were wrong. His true source had been a junior member of the Chinese delegation who had felt grateful to the *Times* for, years earlier, having employed him as a copy boy.[12]

PERKS

Journalist and author Theodore H. White once flashed his press card as he cut to the front of a long amusement park line. "National press," he declared, and bought tickets for himself and other reporters to go through the funhouse.[13]

DRUGS IN THE PRESS

- Reporters covered the White House around the clock after President Eisenhower's 1955 heart attack. To help them keep going, a White House physician distributed amphetamines in the pressroom every morning.

- In the mid-1950s Dan Rather had a Houston policeman inject him with heroin "so I could do a story about it," Rather told a *Ladies Home Journal* interviewer. "The experience was a special kind of hell." Rather also said that he had "tried everything," that he knew "a fair amount about LSD," but that he had not "smoked pot in this country."

- During the 1972 campaign, the reporters and camera crews on a McGovern press plane passed around marijuana, hashish, and cocaine.

- The rumors of drug use in the Carter White House created conflicts for some media organizations. "The reporters who could write the most authoritative account of White House drug habits," Patrick Oster wrote in the *Chicago Sun-Times,* "are engaging in a cover-up of a story that undoubtedly would disturb many Americans, not to mention Jimmy Carter himself." According to Robert Pierpoint of CBS, one network assigned a reporter to track down rumors about White House drug use (Pierpoint didn't identify the network or the reporter). But the reporter, Pierpoint wrote, "had not only smoked pot with members of the White House staff, but had actually supplied the weed." The reporter told his network bosses that, despite his best efforts, he couldn't pin down the story. Similarly, the *Washington Post*'s Diana McLellan claimed that this reference to journalists' drug use was edited out of a *New York Times* article: "Reporters—including at least two employed by the New York *Times*—have smoked marijuana in the presence of and with members of the White House staff and other federal employees." And Jody Powell, Carter's press secretary, heard that a *Times* Washington editor went to considerable lengths to ensure that only drug-free reporters covered the White House drug story.

- In 1984, while on *CBS Morning News* to promote his biography of John Belushi, Bob Woodward of the *Washington Post* said he understood that about forty *Post* people were regular cocaine users. Ben Bradlee, the paper's executive editor, responded: "None of the editors knows what [Woodward] is talking about. Cocaine is illegal, and if I hear of anyone using it around here, it's out the door, goodbye."

- In 1987 Nina Totenberg of National Public Radio revealed that Supreme Court nominee Douglas Ginsburg had smoked marijuana. When reporters called Totenberg to ask about her own drug experience, she said that "I spent my entire youth leaving parties where there was marijuana so that I wouldn't be in a position of being compromised as a reporter." She said she did smoke "one puff" once, and she "almost gagged to death."

- After the Ginsburg episode, a reporter informally surveyed twenty-eight other reporters who were covering a Florida political event. Twenty-one said they had smoked marijuana; four said they had not; and three refused to answer.

- In the '60s *Rolling Stone* offered a free roach clip to every new subscriber. In the '80s its standard employment contract allowed the magazine to test employees for drug use.

- In 1985 an *Albuquerque Journal* reporter was awakened late at night and ordered to come to his office, where a drug-sniffing dog was whimpering at his desk. The reporter unlocked the desk and handed the security men a box of Tylenol.

- When the *Los Angeles Herald* initiated a drug-testing program in 1986, staffers arrived at work to find dozens of cups of what appeared to be urine on top of file cabinets. A sign was posted nearby with a poem that began: "Urine the *Herald* now / You've lost your rights somehow."[14]

CRIMESTOPPERS

In 1966 *The New York Times* reported that "two men were foiled in an attempt to burn their draft cards in front of the Federal Court House in Foley Square by a large crush of newsmen who refused to give the demonstrators enough room."[15]

LAST WORD

On June 24, 1968, the lead story in New Hampshire's *Concord Daily Monitor,* written by editor James M. Langley, began: "I died late yesterday afternoon. It is not unusual for a newspaperman to write his own obituary in advance, but they usually do so anonymously. I prefer the more honest autobiography, even on so sad an occasion (for me)." Langley had written the obituary two years earlier, and instructed his staff to publish it when he died.[16]

JOURNALISM 101

A *Playboy* reporter accidentally left his tape recorder behind when he was interviewing Carl Bernstein. Bernstein returned it. At the end of the tape, Bernstein had added: "Journalism 101. First rule. Never leave behind your notes or your tape recorder in the office or home of the source, because you could get fucked up. I thought it would be funny to give you an 18½-minute gap—but I've been very honest, and all I did was turn the tape over."[17]

DREAM LEADS

Media scholar William L. Rivers once asked Washington correspondents what leads they would most like to write. The responses included:

Richard Valeriani, NBC reporter: "I have just returned from death, and I can report to you that. . . ."

Dan Rather, CBS reporter: "A way was found today that insures that people will be unfailingly kind to other people."

Les Whitten, former assistant to Jack Anderson: "Jesus Christ, whose second coming has been promised for almost two thousand years, landed at Washington National Airport secretly today and confided his plans exclusively to this reporter."

Ralph de Toledano, columnist: "Standing solemnly before an equally solemn audience on the steps of the Capitol, Ralph de Toledano took the oath of office as president of the United States."[18]

LOCAL ANGLE

On a San Fernando Valley radio station, where management had ordered that every newscast open with a local story, one newscast began: "Two high-speed trains collided today between Tokyo and Osaka, Japan. There were 123 people killed and several hundred have been injured. But there were no Valley residents on board."[19]

REMARKS

"The only qualities essential for real success in journalism are ratlike cunning, a plausible manner, and a little literary ability. . . . The capacity to steal other people's ideas and phrases—that one about ratlike cunning was invented by my colleague Murray Sayre—is also invaluable."

—Nicholas Tomalin, London *Sunday Times* writer[20]

"With an expense account, anything is possible."

—Hunter S. Thompson, *San Francisco Examiner* columnist[21]

2

.....

TELEVISION NEWS

EARLY REVIEW

When a prototype television was demonstrated at the 1939 World's Fair, *The New York Times'* reviewer was unimpressed. "The problem with television," he wrote, "is that the people must sit and keep their eyes glued on a screen; the average American family hasn't time for it."[1]

SCRIPT SOLUTION

In the days before Teleprompters, an anchor read from a typed script that lay in front of him, and viewers saw the top of his head much of the time. Don Hewitt, the producer of the CBS evening newscast, once declared that he had solved the problem: Anchor Douglas Edwards should learn Braille. Edwards declined.[2]

ACTOR-REPORTERS

David Hartman of ABC's *Good Morning, America* and Mariette Hartley of CBS's *Morning Program* weren't the first actors to step into news (or seminews) programs. In the '50s Dick Van Dyke hosted CBS's *Morning Show.* NBC considered hiring Jimmy Stewart to do TV commentaries, but ultimately chose Chet Huntley instead. Featured *Today* show on-air talent included Florence Henderson, Betsy Palmer, and, later, Maureen O'Sullivan (whose replacement was a writer, Barbara Walters). In the early '70s CBS talked to Candice Bergen about becoming a *60 Minutes* correspondent. In 1977, after Tom Brokaw left *Today,* NBC tried to hire Alan Alda.

Just as actors moved into news jobs, some newsmen moonlighted as actors. Douglas Edwards, the anchor of the fledgling CBS-TV newscast in the late '40s, spent a few hours a week performing in a radio soap opera called *Wendy Warren and the News.* In 1954 Mike Wallace, famous as the cohost (with his wife) of a Manhattan TV talk show called *Mike and Buff,* spent several months playing an art dealer in a Broadway comedy, *Reclining Figure.*[3]

REMOTE PROBLEMS

In the early days of NBC's *Today* show, a program schedule indicated that a remote segment would originate from the armory at Cleveland. A few hours before the show went on the air, a staff member, Burroughs Prince, discovered that nobody had made the necessary preparations. Prince arranged for a producer, reporter, and mobile unit to be sent to the armory, and then he reserved special phone lines to carry the segment to New York.

When producer Mort Werner arrived at the studio, Prince asked what sort of introduction he should write for the armory remote. Werner didn't know what he was talking about, so Prince showed him the schedule.

"That's Cleveland *Amory,* the author!" Werner said. The typo cost the show three thousand dollars in pointless preparations.[4]

PAVLOVIAN AGGRESSION

The *Today* show's resident chimp, J. Fred Muggs, apparently noticed that whenever a camera's red light was on, his antics went unpunished. J. Fred would sit politely beside host Dave Garroway until the red light appeared, and then lean over and bite Garroway or snatch his glasses.[5]

THE BIRTH OF INSTANT ANALYSIS

After CBS aired its 1957 interview with Nikita Khrushchev, the network came under attack for having given the Soviet leader a soapbox. Jack Gould, *The New York Times* television critic, suggested that CBS should have followed the interview with explanation and criticism by some of the network's "many able and thoughtful commentators." CBS adopted the suggestion, and so-called instant analysis was born.[6]

EDUCATING PALEY

In 1962 CBS president William Paley complimented correspondent Daniel Schorr on his interview with an East German leader. "What impresses me most," Paley said, "was how coolly you sat looking at him while he talked to you like that."

Schorr laughed. "Mr. Paley," he said, "surely you know that those were reaction shots, which were done later?"

Paley, it seemed, didn't know. "Is that honest?" he asked.

"That's a funny question," said Schorr. "I'm uncomfortable answering it. But, no, it's not."

At Paley's instruction, CBS News established a policy prohibiting after-the-fact reaction shots. The policy was soon ignored.[7]

LOSS FOR WORDS

On March 31, 1968, President Johnson gave a televised speech on his Vietnam policy. After describing a plan to stop bombing North Vietnam temporarily, LBJ said that he would not seek reelection.

The surprise announcement stunned NBC's anchor of the postspeech analysis, Edwin Newman. After the President finished, Newman simply said, "And now we switch you to Elie Abel, in Milwaukee, for a reaction."

Abel was equally flabbergasted by the announcement, and he hadn't expected to be called on for several minutes. Viewers saw him sit, frozen. Seconds ticked by. Finally he said: "And now back to Edwin Newman in New York."[8]

SELF-PROMOTION

Starting in the late '60s, local TV newscasts became profitable and stations began competing fiercely for audience shares. In advertising the newscasts, some stations emphasized nonjournalistic elements:

- KGO in San Francisco ran full-page newspaper ads that showed its news staff dressed as cowboys sitting around a poker table. "Feel like you're getting a bad deal from poker-faced TV news reporters?" the ad asked. "Then let the Channel 7 Gang deal you in. They're not afraid to be friendly."
- Later, to promote a series about Soviet spying, KGO ran a TV promo showing Santa's sleigh being shot down by a Soviet missile, a reference to the Soviet shooting of a Korean airliner a few months earlier.
- KGO's competition, KRON, ran full-page ads showing its newscasters dressed up in dogs' heads. The copy: "The Bay Area's pet news team tracking down the news 24 hours a day. Watch the Newshounds of News-watch 4."
- In Boston, WBZ ran a promo showing its muscular anchors, Tom Ellis and Tony Pepper, playing handball.[9]

CONSULTANT'S TRICK

The consultants who redesigned local TV news programs developed a reliable trick. A consultant would convince a client to hire a popular newscaster who, as it happened, worked for a station that competed with another of the consultant's clients in a different city. That way both clients' ratings would improve—one station because it gained talent, and the other station because its competition lost talent.[10]

WHAT THE AUDIENCE WANTS

According to research studies, TV news audiences are most interested in flames, blood, and sex and least interested in ethnic news and labor news.[11]

WHAT THE AUDIENCE REMEMBERS

Researchers at the University of California at Berkeley tried to find out how much information people retain from TV newscasts. In calls made a few minutes after the evening news programs had ended, respondents who had seen a newscast were asked what they could remember. Fifty-one percent could not remember a single story.[12]

WHAT THE ANCHORS KNOW

In 1986 *TV Guide* tested the news-awareness of six local TV anchors. The magazine asked the anchors to name five people: the White House national security adviser, the head of the African National Congress, the Soviet foreign minister, the president of El Salvador, and the most recent Supreme Court appointment. None of the six anchors was able to answer all five correctly, and one anchor got all five wrong.[13]

VON HOFFMAN'S DEPARTURE

Nicholas von Hoffman lost his "Point-Counterpoint" debate slot on *60 Minutes* after he employed a metaphor that seemed too vivid for television. President Nixon, von Hoffman told viewers, was "a dead mouse on the American family kitchen floor and the only question that remains is who is going to have the unpleasant task of picking him up by the tail and tossing him in the garbage." The remark, *60 Minutes* executive producer Don Hewitt told von Hoffman, "set broadcast journalism back thirty years."[14]

TITLE

Fred Friendly was a widely quoted critic of television news. Almost always he was identified as the former president of CBS News (which he was) rather than as a consultant to the Ford Foundation or a Columbia journalism professor (which he also was). Finally Jack Schneider, a CBS executive, sent Friendly a box of business cards that read: "Fred W. Friendly / Former President, CBS News."[15]

WOMEN ON TV (I)

"There's no place for broads in broadcasting."

—A journalism professor to Jessica Savitch, 1964[16]

"We're not looking for a woman. We're looking for a reporter."

—TV news director to Judy Woodruff, 1969[17]

"Christine, our viewer research results are in and they are really devastating. The people of Kansas City don't like watching you anchor the news because you are too old, too unattractive, and you are not sufficiently deferential to men."

—Ridge Shannon, news director of KMBC, to Christine Craft, 1981[18]

BARBARA WALTERS'S SALARY

In 1976 ABC hired Barbara Walters away from NBC, where she had been cohost of the *Today* show, and gave her a five-year, million-dollar-a-year contract. Early responses included these:

"Is any TV journalist worth $1 million a year? No, unless they find a cure for cancer on the side."

—Dan Rather, CBS reporter (Five years later Rather was paid $2.5 million a year to anchor the *CBS Evening News.*)

"I'm really depressed as hell. If Barbara Walters is a five-million-dollar woman, then Walter Cronkite is a sixteen-million-dollar man. This isn't journalism—this is a minstrel show."

—Richard Salant, CBS News president

"There was a first wave of nausea, the sickening sensation that we were going under, that all of our efforts to hold network television news aloof from show business had failed."

—Walter Cronkite, CBS anchor

"We might as well face it. The line between the news business and show business has been erased forever."

—Charles B. Seib, *Washington Post* ombudsman

"DOLL BARBIE TO LEARN HER ABC'S"

—*New York Daily News* headline

"If Barbara had only been a man, everybody would have cheered, or at least chewed their cigars in grudging admiration for such a power play."

—Liz Smith, *New York Daily News* columnist[19]

WOMEN ON TV (II)

"Well, if it's gossip you want, that's why we have a woman here."

—Daniel Schorr introducing Lesley Stahl during *CBS Evening News* coverage of the Watergate hearings[20]

"With rape so predominant in the news lately, it is well to remember the words of Confucius: 'If rape is inevitable, lie back and enjoy it.'"

—Tex Antoine opening the weather segment of the news on New York's WABC, 1976; the public response caused the station to take him off the air[21]

"You just have to, that's all."

—A news executive at KDLH-TV in Duluth, Minnesota, when Pamela Golden asked why she had to wear tight-fitting sweaters and stand sideways while delivering the weather report, 1983[22]

"And ladies, he isn't married."

—Tom Brokaw, NBC anchor, in an on-air reference to John F. Kennedy, Jr., at the 1988 Democratic convention[23]

CRONKITE'S PASSING

During the days leading up to Walter Cronkite's final *CBS Evening News* broadcast in 1981, he was annoyed by the lavish farewell editorials. "Jesus," he said, "I'm not *dead!*"[24]

AMBUSHING THE AMBUSHER (I)

During a break in filming a *60 Minutes* segment, Mike Wallace told the interview subject, a bank officer named Richard Carlson, that consumer credit contracts were particularly hard to understand "if you're reading them over the watermelon or the tacos." Although the CBS cameras were off, the bank had hired its own camera crew to film the interviews, and those cameras were still running.

When the remark began to get attention, Wallace accused Carlson of breaking the rules. Whenever CBS cameras were off, Wallace insisted, *all* cameras were supposed to be off. Wallace first asked Carlson to erase the segment of videotape containing the remark. Later he rescinded the request.

Over the next several months, a few reporters asked Wallace about the incident. He was able to convince the *Wall Street Journal* and *The New York Times* that the story wasn't worth pursuing. When Nancy Skelton of the *Los Angeles Times* called, he told her that he had "a penchant for obscenity and for jokes," and argued that the remark had been partly tactical, intended to elicit "some hint of [Carlson's] feeling toward the minority community." Skelton wrote her story anyway, and the *Times* ran it on the front page.[25]

AMBUSHING THE AMBUSHER (II)

In 1983 Steve Wilson, host of the syndicated TV program *Breakaway,* wanted to interview CBS anchor Dan Rather. Rather never responded to Wilson's written and telephoned requests, so Wilson and a camera crew lay in wait outside the CBS News headquarters in New York. When Rather appeared, Wilson approached him. "Could I see you for just a moment?" he asked. "I've called your office three times. I've sent you a registered letter. . . . I don't know how else to do it."

Rather put his hand on Wilson's shoulder and told a member of the camera crew, "Get that microphone right up, will you?" Then he turned to the camera and said: "Fuck you. You got it clearly?"

The anchor later said he had mistaken Wilson for somebody else, and he apologized for his "inexcusable, rude and un-Christian" behavior. Wilson aired the film, bleeping out the obscenity.[26]

ALTERNATIVE

Burnam Matthews had been wounded in the 1983 bombing of the U.S. Marine barracks in Beirut. On Thanksgiving 1984 he got a call from a TV reporter, who wanted to film Matthews and his family eating Thanksgiving dinner as an illustration of people thankful for their blessings. It was the fourth such request Matthews had fielded that day. As with the others, he declined.

"Oh well," the reporter said, "we know someone whose baby just survived a liver transplant. We'll try them."[27]

WORDS AND PICTURES

For the *CBS Evening News* during the 1984 presidential campaign, Lesley Stahl put together a five-minute segment about President Reagan's reelection effort and its meticulous "orchestration of television coverage." White House advisers, she said in the piece, choreographed presidential TV appearances to help mask the administration's true policies. As Stahl described the various tactics, the screen showed a montage of examples: Reagan talking with farmers, embracing Mary Lou Retton, speaking to veterans at Normandy Beach, surrounded by American flags.

Shortly after the segment aired, Stahl got a call from, in her words, "a very senior White House official." Stahl steeled herself for his protests.

"Great piece," he said.

"What do you mean, 'great piece'?" she said, astonished. "Didn't you hear what I said?"

"I heard what you said," he replied, "but the American people didn't hear what you said. When Ronald Reagan talks and when you run powerful pictures of him before flags and balloons and smiling children and morning in America, the public doesn't hear you. That wipes you out completely."

In recounting the phone call later, Stahl said that "I knew the minute he said it that it was true."[28]

SIX-MINUTE GAP

On September 11, 1987, CBS anchor Dan Rather sat down to deliver the six-thirty *Evening News* feed, which about half of the network's affiliates carry. The program was originating from Miami, where Pope John Paul II was visiting. Rather was told that the newscast would be delayed until CBS Sports completed its coverage of a tennis match. Rather unclipped his microphone, stood up, and marched off to protest the tennis-first decision in a phone call to CBS News president Howard Stringer.

Moments after Rather's departure, the tennis match ended. People in the control room seemed paralyzed. Two CBS reporters in the studio could have begun the newscast. A videotape of the Pope's activities was at hand. So was a "Please Stand By" slide. Instead the network went black while Rather completed his call.

Finally Rather returned to the studio. One witness said he sauntered back slowly, "fixing his tie, deliberately making a statement." Another said Rather rushed back to the anchor desk. After six minutes of dead air, the *CBS Evening News* began.

The incident received considerable publicity, including a front-page headline in the *New York Post* ("TV TANTRUM"). Much of the attention centered on Rather's state of mind. *Newsweek* quoted an unnamed CBS News producer: "To be blunt, I wonder if Dan isn't cracking."

Rather himself said, "I'm at peace." Four months later he said that the incident had been "a bad day. Life goes that way. Man, I wish it hadn't happened."[29]

LIVE EARTHQUAKE

During KNBC's morning news on October 1, 1987, the Los Angeles studio started to shake. As heavy lights and television monitors began to sway overhead, the anchor and weatherman, Kent Shocknek and Christopher Nance, jumped under their desks. From there they continued to broadcast, while viewers saw an empty and shaking desk, until the earthquake had ended.

Accused of having overreacted, anchor Shocknek maintained that he had done the right thing. "I reported the news," he said. "If I disappointed those gore fans who wanted to see a klieg light come crashing down and split my skull open, I'm sorry."[30]

BLACK WEEKS

For a few weeks every year the A. C. Nielsen rating service stopped operating in order to adjust its machines and methods. During the so-called black weeks, the networks often aired political commentaries, cultural shows, and documentaries, in order to get credit for high quality without suffering low ratings. Starting in the mid-1970s Nielsen began operating year-round and the black weeks ended.[31]

SWEEPS WEEKS

Television news programs have always tried to boost their ratings during sweeps weeks, which provide the numbers on which ad rates are based.

- Los Angeles stations offered "news" reports on, among other things, sexual attraction, extramarital affairs, love among the elderly, tanning, kittens, and devil worship.
- A Milwaukee station held a sweepstakes with a million dollars in prizes. To win, players had to answer questions shown during the newscasts. During a subsequent sweeps week the station planned to repeat the stunt until a rival announced plans to broadcast the quiz's answers in *its* newscasts.

- In 1987 a Los Angeles station went too far. KABC heavily promoted a special series about TV ratings and the Nielsen families who, with their viewing diaries, are responsible for producing them. It was a report of disproportionate interest to the diarists, and on the nights that it ran, KABC's Nielsen-measured audience swelled to twice its normal size. The other Los Angeles stations protested, and the ratings company decided not to use the results.[32]

KEEPING IN TOUCH

In the combined newsroom of several Gannett newspapers in New York, a television set is mounted near the city desk. Beneath it is a sign: DO NOT TURN OFF THIS TELEVISION! Editors there had learned of the Challenger space shuttle explosion when a reporter called from home, where he was watching TV. After that, editors ordered that the newsroom set always be kept on.[33]

CRUCIAL INFORMATION

In 1981 Van Gordon Sauter, the president of CBS News, briefed Howard Stringer, the new executive producer of the *Evening News,* on what was expected of him.

"There's one thing you have to know," Sauter said.

"What's that?"

"You see this knob here?" Sauter said, pointing to his TV set.

Stringer nodded.

"Turn it to the right and the sound gets louder."[34]

REMARKS

"Television is a gift of God, and God will hold those who utilize his divine instrument accountable to Him."

—Philo T. Farnsworth,
co-inventor of television[35]

"This instrument can teach, it can illuminate; yes, and it can even inspire. But it can do so only to the extent that humans are determined to use it to those ends. Otherwise it is merely wires and lights in a box."

—Edward R. Murrow, CBS reporter[36]

"If Jesus Christ reappeared on Earth and began to talk to the multitudes, TV would cut away from him for livelier pictures."

—Robert MacNeil, PBS coanchor[37]

"I used to be a reporter."

—James Wooten, ABC correspondent, formerly a *New York Times* reporter[38]

3

COLUMNS, COMICS, AND REVIEWS

POLITICAL AND NEWS COLUMNS

AVOIDING "IT"

After Sinclair Lewis had separated from his wife, columnist Dorothy Thompson, he would sometimes drop by to chat with her. Lewis couldn't abide her obsession with world affairs, which he called simply "It." Before greeting her, he would ask another guest whether his wife was talking about "It." If she was, he would slip away unannounced.[1]

WEIGHING GUILT

On the first day of the 1935 trial of Bruno Richard Hauptmann, columnist Arthur Brisbane arrived at the courthouse. Hauptmann, charged with kidnapping and killing the Lindbergh baby, sat quietly while lawyers discussed preliminary matters with the judge. Brisbane studied the defendant for half an hour, and then rose and walked out. Another reporter asked why he was leaving. "I just wanted to see if he was guilty," Brisbane said. "He is."[2]

EVENING ENTERTAINMENT

In the 1940s Arthur Krock of *The New York Times* would read his column aloud to his family each evening.[3]

COFFEE WITH THE PRIME MINISTER

Columnist Joseph Alsop once visited Golda Meir, the Israeli prime minister. When an aide brought coffee, Alsop asked if it had sugar. Mrs. Meir tasted her cup. Yes, she said. Alsop, put upon, said he didn't take sugar. "Get Mr. Alsop another cup," she instructed the aide.

When he got the second cup, Alsop dropped saccharine tablets into it. He looked around and, seeing no spoon, took off his glasses and used the earpiece to stir the coffee. Mrs. Meir addressed her aide: "Get Mr. Alsop another pair of glasses."[4]

CHANGING TIMES

Fred Friendly, the former CBS News president, liked to tell this story to illustrate the generation gap:

The first day that Friendly taught at Columbia's Graduate School of Journalism, a woman in his class wore a button: MAKE LOVE, NOT WAR. "I don't think that's an appropriate button to wear to class," Friendly chided.

"Oh, Mr. Friendly," she said. "You're so square you think making love is making out."

Friendly thought that over, and later recounted the incident to columnist Walter Lippmann. Lippmann's response: "What the hell is 'making out'?"

When Friendly told his class about Lippmann's remark, one student said: "Who the hell is Walter Lippmann?"[5]

MERRY-GO-ROUND

The investigative column "Washington Merry-Go-Round" has for years been segregated from other columns in Washington newspapers. Cissy Patterson, publisher of the *Washington Times-Herald,* moved the column to the back of the newspaper in the 1940s as part of a vendetta against its coauthor (who was also her son-in-law), Drew Pearson.

Later the column appeared in the *Washington Post,* which put it on the comics page after Pearson criticized some friends of *Post* owner Eugene Meyer. Pearson professed to be unconcerned. "I've always enjoyed being back there," he said in 1969.

After Pearson was succeeded by Jack Anderson, the *Post* continued to run the column with the comics. The placement, Anderson said, didn't bother him either. In fact, the *Post* once talked of moving the column elsewhere, according to Anderson, but he urged that it be left where people expected it.[6]

OVERREACHING?

Jack Anderson's muckraking column has scored some notable exclusives, but apparently not as many as Anderson has claimed. In a 1982 speech Anderson bragged that as early as September 1976 his column had predicted the downfall of the Shah of Iran. Neil Grauer, who was writing a book about columnists, examined Anderson's 1976 columns. None, in September or any other month, contained the prediction.

Grauer asked Anderson's office for a copy of the Iran column. "I can't find the damn thing," Anderson's aide, Joseph Spear, reported back. "Jack described it to me but I can't find it."[7]

FORBIDDEN SUBJECT

Syndicated columnist George Will, a regular panelist on ABC's *This Week With David Brinkley,* once announced that a particular topic would be off limits during the program's "free-for-all" discussion: the previous week's "Doonesbury" comic strips, which had made fun of Will.[8]

WILL'S INVITATION

In a column, George Will called Vice President Bush the "lapdog" of the Reagan administration. A short time later Will invited Bush to lunch. Bush refused and told another journalist that "I draw the line at personal attacks." Will said he found it "astonishing" that the Vice President would take the attack to heart. "If a single newspaper column can rattle a professional politician," Will said, "the man is not at ease with himself."[9]

REMARKS

"If you want to get to the largest number of people, you try to get on television, but if you are trying to scuttle someone's program or get a hearing within the highest levels of the Administration, you go to a columnist."

—Ted Koppel, ABC *Nightline* anchor[10]

"Read the columnists, and if they call a member of your staff thoughtful, dedicated, or any other friendly adjective, fire him immediately."

—President Johnson on how to prevent leaks[11]

"That is what kills political writing, this absurd pretence you are delivering a great utterance. You never do. You are just a puzzled man making notes about what you think."

—Walter Lippmann, columnist, 1915[12]

"How do I know what I think if I can't read what I write?"

—James Reston, *New York Times* columnist, during the 1963 newspaper strike[13]

ENTERTAINMENT COLUMNS

....

PARSONS VS. SKOLSKY

Gossip writer Sidney Skolsky got an angry call from William Randolph Hearst, whose *Los Angeles Herald Examiner* published Skolsky's syndicated column. Hearst said that his star columnist, Louella Parsons, had accused Skolsky of being a Communist. "Are you sure she didn't say 'columnist'?" Skolsky replied. "You know, she has a difficult time pronouncing words." No, Hearst said, he was sure. He added that "when we're through with you, you'll be nothing."

The reason for Parson's accusation, Skolsky suspected, was that a Skolsky column had confidently predicted that Greta Garbo would not marry the conductor Leopold Stokowski. The column appeared on the same day that, unknown to Skolsky, Parsons published an exclusive article predicting that the two *would* marry. (Skolsky, it turned out, was right.) The contradiction, Skolsky thought, enraged Parsons.

Three months later, as he recalled in his autobiography, Skolsky met Parsons for the first time, at a Hollywood restaurant. Parsons sat back and listened as Skolsky talked to others. Then she leaned over and said quietly, "I didn't know you were such a nice man. If I'd known you were so nice, I wouldn't have told Mr. Hearst you were a Communist." The nonchalant confession infuriated Skolsky. He thought it was wrong to strike a woman, but he had to do something. So he bit her. (The autobiography doesn't say where.)

A few days later Parsons's husband, Dockie Martin, asked Skolsky what had happened. Skolsky told him. "And I'll tell you something else, Dockie," Skolsky said. "I had the tooth removed."[14]

WINCHELL VS. SULLIVAN

In Ed Sullivan's first column in the *New York Graphic* in 1931, he set himself apart from some of his colleagues: "The Broadway columnists have lifted themselves to distinction by borrowed gags, gossip that is not always kindly and keyholes that too often reveal what might better be hidden."

The next night Sullivan ran into Walter Winchell in a restaurant. "Did you mean me in what you wrote in your column?" Winchell asked. "No, not exactly," Sullivan replied. "You know, the stage axiom of a big entrance." "Well, Ed," said Winchell, "as long as you've apologized to me, it's all right."

Sullivan hadn't apologized, and Winchell's condescending attitude annoyed him. As he later told the story, he yanked Winchell across the table by the necktie. "Apologize to you?" Sullivan said. "You son of a bitch, I did mean you and if you say one more word about it I'll take you downstairs and stick your head in the toilet bowl." Winchell said nothing, and Sullivan released him.[15]

KILL ORDER

In 1968 the Newsday Syndicate mailed the copy for an upcoming Jeane Dixon astrology column. Among the items: "I still stand on my New Year's 1968 prediction and see no marriage for Jackie Kennedy in the near future. The cloud of grief and disappointment still hangs over her head." Before the column's scheduled publication date, Kennedy wed Aristotle Onassis. The syndicate rushed an advisory to its clients, asking them to delete the item and substitute instead a prediction that Mrs. Onassis's "greatest happiness is all ahead of her." The letter also explained the mix-up: Jeane Dixon's "negative vibrations" had concerned Lord Harlech, whom Jackie Kennedy had been seeing, and not Onassis.[16]

SHORTEST COLUMN

A 1973 column by Bob Considine probably stands as the shortest on record: "I have nothing to say today."[17]

SOVIET REPRINTS

Soviet newspapers have reprinted some of Art Buchwald's satirical columns, presenting them as straightforward reportage on the outrageous American system.[18]

OVER THE EDGE

In 1982 humorist John Bloom went too far in his *Dallas Times Herald* column. Bloom, writing as redneck Joe Bob Briggs, parodied the USA for Africa song "We Are the World." Bloom's "We Are the Weird" went: "We are the weird, / We are the starvin' / We are the scum of the filthy earth." The column said that the song would aid "the United Negro College Fund in the United States, 'cause I think we should be sending as many Negroes to college as we can, specially the stupid Negroes."

In response, more than five hundred readers threatened to cancel their subscriptions, and three hundred people gathered and confronted *Times Herald* editor Will Jarrett. Jarrett said that the particular column should never have gotten past editors; that "Joe Bob Briggs" would never appear again in the *Times Herald;* that the newspaper's pages would reflect increased racial sensitivity; and that the editorial staff would add at least twelve blacks and other minorities during the coming year. The announcements, Jarrett insisted, were not evidence of capitulation. "This was a move we intended to make anyway," he said. "We just took this opportunity to announce it." Columnist Bloom resigned, saying he was disappointed that the *Times Herald* had given in to people who didn't understand satire.[19]

COMICS

. . . .

FIRST COMIC

The first regularly appearing newspaper comic was the "Yellow Kid," the creation of Richard Outcault. It appeared under the title "Hogan's Alley" in Joseph Pulitzer's *New York World* in 1895 and became an instant success. William Randolph Hearst hired away dozens of the *World*'s most popular writers and artists, including Outcault, for his *New York Journal.* Both newspapers continued to run the strip (George Luks drew the *World*'s one) while fighting over who owned the rights to the character. As the Hearst-Pulitzer circulation war continued, both sides descended into sensationalism and demagoguery. The "Yellow Kid" came to symbolize the jangling, hyperbolic style, and the term "yellow journalism" was born.

Although the "Yellow Kid" earned Outcault's fame, he found fortune elsewhere. He moved to the *New York Herald* and started another strip, "Buster Brown." This time Outcault made sure to keep the legal rights, and he became wealthy from the licensing fees. He put his first creation behind him. "When I die," he said, "don't wear yellow crepe, don't let them put a Yellow Kid on my tombstone and don't let the Yellow Kid himself come to my funeral."[20]

FIRST COMICS SECTION

The first color comics section ran in 1896 in the *New York Journal* and featured, among others, "The Katzenjammer Kids," "Happy Hooligan," and "Alphonse and Gaston." The *Journal* advertised it as "eight pages of iridescent polychromous effulgence that makes the rainbow look like a lead pipe."[21]

CARTOONIST'S BYLINE

When the *New York World* started giving its reporters bylines, its cartoonist wanted the same recognition. Harry Hershfield, who drew the successful "Desperate Desmond," asked Arthur Brisbane, the paper's editor, if he could begin signing his work.

"No," Brisbane said. "Only newspapermen are getting bylines."

"But my strip appears in the papers," Hershfield argued. "Doesn't that make me a newspaperman?"

Brisbane replied, "Is a barnacle a ship?"[22]

RESPONSES

- When Al Capp asked "Li'l Abner" readers what Lena the Hyena's "most gruesome" face should look like, nearly a million people sent in drawings.

- One and a half million people submitted entries to a contest announced in "Ripley's Believe It or Not."
- Four hundred thousand readers suggested names for Dagwood and Blondie's second child.
- During World War II a columnist wrote that in an upcoming "Gasoline Alley" strip, Skeezix would be wounded. To stem the flood of phone calls and letters, the *Pittsburgh Post-Gazette* ran a front-page story saying the columnist had been wrong.
- In 1933 Henry Ford sent a telegram to Harold Gray, the artist of "Little Orphan Annie," after Annie had lost her dog. "Please do all you can to help 'Annie' find 'Sandy,' " Ford wrote. "We are all interested."[23]

PRESIDENTIAL INTERVENTION

After an argument with his manager, Ham Fisher's "Joe Palooka," a prizefighter, joined the French Foreign Legion in Africa. The setting allowed for some new plotlines for the comic strip, but Fisher soon concluded that the opportunities were drying up. How, he wondered, could he get Palooka released from the Foreign Legion?

Fisher decided that only President Franklin Roosevelt could help. He wrote to FDR's aide, Stephen Early, and asked if he could draw the President in the strip. Early said yes, so long as it was done tastefully.

With that, the problem was solved. In the strip President Roosevelt wrote a letter to the president of France asking for Palooka's release, and Palooka returned to the United States to resume boxing. President Roosevelt got word to Fisher that he had enjoyed his guest appearance.[24]

DRAWING THE FUTURE

More than twenty years before President Reagan proposed the "Star Wars" missile defense system, Daddy Warbucks of "Little Orphan Annie" told Annie that he had developed an "electronic umbrella" to protect cities from nuclear missiles. Replied Annie: "Wow, am I happy to know that!"[25]

ADDRESSING THE ENEMY

In the mid-1960s "Li'l Abner" ridiculed antiwar singers (with a character named Joanie Phonie) and college protesters (with a group called Students Wildly Indignant About Nearly Everything, or SWINE). After "Li'l Abner" artist Al Capp finished a lecture at one college, a student asked why, feeling as he did about students, he continued to speak at more than forty colleges a year. "For the $3,000 fee," Capp said, "and I wouldn't spend an hour with a bunch like you for a nickel less."[26]

THE "DOONESBURY" WEAPON

In 1979 Time Inc. bought a share of Universal Press Syndicate, and as a result the syndicate's comic strip "Doonesbury" moved from the *Washington Post* to the Time-owned *Washington Star.* The *Star* started an advertising campaign around the slogan "I'm following Doonesbury to the Washington Star." *Post* editors, annoyed, stopped running the comic strip three weeks before the contract ran out. The *Star* couldn't start running it early, so Washington got "Doonesbury" where it could. Radio announcers read it aloud over the air, and the White House added it to the daily news summary prepared for President Carter.[27]

"BLOOM COUNTY" PULITZER

In 1987 Berke Breathed's "Bloom County" won the Pulitzer for editorial cartooning, setting off a fierce controversy. In the past the award had almost always gone to an editorial-page cartoonist. The two exceptions—Garry Trudeau and Jules Feiffer—had been heavily political comic strips, which, in fact, many newspapers run on the editorial or Op Ed page.

The strongest critic of the Breathed award was Pat Oliphant, an editorial cartoonist who had won a Pulitzer in 1967. Oliphant called Breathed "the darling of the gift-shop merchandisers and the readers of *People* magazine," and said that giving Breathed a Pulitzer was like giving "the investigative reporting or editorializing award to Ann Landers." Oliphant added: "This year, 'Bloom County.' Next year, 'Garfield.' "

Responded Breathed: "I think Pat Oliphant is the greatest cartoonist who ever lived. I also just wrote him a letter to tell him that the next time we met I'd be hitting him in the honker."[28]

"DOONESBURY" BLACKOUTS

A number of newspapers have refused to run Garry Trudeau's "Doonesbury" strips for various reasons.

During the Watergate furor, the *Washington Post, Baltimore Sun,* and *Boston Globe,* among others, held back a strip in which a character says of former Attorney General John Mitchell: "It would be a disservice to Mr. Mitchell and his character to prejudge the man, but everything known to date could lead one to conclude he's guilty. That's guilty! Guilty, guilty, guilty!!" Howard Simons, the *Washington Post* managing editor who made the blackout decision, said, "We cannot have one standard for the news pages and another for the comics."

Political sensitivities have led to other "Doonesbury" omissions. Several newspapers, including the *Los Angeles Times,* refused to use a "Doonesbury" series about Frank Sinatra that includes photos of Sinatra with alleged mobsters. The *Los Angeles Times* and other papers also omitted strips describing a trip through Ronald Reagan's brain and strips suggesting that California Governor Jerry Brown was linked to organized crime. In 1987 more than thirty newspapers refused to run a "Sleaze on Parade" series, which lists Reagan administration people who had been indicted or investigated.

Other sensitivities have also blacked out "Doonesbury." The *Boston Globe* and two dozen other papers refused to run a strip that shows two then-unwed characters, Rick Redfern and Joanie Caucus, sharing a bed. Several newspapers skipped a 1987 series about spring break promiscuity in Fort

Lauderdale. The *New York Daily News* refused to run a week-long series that hit too close to home, satirizing *News* columnist Jimmy Breslin's role in the Son of Sam case. In one strip the would-be killer, called "Son of Arnold and Mary Leiberman," wants to see Breslin, but the columnist is too busy with agents and movie deals. In 1988 the *Winston-Salem Journal* refused to run a strip that, the newspaper said in an editorial page statement, "singled out for unfair attack the city's largest company." In the strip, an employment applicant at R. J. Reynolds Tobacco Co. doesn't get the job because he's unable to say with a straight face "Cigarettes do not cause cancer."

One "Doonesbury" series touched on so delicate a matter that the strip's distributor, Universal Press Syndicate, convinced Trudeau to replace it with tamer stuff. The "Doonesbury" *Silent Scream II,* a take-off on the antiabortion film *Silent Scream,* concerns a twelve-minute-old fertilized egg called Timmy. The *New Republic, Ms.,* and about forty newspapers made special arrangements to publish the series. The syndicate's caution may have been unwarranted: The executive producer of *The Silent Scream,* Donald Smith, praised the strips, and perhaps missed the satire.[29]

OTHER BLACKOUTS

- In the '40s several newspapers dropped "Little Orphan Annie" for, among other things, the strip's raucous opposition to unions and gasoline rationing and its advocacy of capital punishment and President Roosevelt's impeachment. "Perhaps," the *Nation* commented, "the Society of the Prevention of Cruelty to Children should take her under control until her syndicators, Hearst and the *Chicago Tribune,* can demonstrate their moral fitness to be the guardians of a child as impressionable and dull as Annie."
- In the '50s "Pogo" belittled Senator Joseph McCarthy, prompting several newspapers to cancel it. Politics, the publishers explained, was not permitted on the comics page. "But I notice," artist Walt Kelly remarked, "that

when I poked fun at the Communists in 'Pogo,' nobody canceled."

- Mort Walker's "Beetle Bailey" generated several controversies. An early conflict centered on navels. Walker's syndicate ordered Walker not to draw them, but he refused to comply. For a time the syndicate snipped navels out of the strip, and finally gave up. Another time, Walker came up against the Pentagon. The army's newspaper, *Stars and Stripes,* dropped the strip when Walker added a black officer, Lieutenant Flap. The integrated comic strip, army officers said, might increase racial tension. When the Senate began looking into the problem, the army backed down.

  Other "Beetle Bailey" strips were accused of insensitivity to women. The *Minneapolis Tribune* and several other papers pulled a 1981 strip in which General Halftrack's secretary, Miss Buxley, complains that she's "just not all here today." Watching her leave, the general remarks, "If there was any more of her here, I don't think I could take it." Mort Walker insisted that he was merely "trying to show how much of a jerk the general is." The protests did prompt Walker to raise Miss Buxley's neckline and lower her skirt.

- Episodes in Berke Breathed's "Bloom County" troubled some editors. In 1987 the *Miami Herald, Newsday,* the *Boston Globe,* and several others refused to run a strip in which a character says "Reagan sucks!" Some other newspapers changed "sucks" to "stinks." The following year Breathed drew a two-week series in which Opus visits two companies, Gillette and Mary Kay Cosmetics, and discovers animals undergoing various torturous tests in the name of product safety. Breathed called the series "reality comics." Editors at three newspapers, including the *Los Angeles Daily News,* found the strips a bit too real for the comics page, and refused to run the series.

- Politics created troubles for "Cathy" in 1988. The *Los Angeles Times, Dallas Morning News,* and other newspapers refused to run a two-week series in which a character campaigns energetically for Michael Dukakis. One small paper, the *Cullman Times* in Alabama, went further: it replaced the pro-Dukakis strips with the boxed headline VOTE FOR BUSH. Of the controversy, "Cathy" author Cathy Guisewite said, "I occasionally venture into serious issues that women think about. It's not always cellulite. . . ."

- Bill Watterson's "Calvin and Hobbes" ran into problems over taste in 1988. In one strip Calvin boasts that he has brought a Thermos of phlegm for lunch. That was too much for the *Daily Oklahoman,* which announced that it was canceling the strip permanently.
- Some comics have been censored for more arcane reasons. In a 1936 "Dick Tracy" comic strip, Chester Gould drew the detective hero trapped behind a gigantic boulder in a mine shaft. Tracy looks toward the reader and says "Gould, you have gone too far." In the last frame a giant eraser appears and starts to erase the boulder. The touch of surrealism went too far for the *Chicago Tribune,* which refused to run the strip. For years the Mormon Church–owned *Deseret News* in Salt Lake City deleted any references to smoking, leaving some characters mysteriously holding their fingers before their lips. In 1975 the *Omaha World-Herald* blacked out a remark that disparaged the press: A reporter in a "Steve Canyon" strip says to an editor "But you always said 'never let the truth interfere with a good story'!"[30]

EDITORIAL CARTOONS

....

NAST'S CONTRIBUTIONS

Thomas Nast, who drew cartoons for *Harper's Weekly* in the late nineteenth century, not only enriched popular culture (he invented the Democratic donkey, the Republican elephant, and the modern image of Santa Claus); he also helped destroy New York City's corrupt political boss, William Marcy Tweed. At one point Tweed said that most of his constituents couldn't read, so it didn't much matter what the newspapers (mainly *The New York Times*) wrote about him, but his constituents *could* understand Nast's razor-sharp cartoons. The Tweed ring tried to bribe Nast, offering him money to "go abroad and study art." Nast refused.

Later Tweed himself went abroad, but Nast's handiwork followed him. After finishing one prison term, Tweed was awaiting trial on various corruption charges when he slipped away from his jailers and sailed to Spain. There, American authorities arrested him. They had been tipped off by someone who had recognized Tweed from a Nast cartoon.[31]

MORGAN'S NOSE

Financier J. P. Morgan once wrote a note to Joseph Pulitzer, asking if the editorial cartoonist at Pulitzer's *New York World* might stop exaggerating the size of Morgan's nose quite so much. Pulitzer, who was self-conscious about his own nose, instructed the artist to be gentler when caricaturing Morgan.[32]

REGULATION

After a *Philadelphia North American* cartoon depicted him as a portly parrot in 1902, Pennsylvania Governor Samuel Pennypacker pushed a bill through the state legislature making it illegal to depict men "as birds or animals." The cartoonists complied, depicting politicians as vegetables instead.[33]

EXCESSIVE VERISIMILITUDE

In 1983 Paul Szep, the Pulitzer-winning editorial cartoonist of the *Boston Globe*, drew Soviet leader Yuri Andropov responding indignantly to an MX missile proposal. Szep first drew "@*!!@" coming out of Andropov's mouth, but he wanted more accuracy, so he asked a Russian-speaking reporter for a phrase. Szep added the reporter's suggestion, "HA

XYNA," to the cartoon—without, Szep later said, knowing what it meant. Within hours of publication, Russian-speaking readers called to complain that the *Globe* had published an obscenity, variously translated as "what the fuck" and "suck my cock." The newspaper reprimanded Szep and suspended him without pay for a week.[34]

HHF

Officials in the Reagan Defense Department sometimes referred to proposals as suffering from "HHF"—"high Herblock factor," meaning that the program would be especially susceptible to caricature by the *Washington Post*'s editorial cartoonist.[35]

REMARKS

"Political cartoonists violate every rule of ethical journalism—they misquote, trifle with the truth, make science fiction out of politics. . . . But when the smoke clears, the political cartoonist has been getting closer to the truth than the guy who writes political opinions."

—Jeff MacNelly, political cartoonist[36]

"I'm glad Walter Lippmann can't draw."

—Lyndon Johnson[37]

REVIEWS

. . . .

MARGARET FULLER AND HORACE GREELEY

In the 1840s Margaret Fuller became the first woman to write literary criticism for a newspaper and one of the first women to join a newspaper staff in any substantial capacity.

She came to the attention of *New York Tribune* editor Horace Greeley by way of one of her literary-magazine essays, which, Greeley thought, showed an "un-American richness of culture and ripeness of thought." He invited Fuller to leave her home in Boston and take a job on the *Tribune*. Fuller accepted and, at the urging of Greeley's wife, moved into the Greeley household.

Although they lived and worked together, Fuller and Greeley maintained a relationship of, in Greeley's phrase, "friendly antagonism." Fuller's articles often came in well after the deadline, sometimes because of her incapacitating migraines. Greeley attributed the headaches to her taste for strong tea, and chided her once at the breakfast table. Fuller coolly asked him to keep his suggestions to himself. Greeley never raised the subject again, but he continued to glare his disapproval when she drank the tea, creating, he wrote, "a perceptible distance between us."

Greeley also differed with Fuller on the subject of women's rights. Fuller supported absolute social equality, a position that Greeley shared, but she expected chivalry from men, which struck Greeley as inconsistent. Whenever she would reach for Greeley's arm or ask him to arrange an escort to walk her home after dark, he would brightly recite from her book *Woman in the Nineteenth Century:* "Let them be sea-captains if they will!" The sarcasm, Greeley admitted, "did not tend to ripen our intimacy."

Greeley did respect Fuller's "original, vigorous and earnest mind." As a literary critic, her first article was a thoughtful critique of Emerson's essays. She was one of the earliest admirers of Robert Browning. She also reported news, writing about the savage conditions she found in visits to an insane asylum and a prison.

After two years in New York, Fuller sailed to Europe, where she continued to write for the *Tribune* about literature, politics, and war. She had a son with an Italian marchese (accounts differ on whether they married). Five years later the three of them sailed for the United States. The ship hit a storm and sank a few miles from New York harbor, killing everyone on board. The *Tribune* reported that "[a] great soul has passed from this mortal stage of being."[38]

SELF-REVIEW

Charles Ashman, a lawyer and author, managed to review his own book for *The New York Times Book Review* in 1973. He phoned the *Times* and identified himself as Melvin Belli, the flamboyant San Francisco lawyer who was a friend of Ashman's. Ashman-Belli said he had just read a book called *The Finest Judges Money Can Buy* by Charles Ashman, and he proposed to write a review that would comment on the book and discuss other episodes of the bribery of judges. John Leonard, the *Review*'s editor, okayed the proposal because, he later wrote, "a solemn literary journal is always on the lookout for evidence of sin in high places." Ashman submitted a laudatory review with Belli's byline, and the *Times* published it. Belli saw the article when it was published but decided not to do anything.

A few weeks later the *Times* published an apology that demonstrated that the editors still didn't know what had happened. The apology said that in the future, the *Times* would not allow a friend of an author to write a review, as had happened when Belli reviewed Ashman's book.[39]

SUPPLEMENTARY INCOME

Some book reviewers for New York newspapers have made as much as a thousand dollars a month by selling review copies to secondhand bookstores, according to a story by Michael Cordts in the *Rochester Democrat and Chronicle.* To get the story, Cordts took a temporary job in New York City's Strand Bookstore, where he saw boxes of books originally addressed to book editors. Cordts took down names and phoned the editors. When they denied selling the review copies, he told them what he had seen. As a result of the story, several book editors were fired or reassigned. The Strand's managers said the publicity had been a boon—the store was receiving more review copies than ever before.[40]

SULLIVAN'S START

In his first outing as a theater critic in the 1920s, Ed Sullivan wrote a biting review of August Strindberg's *The Father.* Unaware that the playwright had died in 1914, Sullivan wrote that Strindberg ought to rewrite the second act from scratch.[41]

SURE THING

Exasperated by negative reviews of their productions, the Shubert brothers started their own weekly newspaper. The *New York Review* guaranteed that each Shubert production would get at least one rave notice.[42]

SLIPPING PAST THE SHUBERTS

The Shuberts also tried to stop negative reviews of their plays by barring hostile reviewers from their theaters. One excluded journalist, Walter Winchell, fired back in his column: "A certain critic, barred from Shubert openings, says he'll wait three nights and go to their closings."

When sarcasm had no effect, Winchell and other critics resorted to trickery. Winchell managed to see a Marx Brothers show from backstage. He had appeared at the stage door disguised as Harpo, and the guards had waved him in. Another banned reviewer, Channing Pollock of the *New York Morning Telegraph,* developed a wide repertoire of disguises, including false beards and nose putty.

Other critics tried to use the law. When the Shuberts announced that none of their theaters would admit *New York Times* critic Alexander Woollcott, he got an injunction ordering them to let him in, and the *Times* notified the Shuberts that their advertising was no longer welcome. Although the injunction was later overturned, the Shuberts were so desperate to resume advertising in the *Times* that they agreed to admit Woollcott. In Boston critic George Holland had the city make him an acting fire marshal. He would show up at opening nights and announce that it was time for another fire inspection. Under the law, the theater had to let him in.

In New York the Shuberts' practice came to an end after

they refused to admit columnist Leonard Lyons. Lyons, a lawyer, successfully lobbied the legislature for a bill that required theaters to admit any sober person with a ticket. Woollcott had started down the same road with a proposal called the "Drama Critics Protection Bill," but the Shuberts had defeated it. Lyons pursued the matter more forcefully, and a few years later the bill became law. Insisting that it was unconstitutional, the Shuberts took the case to the Supreme Court, where the law was upheld.[43]

SHORTEST REVIEW

Clive Barnes of *The New York Times* wrote a one-word review of the play *The Cupboard:* "Bare."[44]

REVIEWER STUMBLES

In 1987 the *San Francisco Chronicle* published a review of the San Francisco ballet's performance of *Bizet pas de Deux.* The review, headlined "S.F. Ballet Misses a Step at Stern Grove," slammed the performance. It nicknamed the principal dancer, Ludmila Lopukhova, "Lumpy," and referred to her "potato-drenched Russian training." Soon after publication the newspaper began getting calls from irate ballet patrons. The program, they said, had been changed at the last minute to *Ballet d'Isoline,* performed by five male dancers; Lopukhova had not appeared.

Critic Heuwell Tircuit blamed poor health. He said he had been so sick during the performance that he hadn't noticed the change in program and dancers. When he wrote his review, he said, "I sat at the machine and my fingers moved." William German, the newspaper's executive editor, said he had reason to believe that Tircuit's explanation was "not a credible one." Tircuit was fired.[45]

TURNING TABLES

A restaurant owner once proposed that *Chicago Tribune* restaurant critic Fran Zell cook a meal and that several restaurateurs review it. Zell agreed. The restaurateurs, given the chance for vengeance, produced unfavorable reviews. One called her meal "a cop-out." Another said it was "a disappointment." A third wrote: "In my restaurant, we cook the pasta before we serve it. It's sort of a tradition." "The meal was a flop," Zell said afterward, "but I learned a lot about what it's like to cook under pressure."[46]

INVESTIGATIVE COMPETITION

In 1988 the *Detroit News* published a photo of *Detroit Monthly*'s new, previously unrecognized restaurant critic, urging restaurant managers to "clip and save" the page.[47]

CHECK, PLEASE

According to a 1987 estimate, *The New York Times'* food critic, Bryan Miller, spends some $90,000 a year of *Times* money in restaurants.[48]

REMARKS

"[W]e're less corrupt than literary critics, because they want to write whereas we have no ambition in movie making."

—Andrew Sarris of the *Village Voice* on his fellow film critics[49]

"I can't tell *you the number of critics who slip me scripts on the side. Then they rip you apart as an actor because you haven't responded to their screenplay."*

—Robert Redford[50]

"Frank Rich and John Simon are the syphilis and gonorrhea of the theater."

—David Mamet, playwright[51]

"I don't know about the siff, but a theater without a clap or two would be a pretty lonely place."

—John Simon, *New York* magazine theater critic[52]

4

THE NEWS PACKAGE

CHOOSING THE NEWS

WHAT'S NEWS?

"When a dog bites a man," *New York Sun* city editor John B. Bogart once said, "that is not news, but when a man bites a dog, that is news." Some other definitions of *news:*

"What protrudes from the ordinary."

—Walter Lippmann, columnist

"The departure from normal."

—Leo Rosten, political scientist
and author

"What interests a good newspaperman."

—Gerald Johnson, *Baltimore Sun* editorial writer

"What one's colleagues have defined as news."

—Douglass Cater, former journalist and White House aide

"What I *say it is. It's something worth knowing by* my *standards."*

—David Brinkley, NBC coanchor

"Anything that will make people talk."

—Charles A. Dana, *New York Sun* editor

"Anything that makes the reader say, 'Gee Whiz!'"

—Arthur McEwen, *San Francisco Examiner* editorial writer

"What a chap who doesn't care much about anything wants to read."

—Corker, a character in Evelyn Waugh's novel *Scoop*

"Women, wampum, and wrongdoing."

—Stanley Walker, *New York Times* city editor

"Things that people don't want to be known."

—Nichols Tomalin, London *Sunday Times* writer

"What somebody somewhere wants to suppress. All the rest is advertising."

—Lord Northcliffe, *Times* of London owner[1]

BACKLOG

The *Boston News-Letter,* the first newspaper in the American colonies to publish more than once, printed European news in the order in which it was received. The volume of information quickly exceeded the allotted space. Rather than pruning the European news, John Campbell, the newspaper's publisher, allowed the backlog to grow. By 1718 he was more than a year behind; to catch up, he had to increase the newspaper's size.[2]

WASHINGTON'S ORDERS

During the Revolutionary War, General Washington communicated with his dispersed army via newspapers. Many papers published Washington's orders verbatim, particularly notices of courts-martial, which were intended to stiffen the resolve of troops. When the army occupied one region that lacked a satisfactory newspaper, Washington helped start the *New Jersey Gazette.*[3]

EASING MONDAYS

In the '20s, responding to criticism that it overemphasized stories of crime and other bad news, the *Boston Globe* instituted a policy of good-news Mondays. Except in extraordinary circumstances, the Monday morning lead story would be upbeat and "constructive." After a few years the bad-news critics stopped complaining and the practice died out.[4]

NO NEWS

President Johnson once complained to *Time* founder Henry Luce about the magazine's bad-news focus. "Look at this," LBJ said, waving a copy of *Time.* "This week two hundred thousand blacks registered in the South, thanks to the Voting Rights Act. Three hundred thousand elderly people are going to be covered by Medicare. We have a hundred thousand young unemployed kids working in neighborhoods. Is any of that in there? No." *Time* was reporting, Johnson added, only riots, Vietnam, and similar bad news.

"Mr. President," Luce replied, "good news isn't news. Bad news is news."[5]

BLACKOUTS: FRIENDS AND ENEMIES

- In the 1920s Senator Magnus Johnson of Minnesota walked into the Senate press gallery and delivered a blistering critique of the press. After he had left, the reporters agreed to stop mentioning Senator Johnson in their articles. The blackout caused Johnson, in the view of a contemporary observer, "inestimable" political damage.

- George Richards, who owned more than thirty radio stations in the 1940s, ordered his staff to carry only unfavorable items about President Franklin Roosevelt and his family.

- Walter Annenberg instructed editors at his *Philadelphia Inquirer* to kill any references to people he disliked. One person on "Annenberg's shit list," as reporters called it, was the president of the University of Pennsylvania. News stories referred to him simply as a "high university official." Another person on the list was Dinah Shore, whose popular program was identified only generically—"Variety Show"—in the *Inquirer* and in Annenberg's *TV Guide.* When the Philadelphia '76ers made the list, the *Inquirer* gave the team no pregame coverage and minimal postgame coverage.

- During the civil rights tensions of the '60s, NBC news executives imposed a ban on film of two black militants, Stokely Carmichael and H. Rap Brown, because of their inflammatory rhetoric.
- According to some Associated Press reporters, AP held back a story about possible wrongdoings by Colonel Oliver North of President Reagan's National Security Council staff. North and AP executives were meeting frequently to discuss the plight of Terry Anderson, an AP correspondent held hostage in Lebanon, and some AP reporters claimed that the wire service postponed its North story in order to maintain good relations with him. Executive editor Walter Mears denied the allegation.[6]

EVALUATING FATALITIES

When Susan Watson, a black reporter, joined the *Detroit Free Press* in 1965, she sometimes heard editors talk about a "cheap murder." It referred, she realized, to a black killing another black. Similarly, Robert Keane, a black reporter at the *New York Daily News* in the late '60s, noticed that editors asked two questions about fatal fires—how many people were dead, and what race they were. If the victims were black, Keane found, the story was less likely to get into the paper.[7]

BLACKOUTS: PRESS NEWS

- In 1893 Charles H. Taylor, Jr., business manager of the *Boston Globe* (and son of its owner), ordered editors never to mention the city's other newspapers in print.
- Diana McLellan, the *Washington Post*'s gossip columnist, tried three times to publish an item about the pregnancy of a Washington woman. Each time editors killed it. The pregnant woman was Sally Quinn, the wife of *Post* executive editor Ben Bradlee.
- In a summary of Supreme Court actions in 1973, *The New York Times* omitted one Court decision. The Justices had announced that they would not revive a paternity suit in

which the defendant was *Times* publisher Arthur Ochs Sulzberger.

- In 1983 the National News Council ruled that a *New York Times* article had "committed factual errors and presented information selectively." The *Times,* which had opposed the creation of the nonpartisan News Council and had refused to cooperate with it, ran no mention of the ruling.
- In 1987 *The New York Times* asked the declared presidential candidates to allow *Times* reporters to examine confidential FBI and CIA files about them. The candidates refused, and *Times* executives decided not to press the matter. Many articles were published about the controversy, but none in the *Times.*
- A 1985 regulatory ruling got almost no press coverage. The Occupational Safety and Health Administration had concluded that the oils in newspaper inks cause cancer and that ink barrels should include printed warnings.[8]

RESCINDED ORDER

In 1971 *Washington Post* columnist Maxine Cheshire wrote an item about Henry Kissinger's relationship with Judy Brown, an actress who had appeared in X-rated movies. As the final deadline approached, *Post* executive editor Ben Bradlee decided to kill the item. It was inappropriate, he said, for the *Post.*

Just then Kissinger called and pleaded with Bradlee not to publish anything about the woman. Bradlee hung up and told Cheshire to put the item back in. "If he is *that* concerned about it, and that upset about it," Bradlee said, "I think we should run it."[9]

WHERE'S NEWS

- One study of the network newscasts examined the amount of time devoted to different regions of the United States relative to their population. It found the Pacific to be the most overcovered, followed by the Northeast. Most undercovered was the Midwest.

- "A hundred Pakistanis going off a mountain in a bus make less of a story than three Englishmen drowning in the Thames." —Mort Rosenblum, former editor of the *International Herald Tribune*
- "A dogfight in Champa Street is better than a war abroad." —Saying among reporters at the *Denver Post,* which was situated on Champa Street[10]

THE NATION'S PULSE

The choice for lead story in *USA Today*'s September 15, 1982, inaugural edition was based on an informal survey undertaken by the newspaper's founder, Al Neuharth. Bashir Gemayel, the president-elect of Lebanon, had been murdered, and most *USA Today* editors assumed that story would lead the paper, as it did other papers across the country. But Monaco's Princess Grace had died in a car crash, and Neuharth suspected that her death was, for most Americans, the more important story.

To find out, he visited a bar and a political gathering. In both places nearly everyone was talking about Princess Grace. When Neuharth mentioned the Lebanon assassination, people shrugged. The next morning, *USA Today*'s lead story was headlined "America's Princess Grace dies in Monaco." Gemayel ended up on an inside page.[11]

REMARKS

"And I am sure that I never read any memorable news in a newspaper. If we read of one man robbed, or murdered, or killed by accident . . . we never need read another. One is enough. If you are acquainted with the principle, what do you care for a myriad instances and applications?"

—Henry David Thoreau[12]

"Surely ninety percent of all so-called news is old stuff, some of it two or three thousand years old. Public servants serve; felons act feloniously; demagogues croak their froggy tunes; echo answers echo. . . ."

—E. B. White[13]

"After I finished high school I went to Kansas City and worked on a paper. It was regular newspaper work: Who shot whom? Who broke into what? Where? When? How? But never Why, not really Why."

—Ernest Hemingway[14]

"The power to determine each day what shall be important and what shall be neglected is power unlike any that has been exercised since the Pope lost his hold on the secular mind."

—Walter Lippmann, columnist[15]

"Newspaper editors are men who separate the wheat from the chaff, and then print the chaff."

—Senator Adlai Stevenson[16]

LANGUAGE

. . . .

PASSIONLESS TIMES

In its first issue in 1851, *The New York Daily Times* (it later dropped "Daily") announced that it would avoid sensationalism: "We do not mean to write as if we were in a passion, unless that shall really be the case; and we shall make it a point to get into a passion as rarely as possible. There are very few things in this world which it is worth while to get angry about; and they are just the things that anger will not improve."[17]

KEEPING BENNETT HAPPY

After James Gordon Bennett, Jr., decreed that the word "Herald" must always appear in italics in his *New York Herald,* a holiday item referred to "Hark the *Herald* Angels Sing."[18]

CLOSE EDITING

On the English-language *Paris Herald* (the predecessor of the *International Herald Tribune*), British copy editor Eric Hawkins once changed a slang phrase in an American reporter's article: "So's your old man" became "Your father is also."[19]

WHAT'S GAY

In 1981 free-lance reporter Sidney Zion wrote this lead for an article about the resurgence of big-band jazz: "Between the rock and the hard disco, the melody began to slip back in. A piano bar here, a big band there, a touch of Gershwin, a spot of Kern. In gay places and out of the way places."

An editor at *The New York Times Magazine* told Zion that, according to the *Times* stylebook, the last sentence had to be changed to "In homosexual places and out of the way places." Zion complained that the change wrecked the meter and shifted the tone. The editor replied that if Zion meant "happy," "gay" could stay; but if he meant sexual preference, it had to be "homosexual."

"They knew very well what I meant," Zion later said, "but I said 'Okay, if that makes you feel better.' " The sentence was printed as Zion had written it.[20]

NEW WORDS

- Columnist Walter Winchell coined a number of words and phrases. In *The American Language,* H. L. Mencken catalogued them and predicted that several would permanently enter the language. Winchellisms include

Chicagorilla (gangster), *moompitcher* (moving picture), *wildeman* (homosexual), *giggle water* (liquor), *radiodor* (radio announcer), *debutramp, infanticipating, messer of ceremonies, make whoopee, blessed event,* and *intelligentleman.*

- Another gossip column invention is *jet set,* the creation of Igor Cassini of the *New York Journal-American.*
- In addition to onomatopoeia *(bam, glug, grr, oof, whap),* comic strips invented or popularized such words as *piker* ("Mutt and Jeff"), *dingbat* ("The Dingbat Family"), *jeep* ("Popeye"), *G.I. Joe* ("Private Breger"), and *heebie-jeebies* ("Barney Google").
- Finley Peter Dunne, at the time a sportswriter for the *Chicago Telegram* (later the creator of the savvy saloonkeeper Mr. Dooley), coined *southpaw.*
- Frank Ward O'Malley, a reporter for the *New York Sun* at the turn of the century, created *brunch.*
- In politics, journalists have coined *cold war* (Herbert Bayard Swope, executive editor of the *New York World*), *egghead* (columnist Stewart Alsop), and *hawks and doves* (Stewart Alsop and Charles Bartlett).[21]

REVISED SPELLING

Starting in 1934, the *Chicago Tribune* adopted phonetic spellings for some words, including *frate, tho, thru, telegraf,* and *geografy.* The new style was flexible: When readers complained about one phonetic spelling, *iland* (some said it reminded them of an African antelope), the newspaper restored the *s.* "[T]he same kind of people who today fuss about *frate,*" an editorial said, "used to throw fits about *honor* and *labor,* which, they thought, must be spelled *honour* and *labour.* Maybe in a few years, people will think *freight* is a silly way to spell the word."

After more than twenty years, phonetic spelling still wasn't catching on and the *Tribune* abandoned its campaign. An editorial in 1955 said that the newspaper had stopped using the phonetic spellings a week earlier. "To our surprise," it continued, "not one reader, so far as we are aware, noticed. . . ."[22]

EMPLOYE

In early 1988 the *Washington Post* announced that it was shifting a spelling, from *employe* to *employee. Employe* had generated thousands of complaints, but, a *Post* editor remarked, it had also saved newsprint: Had the newspaper used *employee* over the past ten years, the additional *e*'s would have taken up an extra 185 pages.[23]

MR. AT THE SUN

A *Baltimore Sun* article on the philosophy of music followed the stylebook rule that every man's name requires a "Mr." Among the results were Mr. Augustine, Mr. Beethoven, and Mr. Plato.[24]

MS. AT THE TIMES

In 1986 *The New York Times* bowed to feminist pressure and began permitting the title "Ms." to appear in news columns, prompting Gloria Steinem to say "I will no longer be referred to as Miss Steinem of *Ms.* magazine."[25]

LOADED WORDS

In 1970 women writers on the *Washington Post* protested the sexism that they said was implicit in many of the newspaper's features. To make the point, they distributed the following:

> Ben Bradlee, slim, attractive, but complex executive editor of the *Washington Post,* is 49 years old today, but he doesn't look it. How does he manage to combine a successful career with the happy home life he has created in his gracious Georgetown home?

In an interview today, pert, vivacious Mr. Bradlee revealed his secret. He relaxes after a day of whirlwind activity of the newspaper world by whomping up a batch of his favorite pecan-sauerbraten cookies for his thriving family. . . .

What does Mrs. Bradlee think of her debonair husband's flair for journalism? "I think it's great," she said. "Every wife should let her husband work. It makes him so well-rounded. Now he has something to talk about at the dinner table."

She appreciates the extra effort he takes to maintain his youthful looks and figure despite his busy, busy day. Mr. Bradlee loves his work, but he is aware of the dangers involved. So far he does not feel that he is in competition with his wife.

"When that day comes," he said with a shudder, "I'll know it's time to quit."

Mr. Bradlee's quick and easy recipe for pecan-sauerbraten cookies appears in tomorrow's bulletin.[26]

WORD CHOICES

- *New Yorker* press critic A. J. Liebling noted that in newspaper coverage of strike stories, management makes *offers* and labor makes *demands.*
- Some colorful writing, CBS correspondent Daniel Schorr suggested, must end at the water's edge. "I know that if I refer in a broadcast to 'Crusty old Chancellor Adenauer,' that will be regarded as vivid writing," he wrote. "And if I refer to 'Crusty old General Eisenhower,' I'll soon be hearing about it. Objectivity varies with geography."
- In covering a dictator, the choice of adjectives may depend on the ruler's political orientation, in the view of Alexander Cockburn of the *Nation.* "If he is one of *our* dictators," Cockburn wrote, "then use words like *dynamic, strong man, able.* He *laughs* a great deal, is always *on the move, in a hurry.* . . . If, on the other hand, he is one of *their* dictators, then use words like *unstable, brooding,*

erratic, bloodthirsty, indolent. He seldom ventures out of his palace unless under *heavy guard.* He is *rumored to be ailing.*"[27]

MORE CLICHÉS, PLEASE

A UPI editor argued that newspapers would publish the wire service's stories more often if the writers used more clichés. "The AP is much better than we are at getting the good old cliché buzz words in their leads," Gerry Loughran, UPI's foreign editor, instructed his staff in 1980. "Editors feel comfortable with them. They look for them." As examples he cited *deadline, ultimatum, landslide, reverse, defeat, setback,* and *victory.*[28]

JOURNALESE

Paul Dickson, a Maryland lexicographer, has catalogued and explained some of the terms that often appear in news stories:

> *Blue ribbon:* Phrase applied to any panel or commission containing a former governor of Pennsylvania.
>
> *Little-known:* Used when a reporter is showing off and saying, "Here is something I know, but you don't." Example: "This violates the provisions of a little-known law that prohibits the reuse of cat-food cans."
>
> *Presumably:* Code word telling the reader that the writer is about to make a wild guess.
>
> *Reputed:* Known to all living things, as in the phrases "reputed Mafia kingpin" or "reputed underworld chieftain."
>
> *Wag:* Almost always used when the writer quotes his own cynical or funny line. "As one city-hall wag observed, 'It was the first time an alderman had been seen with his hands in his own pockets since last winter's cold snap.' "
>
> *Watershed:* Important. Usually applied to whatever political race or piece of legislation a reporter is assigned. "A

watershed bill now before the legislature would, for the first time in the history of the state, make it illegal to sell night crawlers without a permit."[29]

SIMPLIFY

In the mid-1950s *The New York Times* tried to get reporters to write shorter, simpler sentences. Turner Catledge, the managing editor, told reporters to imagine that they were writing letters to a "curious but somewhat dumb younger brother." In *Winners and Sinners,* the paper's in-house newsletter, Theodore M. Bernstein instructed writers to limit themselves to one idea per sentence. Another *Times* editor, Lester Markel, replied by memo: "I have read your edition of Winners & Sinners. It is a special edition. It interests me. No end."[30]

REMARKS

"I never write metropolis *for seven cents, because I can get the same price for* city. *I never write* policeman, *because I can get the same money for* cop.*"*

—Mark Twain on being paid by the word[31]

"Journalism is a license to dabble at the margins of great writing, without the risks."

—Robert MacNeil, PBS *MacNeil-Lehrer Newshour* coanchor[32]

"New clichés are being made—shouldn't we be making them?"

—Harry Rosenfeld, *Washington Post* national editor, on the search for new metaphors in journalism[33]

HEADLINES AND COVERS

....

HISTORY IN HEADLINES

"The TIMES are / Dreadful / Dismal / Doleful / Dolorous, and / DOLLAR-LESS"

—*Pennsylvania Journal and Weekly Advertiser*'s final edition in 1765, after the passage of the Stamp Act

"AWFUL EVENT"

—*New York Times'* top-most headline on Lincoln's assassination

"HOW DO YOU LIKE THE JOURNAL'S WAR?"

—*New York Journal* on the Spanish-American War, 1898; the newspaper had been noisily lobbying for war

"WALL STREET LAYS AN EGG"

—*Variety* on the 1929 stock market crash

"HUMPHREY IN A SHAMBLES"

—*Chicago Daily News* on the raucous 1968 Democratic convention

"FORD TO CITY: DROP DEAD"

—*New York Daily News* on
President Ford's 1976
decision not to use federal
funds to alleviate New York
City's fiscal crisis[34]

MISCOMMUNICATION

When President Carter called for economic self-discipline, a *Boston Globe* editor looked over the newspaper's editorial on the subject and jokingly suggested a headline. Someone thought he was serious, and in the *Globe's* early edition the editorial appeared under the headline "Mush from the wimp."[35]

DULLEST HEADLINE

The reporters who worked nights at the London *Times* in the '30s amused themselves with competitions for the dullest imaginable headline. Claud Cockburn won one round with this: "Small Earthquake in Chile / Not Many Dead."[36]

TABLOID WORDS

A 1987 computer analysis found that these words most frequently appear in *New York Post* headlines (in descending order): COP, KILL, JUDGE, WALL STREET, DEATH, NO, SLAY, U.S., SOVIET, COURT.

A British tabloid editor provided a different list of his top headline words: FREE, SEX, WIN. "If we could just say WIN FREE SEX," said the *Star*'s Nigel Blundell, "we'd really have it made."[37]

NOTABLE HEADLINES AND TEASERS

"Sum Fu Wurds, Fonetic, As Tu the Nu Spelin"

—*Washington Post* on
Theodore Roosevelt's effort
to simplify spelling

"BRONX MAN LEADS RUSSIAN REVOLUTION"

—*Bronx Home News* on the November 1917 revolution; Leon Trotsky had lived in the Bronx for three months

"CHARGES GINA WAS OBSCENA ON LA SCREENA"

—*New York Daily News* on Gina Lollobrigida's 1967 Italian prosecution for indecency

"Rocky Won't Roll"

—*Boston Globe* on Nelson Rockefeller's withdrawal from the 1960 presidential campaign

"Castro Narrowly Escapes Drowning: Too Bad! Too Bad! Too Bad! Too Bad!"

—*El Paso Times*

"Hirohito Dead, Joins Hitler in Hell"

—Everett, Massachusetts, *Leader Herald-News Gazette*

"HEADLESS BODY IN TOPLESS BAR"

—*New York Post*

"Sheik, your booty!"

—*NBC Overnight* teaser on judge's ruling about Sheik Al Fassi's alimony debt

"Male genitals found on railroad track. Stay tuned to the eleven o'clock news for details."

—News teaser during prime time on KGO-TV, San Francisco[38]

REMARKS

"My favorite word is 'coed.' When you see coed, people want to buy the paper. I don't know why—just some young, innocent girl getting into a lot of trouble."

—Vincent Musetto, *New York Post* headline writer[39]

"If the headline is big enough, it makes *the news big enough."*

—Charles Foster Kane[40]

THE NEWS PRESENTATION

....

READERS AS WRITERS

Early newspapers were often passed from person to person. Some papers contained one or more blank pages, which a subscriber could fill with his own news before sending the newspaper on to friends.[41]

PRIVATIONS

In the mid-nineteenth century, when the price of newsprint shot up, some printers published their newspapers on sacks, wrapping paper, tissue paper, and the blank side of wallpaper.[42]

MYSTERY

Starting in 1899 and continuing for nearly twenty years, the *New York Herald* published this letter every day on its editorial page:

> To the Editor of the *Herald*:
>
> I am anxious to find out the way to figure the temperature from centigrade to Fahrenheit and vice versa. In other words, I want to know, whenever I see the temperature designated on the centigrade thermometer, how to find out what it would be on Fahrenheit's thermometer.
>
> Old Philadelphia Lady
> Paris, December 24, 1899

The publisher, James Gordon Bennett, Jr., never told anyone why he kept reprinting the letter.[43]

TIMES MOTTO

In the late 1890s Adolph Ochs, owner of *The New York Times,* decided that the newspaper deserved a better motto than "All the News That's Fit to Print," Ochs's own creation. He announced a contest and offered a hundred-dollar prize. The winner was "All the World's News, But Not a School for Scandal." Ochs paid the prize money but decided to leave the old motto in place after all. When someone asked him just what news was *not* fit to print, he replied, "What's untrue."[44]

MOTTOS

"This is Published to Prevent False Reports"

—*The Present State of New-English Affairs*

"It Shines for ALL"

—*New York Sun*

"The World's Greatest Newspaper"

—Chicago Tribune

"America's Greatest Evening Newspaper"

—New York Journal

"To Injure No Man But to Bless All Mankind"

—Christian Science Monitor

"An eight-page journal containing statements almost TOO GOOD TO BE TRUE"

—Danbury (Connecticut) *News*

"The Paper With a Heart and Soul"

—Denver Post

"The Newspaper You Can Spend an Evening With"

—New York World Journal Tribune

"Independent in All Things, Neutral in Nothing"

—San Francisco Chronicle

"A Relatively Independent Newspaper"

—Bettendorf (Iowa) *News*

"Not For Love, Honor, or Fame, But For Cash"

—Marble Hill (Indiana) *Era*

"The Only Newspaper in the World That Gives a Damn About Jacksonville, N.C."

—*Jacksonville Daily News*[45]

REVERE'S LEGACY

In the days before broadcasting, the *Boston Globe* borrowed a technique from Paul Revere, instructing readers to watch the tower spotlight on the Boston custom house for the latest election results. In 1916, for example, the *Globe* announced that one flash every thirty seconds would mean that President Wilson had been reelected; two flashes, that Charles Evans Hughes had won; and three flashes, that the election was too close to call.[46]

COMPOSOGRAPHS

In the '20s the *New York Graphic* (motto: "Nothing But the Truth") invented the "composograph," a genuine-looking photo of a restaged news event. Reporters or professional models would pose for the photographer, and then an art director would superimpose celebrities' faces on the photo. With composographs the *Graphic* was able to show a wealthy real estate magnate shouting "Woof! Woof! Don't be a goof!" at his fifteen-year-old bride (their pet goose interjects "Honk! Honk! It's the bonk!"); a showgirl bathing in champagne while Broadway producer Earl Carroll and others look on; and Enrico Caruso greeting Rudolph Valentino in Heaven. For its composographs and other sensationalist antics, the *Graphic* was nicknamed the *Porno-Graphic.*[47]

HYPING ACCIDENTS

At auto accidents, newsreel camera crews would sometimes pour several gallons of water on the roadway before filming. In black-and-white film, water looked like blood.[48]

MURDER ANGLE

Following diet doctor Herbert Tarnower's murder, a *New York Post* writer urged publisher Rupert Murdoch to begin running excerpts of Tarnower's book in a series called "Dr. Tarnower's Diet Tips from the Grave." The idea was not pursued.[49]

TASTE

....

1830s Standards

James Gordon Bennett's *New York Herald* was criticized for violating community mores when it published the words *shirt, leg,* and *trousers,* rather than the preferred *linen, limb,* and *unmentionables.*[50]

GREELEY'S POLICY

As a young New York editor, Horace Greeley enforced strict standards of taste. In the weekly *New-Yorker* in the 1830s, Greeley announced: "We do not care to publish accounts of murders except where they can be made to tell against that infernal scourge of the country—ardent spirits." Suicides, too, had to be alcohol-related to get into the *New-Yorker.* A typical one read: "A man by the name of Tibbetts, a short time since, jumped into eternity and the Kennebec River at one and the same time! Cause, intemperance."

Greeley maintained his righteous approach at the *New York Tribune,* which he founded in 1841. He banned "immoral and degrading police reports" from the paper. Newspapers that published such reports were, he wrote, "the Satanic Press" that "pander[s] to whatever is vile and bestial in a corrupted and sensual populace." He also denounced the theater as unwholesome, writing that "a large proportion of those connected with the stage are libertines or courtesans." The *Tribune* initially refused to accept theater advertisements, but Greeley's business partners convinced him that the newspaper needed the revenue.[51]

COUNTERPROGRAMMING

As a contrast to the yellow journalism of the *World* and the *Journal* at the turn of the century, *The New York Times* promoted itself by advertising "It does not soil the breakfast cloth."[52]

DOUBLE STANDARD

Later, when someone asked *New York Times* owner Adolph Ochs why the *Times* was devoting as much space as the tabloid *Daily News* to a grisly slaying, Ochs explained: "If a tabloid prints that sort of thing, it's smut; but when the *New York Times* prints it, it's a sociological study."[53]

OFFICIAL CODES

In the 1910s and 1920s, several newspapers and press associations promulgated codes of professional conduct. Among the provisions:

"A newspaper cannot escape conviction of insincerity if while professing high moral purpose it supplies incentives to base conduct, such as are to be found in details of crime and vice. . . ."

—American Society of
Newspaper Editors

"Don't use the words 'murder,' 'scandal,' 'divorce,' 'crime,' and other rather offensive phrases when it is possible to tell the story without them."

—William Randolph Hearst's
instructions to his editors

"The physiology of conception and childbirth and all matters relating thereto will not be discussed in the columns of The Times."

—*Seattle Times*

"Be extremely careful of the name and reputation of women. Even when dealing with the unfortunate, remember that so long as she commits no crime other than her own sin against chastity, she is entitled at least to pity."

—Sacramento Bee

"No story is worth ruining a woman's life."

—Detroit News[54]

SELECTING BEST-SELLERS

In the 1950s and early 1960s the *Chicago Tribune* published "Among the Best Sellers," instead of a list of all best-sellers, so that editor Don Maxwell could omit risqué books like *Tropic of Cancer* and *The Carpetbaggers.*[55]

RETOUCHING

After D-Day, many newspapers published a photo of Normandy Beach showing a dead soldier in the foreground. In the *Christian Science Monitor* the photo was retouched so that the body became a log.[56]

WEDDING KISS

Alongside its story about the Marilyn Monroe–Joe DiMaggio wedding, *The New York Times* ran a photo of Monroe and DiMaggio about to kiss. The next day John Randolph, the photo editor who had selected the picture, was told he was being demoted to copyreader. The photo, showing Monroe's open mouth, was too indecent for the *Times.*[57]

PAGE THREE

Page three of Rupert Murdoch's London *Sun* regularly features a photo of a topless woman. Murdoch thought about introducing the same feature to his *New York Post,* but his wife objected so strongly that he dropped the idea.[58]

FORBIDDEN NUMBER

A *Los Angeles Times* headline in 1972 read "70-Car Fog Pileup." In fact, sixty-nine cars had crashed. An editor changed it, reasoning that sixty-nine was a smutty number.[59]

ALTERED MOVIE AND PLAY ADS

- When the Yale Drama School presented *'Tis Pity She's a Whore* in 1967, the *New Haven Register* ran ads for *'Tis Pity She's Bad.* In the *Hartford Courant* it became simply *'Tis Pity She's.*
- In 1975 the *Buffalo Evening News* changed *The Happy Hooker* to *The Happy Hoofer.*
- A different concern motivated a South Carolina newspaper, the *Spartanburg Herald-Journal,* to alter an ad for the 1975 movie *Mandingo.* The original ad showed a black man embracing a white woman and a white man holding a black woman. The *Herald-Journal* cut and pasted in order to unmix the races.
- The 1986 movie version of David Mamet's play *Sexual Perversity in Chicago* was called *About Last Night. . . .* The production company had found that many newspapers and TV stations would refuse to advertise anything with "sexual perversity" in the title.
- In 1987 several newspapers, including *The New York Times* and the *Los Angeles Times,* sliced the last two words off the title of the movie *Sammy and Rosie Get Laid.*
- The *Chicago Sun-Times, Dallas Morning News,* and *San Francisco Examiner,* among other papers, refused to publish the ad slogan of Stanley Kubrick's 1987 film *Full Metal Jacket:* "In Vietnam, the wind doesn't blow—it sucks."[60]

BUTZ'S FAREWELL

In 1976 Earl Butz, the secretary of agriculture, resigned after it was widely publicized that he had made a racist remark.

Butz's statement had been: "I'll tell you what coloreds want. It's three things: first, a tight pussy; second, loose shoes; and third, a warm place to shit."

Most people watched Butz make his exit without knowing exactly what he had said. The Associated Press sent out the uncensored quotation but, according to *Columbia Journalism Review,* only two newspapers printed it: Wisconsin's *Madison Capital Times* and Ohio's *Toledo Blade.* Other newspapers said Butz had derogatorily described blacks' "sexual, dress, and bathroom predilections," or that he had said "a tight [obscenity] . . . a warm place to [vulgarism]," or otherwise cleaned up the language. ("Courageously," David Shaw of the *Los Angeles Times* commented, ". . . no editors dropped 'shoes' from Butz' remarks and substituted 'an article of footwear.' ")

Two newspapers provided ways for readers to see Butz's uncensored remarks. The *Lubbock Avalanche-Journal* in Texas announced that the original statement was available in the newspaper office, and more than two hundred people came to read it. The *San Diego Evening Tribune* offered to mail a copy to anyone who requested it, and more than three thousand people did so.

Some editors explained that Butz's office wasn't high enough to justify waiving the usual policy against printing obscenities. Ben Bradlee said the *Washington Post* would publish an obscenity spoken by a president or vice president, but "it gets harder and harder when you come to cabinet members" like Butz. At *The New York Times,* executive editor A. M. Rosenthal said, "We'll take 'shit' from the president of the United States, but from nobody else."[61]

"ASS" POLICY

In 1980, when President Carter said that if Ted Kennedy ran for President, "I'll whip his ass," *The New York Times* replaced *ass* with dashes. Four years later, when Vice President Bush said of his debate with Geraldine Ferraro, "We tried to kick a little ass," the *Times* reported that Bush had spoken "a locker-room vulgarity." But when the commander of the Iran rescue mission said he hadn't wanted to be part of a "half-assed" mission, the *Times* published the remark as spoken. Some reporters concluded that an ass isn't fit to print, but half an ass is.[62]

REMARKS

"A newspaper can send more souls to Heaven, and save more from Hell, than all the churches or chapels in New York—besides making money at the same time. Let it be tried."

—James Gordon Bennett in his year-old *New York Herald,* 1836[63]

"I want this paper to be so conducted that it can go into any home without destroying the innocence of any child."

—Warren G. Harding, publisher of Ohio's *Marion Star* and future President[64]

"Newspapers are read at the breakfast and dinner tables. God's great gift to man is appetite. Put nothing in the paper that will destroy it."

—William Rockhill Nelson, *Kansas City Star* founder[65]

"Whatever Divine Providence permits to occur I am not too proud to report."

—Charles A. Dana, editor of the *New York Sun*[66]

"When you run a picture of a nice clean-cut all American girl like this, get her tits above the fold."

—Al Neuharth, founder of *USA Today,* at a page-one meeting[67]

II

NEWS BEATS

nvicted on
ad been impli-
ifferies, the for-
kerage firm that
Jefferies agreed
curities law viola-
e with the Govern-
on of crime on Wall
as implicated by Mr.

ent charged that Mr.
millions of dollars by
stock in takeover tar-
his ownership in those
y using secret accounts
& Company, a West Coast
and later selling his hold-
he stock price had risen.

x Losses

zerian is al
ud for eng
n two securi
sses. The ch
Mr. Bilzer

Jersey when a became a
en Auto Body City heard a Superior Court
ue a restraining Body's lawyer to have the request from
om entering order preventing
en Towing. Judge James Dow-
into an agreement
he request, but scheduled
ve the matter

ASHINGT
Federal
approve
ver Tru
New Y
acco
ne of

contract specifications.
The city's response to the alle-
that when it rejected Hoboken
sole bid on the contract
because it thought
favorable offer
tised, and
bid

ing could comply
The Goldome offices that Manu-
turers Hanover is acquiring in
York, Nassau, Orange and Su-
counties hold total deposits of
billion.

In approving the purchase, th
rejected arguments that Manuf
ers Hanover had failed to me
credit needs of low- and moder
come communities, primar
klyn. The complaint was
the Workers of
ociation of Con
s for Reform No

The Fed said
greed to
its
of drug profit
ons."
detection i
enormou
the general
border.

r. charges
e, Peabody & Company, and the
ertson & Company, as well as a
ermill Paper Company, involving securities
ock transaction
f Armco Inc.

rison and $2.25 mil-
case was the first
illegal stock parking,
ership of securities is
avoid disclosure or other

erian was charged with two
securities fraud, five counts
false statements with the
nment and two counts of con-

Worth Put at $81 Million

Yesterday's sentence capped the
undoing of the career of a man who
appeared seemingly from nowhere to
engineer some of the most lucrative
that should
ing to cooperate.

ek

ls are scheduled to
and are expected to
the subcommittee
ministration's views
g Canadian problem.
National Drug Control
s directed by William
pected to announce the
committee next month
ional and domestic
The

form the basis for policy
regulatory recommend

ted States, banks
r currency transac
re than $10,00
uch law.
st year Ca
it permit
assets
or conv
The new law
ering a crime
Canada, though
believe the
as effective as those in
United States.

Several recent investigations have
disclosed significant ties between
money laundering operations by drug
dealers in the United States and Latin
America who have made use of Cana
dian banks, many of which ha
branches throughout Latin Ame
Federal authorities say that C
tion Polar Cap, the largest
laundering investigation in A
history, uncovered more th
lion that was laundered
month period, some of
through banks in Toro

Panama Bank Conv

In that case, Ca
authorities

Years of Publicizing Report

The report, which officials of the
drug agency said they had hoped to
keep confidential out of
publicity would further
drug traffickers to use
banks, came to light at
the Senate Foreign Rela
mittee's subcommittee o
narcotics and internat
tions. John F. Kerry, a M
Democrat who is chai
committee, obtained a c
port and cited it as
friendly country whose
thumbing their noses a
banki

Continued From

he wrote. "I wish I co
the clock of time and
ever mistakes I may hav
a statement to the court,
rian said his letter was he
declined to say anything fur
However, Judge Ward sa
lieved Mr. Bilzerian had be
guided by the desire for mon
had begun to misrepresent the
to obtain it.

'In Short, He Lies'

"I have no doubt that in his
years, he has done good things f
other people, but there is another sid
to the defendant," Judge Ward said.
"The allure of money has caused him
to lose what I believe to be proper
perspective. In short, he lies."
Judge Ward added that the case
was "replete with false documents"
that supported his opinion.
While Mr. Bilzerian was not
charged with perjury, a Federal
judge can be permitted to consider
such a possibility when announcing
sentence.

During his testimony
spoke as though
about

5

LAWMAKERS AND OFFICIALS

EARLY DIGS

John Peter Zenger's libel prosecution in 1734 came about partly because of mock advertisements and announcements that belittled politicians. One advertisement in Zenger's *New York Weekly Journal* asked readers to help locate a lost spaniel. The ad's description of the dog, as it happened, closely matched the appearance of a governor's aide. Another jab was an item in the *Journal*'s listing of ships and their cargoes, announcing the arrival of a "choice parcel of new authorities" imported from "God knows where."[1]

BOSS TWEED AND THE *TIMES*

In the 1870s New York City's Tweed ring tried repeatedly to buy the silence of *The New York Times.* When the newspaper started its crusade against William Marcy Tweed, making daily references to the "swindlers" and "thieves" who worked for him, Tweed's men first tried to buy the newspaper outright.

Publisher George Jones refused to sell. *"No money,"* he thundered in an editorial, could buy a single share of the *Times* for the Tweed ring.

Soon the *Times* began publishing financial records that showed precisely how Tweed had swindled the city government. Tweed's men tried again, this time proposing a bribe instead of a purchase. Richard B. Connolly, the city comptroller, made the offer to the publisher. "Wouldn't it be worth, say, five million dollars, Mr. Jones, to let up on this thing? Five million dollars, sir!"

Jones answered, "I don't think that the devil will ever bid higher for me than that."

Connolly interpreted the response as a sign of interest. "Think of what you could do with five million dollars! Why, you could go to Europe and live like a prince."

"True, sir," Jones replied. "But I should know while I lived like a prince, that I was a rascal."

The *Times* continued its exposé and then reprinted the articles along with supporting evidence in a special supplement. A citizens' committee, spurred on by the *Times* articles, initiated an investigation. Tweed was indicted, convicted, and imprisoned. "The theory that government is only organized robbery," a *Times* editorial asserted, "has received its death blow."[2]

LONG'S THANKS

In the 1930s Louisiana police sometimes pulled cars to the side of the highway, not to issue tickets but to urge drivers to subscribe to the *New Orleans Tribune.* The policemen carried subscription forms, with which they could sign people up on the spot. The campaign was Governor Huey Long's way of thanking the newspaper for its friendly coverage.[3]

SPACE FOR SALE

In 1935 scores of reporters descended on Flemington, New Jersey, for Bruno Richard Hauptmann's trial on charges of kidnapping and murdering Charles Lindbergh's baby. The local sheriff charged each reporter ten dollars for admission.

The money, he said, was needed to pay for the press bleachers he had installed in the courtroom.[4]

CLOAKROOM ASSAULT

At Washington's Sulgrave Club in 1950, Senator Joseph McCarthy ran into columnist Drew Pearson, one of the press's strongest McCarthy critics. McCarthy said that he planned to deliver a speech from the Senate floor, where he would be immune from a defamation lawsuit, that would "put Pearson out of business." Pearson replied, "Joe, have you paid your income taxes yet?" McCarthy challenged Pearson to step outside. Pearson declined. Later, during dinner, McCarthy slipped behind Pearson and, in passing, grabbed him by the neck.

In the cloakroom after dinner McCarthy struck harder, though accounts differ as to just how hard. McCarthy said he gave Pearson a light slap. Pearson said McCarthy kicked him twice in the groin and then began punching his head. Senator Richard Nixon, who broke up the fight, agreed with Pearson's account. Nixon later said that if he hadn't intervened, the columnist might have been killed.

Afterward several senators congratulated McCarthy. One said he had heard two different stories as to where Pearson had been hit, and he hoped both were accurate.[5]

"RUDE PISSANT"

In 1955 Senate Majority Leader Lyndon Johnson announced that he would hold a news conference at his Texas ranch. Dan Rather, then a reporter for a Houston TV station, shared a ride to the LBJ Ranch with a fellow reporter. After an hour Johnson hadn't appeared, and Rather decided to call his station for guidance.

Someone told him there was a phone just inside Johnson's house. Rather slipped in an open door and called the station. He told his boss that LBJ might have decided to postpone the news conference a few hours so the morning papers would play it more prominently.

Just then the phone was grabbed out of Rather's hand. He turned and saw Senator Johnson, who bellowed into the phone: "This is Lyndon Johnson. I don't know who the hell you are, and I damned well don't know who this rude pissant is. But I can tell you this: He doesn't belong here, I'm throwing his ass out, what he just told you is bullshit and if you use it, I'll sue you." Rather ran from the house and continued down the road at top speed.

Several minutes later a white Lincoln Continental pulled alongside him, and Lady Bird Johnson leaned out. "Whatever he said," she shouted, "he didn't mean anything by it, honey. It's just his way." Rather got in, and she drove him back for the news conference.[6]

PUBLISHER'S CONTRIBUTION

In 1971 the publisher of the *Boston Globe,* Davis Taylor, gave Congressman Thomas P. "Tip" O'Neill's campaign five hundred dollars and asked that he not be identified as a contributor. O'Neill complied by putting the money in an account that was exempt from disclosure requirements.

A short time later a *Boston Globe* reporter called O'Neill and asked for the names of contributors to the account. O'Neill refused. The *Globe* ran a story under the headline: "O'NEILL 'HID' CAMPAIGN NAMES IN LEGAL D.C. LIST." Troubled by the implication of wrongdoing, O'Neill sent the list of contributors to *Globe* publisher Taylor. "You have my permission," O'Neill wrote, "to use it—in full—or give it to any other newspaper." The list remained unpublished.[7]

A RUMOR'S GENEALOGY

In early 1981 (a few weeks before President Reagan was shot), a half-dozen news organizations pursued the same remarkable story: Vice President George Bush had been wounded and, for some reason, the government was engaged in a huge cover-up. The story originated, according to a *Washington Post* analysis, late one night when a Capitol Hill woman heard a car accident. She ran to the street to see if she could help. There she heard a policeman say that the Vice President had been shot. She went back to her apartment and turned on the television for a bulletin, but none came. She called reporters at the *Post* and a TV station to ask what had happened. Her story came as news to them.

The rumor gained in strength. Everyone the woman called passed the story on to other people, who passed it on to still others. By different streams it kept coming back to reporters, and the repetitions seemed like confirmation. Misunderstandings further amplified the rumor. When two *Post* reporters visited a police official, he insisted that no such incident had occurred. But the reporters saw on his notepad Bush's name, a date and place, and "assault," and they concluded that the official was part of the cover-up. In fact, the jottings concerned a call from another reporter chasing the rumor. Groups of reporters staked out the townhouse owned by the original source of the story. Increasingly nervous about her role in an apparent scandal, she stopped answering questions and then went into hiding. That too struck reporters as reliable evidence of a cover-up.

As the rumor passed from person to person, it split into several variations. In one version, Bush had been emerging from his supposed mistress's townhouse (hence the cover-up) when a mugger shot and wounded him. In another version it was the mugger, wrestling with Bush, who had been wounded by a Secret Service agent.

By this time, although nothing had been published or broadcast, the story was being pursued by CBS, NBC, *Newsweek, Time, The New York Times,* and the *Post.* Questions about it had arisen at the daily White House press briefing. The tale had become, Bush's press secretary Peter Teeley said, "cocktail talk" all over Washington. Bush, angry and frustrated, arranged for the FBI to interview him in order to make his adamant denials part of an official record. Bush's wife Barbara suggested an additional step. The Vice President, she said, should stand naked before a news conference and let reporters see for themselves that he hadn't been wounded. "He was not amused," she later said.

Finally the *Post* convinced the Capitol Hill woman to talk. She told what she knew—that she had heard a policeman say that Bush had been shot, but that she hadn't seen anything herself. The policeman, contacted by the *Post,* said, "I didn't say it and I didn't hear it." In a front-page article the *Post* debunked the story. "As far as anyone can go in proving a negative," the *Post* said, "the story has no basis whatsoever."[8]

SHAPING COVERAGE

- Chicago Mayor Richard J. Daley made a practice of announcing news conferences only a few moments before they took place, in order to keep reporters close to the press office and away from potentially damaging sources elsewhere.

- George Regan, the press secretary to Boston Mayor Kevin White, would sometimes tell a TV reporter about a secret meeting involving top city officials. The reporter and camera crew would burst in, and Regan would eject them. From the episode the reporter would get a few seconds of dramatic film and new respect from his bosses for his investigative abilities; Regan would get the reporter's gratitude and a brief TV appearance.

- In 1988 Mayor Marion Barry of Washington tried, through intermediaries, to make a deal with *Washington Post* columnist Carl Rowan. According to Rowan, he was told that if he would stop accusing the city administration of corruption in his column, then the city would drop charges pending against him for possessing an unregistered weapon. (Rowan had used the gun to wound a trespasser.) Rowan refused the offer. His trial ended in a hung jury, and the prosecutor decided not to hold a second trial. Afterward Rowan said that "my column and my commentaries are not for sale to any craven politician."

- New York Governor Mario Cuomo told *New York Times* reporter Jeffrey Schmalz: "I could end your career. Your publisher doesn't even know who you are."

- Before his 1988 impeachment, Arizona Governor Evan Mecham decided that a troublesome reporter no longer existed. When *Phoenix Gazette* columnist John Kolbe asked questions at the governor's news conferences, Mecham behaved as if no one had spoken and waited for the next question. On one occasion another reporter repeated Kolbe's question. Mecham abruptly ended the news conference and walked out.

- In 1965 the State Department gave reporters a background paper alleging that Communists had influenced the rebellion in the Dominican Republic. The paper's ground rules were unorthodox. "There should be no direct quoting of it," an attached note said, "meaning you can use the language that appears in front of you but it should not be put in quotes. It is not to be called a document. It is not an official paper and should not be regarded as such. You should not use the word 'document.' "
- Congress has declared one area of the Capitol building off-limits to photographers: the doorway to the House floor, where lobbyists stand behind a rope and use hand signals to tell members of Congress how to vote.[9]

KISSINGER RULES

As Secretary of State, Henry Kissinger routinely briefed the reporters who covered his trips abroad, but he insisted that he be identified as a "senior U.S. official."

Some reporters dropped clues in their stories. On CBS radio, Bob Schieffer referred to the mysterious official "who often shows up in various parts of the world where Henry Kissinger is visiting," an official who "knows a lot about foreign policy." On another occasion CBS described the senior official as stout and wearing glasses. In the *Boston Globe,* William Beecher wrote that "the senior U.S. official was last seen entering a long black limousine with Nancy Kissinger."

The "senior U.S. official" bowed out during Kissinger's final trip abroad, when Kissinger asked reporters to attribute his briefing to "a State Department source" instead. Barry Schweid filed an obituary with the Associated Press: "America's second most famous diplomat—the 'senior U.S. official' who always travels aboard Secretary of State Henry A. Kissinger's jet—disappeared Tuesday somewhere across the Atlantic."[10]

WHY LEAK?

In a 1983 survey 42 percent of government officials admitted that they sometimes leaked information to the press. Among leakers, justifications included to get attention for an issue or option (73 percent), to send a message to someone else in the government (32 percent), and to undermine an opponent (19 percent).[11]

SKEPTICS

"I have this abiding reservation about 'aides close to the Governor said.' Sometimes I think that's made up."

—New York Governor Mario Cuomo

"I haven't much faith in an unnamed source. Sometimes I wonder if there is such a thing. . . ."

—President Reagan[12]

FIRE THE REPORTER

- During World War I, General John J. Pershing forced United Press to replace a young correspondent, Westbrook Pegler, who had written about the army's botched attempts to censor the news.
- President Hoover, obsessed with leaks, complained to publishers. As a result, several reporters were fired or transferred.
- In 1940 Joseph P. Kennedy, the American ambassador to Britain (and father of John F. Kennedy), talked with Louis M. Lyons of the *Boston Globe* and two men from the *St. Louis Post-Dispatch.* The St. Louis men had requested an

off-the-record briefing, but Kennedy failed to explain that restriction to Lyons. Lyons's detailed story, headlined "Kennedy Says Democracy All Done in Britain, Maybe Here," created a furor and hastened Kennedy's departure from diplomatic service. Kennedy told the *Globe* to fire Lyons, insisting that the interview had been off the record for all participants. When the paper refused, Kennedy arranged for Boston businesses to cancel thousands of dollars in *Globe* advertising.

- At a White House meeting, President Kennedy told Arthur Ochs Sulzberger, publisher of *The New York Times,* that the *Times'* Saigon correspondent, David Halberstam, was too close to the Vietnam War to report it objectively. Sulzberger demurred. Kennedy asked if the *Times* had given any thought to transferring Halberstam elsewhere. No, Sulzberger said. Back in New York, Sulzberger canceled Halberstam's scheduled two-week vacation, in order to keep the disappearance of Halberstam's byline from giving Kennedy a false sense of victory.

- President Kennedy urged Blair Clark, the news director of CBS, to take correspondent Daniel Schorr out of Germany. Schorr was, the President said, overplaying the Germans' criticism of American foreign policy. Schorr remained in place.

- When he was running for governor of California, Richard Nixon tried unsuccessfully to get *Newsweek* to fire its San Francisco bureau chief, Bill Flynn, by charging that Flynn was too close to the Democratic candidate, Pat Brown.

- Nixon White House officials tried and failed to get PBS to remove Peter Lisagor, an outspoken *Chicago Daily News* reporter, from the program *Washington Week in Review.*

- During the 1988 presidential race, officials in the Michael Dukakis campaign tried to get ABC to reassign Sam Donaldson, who they said had been unfairly negative toward Dukakis. ABC refused.[13]

CONFESSION

In 1983 John C. Danforth, a U.S. Senator from Missouri and an ordained Episcopal minister, delivered an unconventional sermon at Princeton University's chapel. His topic: How the press affects politics.

"Here is a personal confession," Danforth said. "I serve on both the Senate Finance Committee and the Governmental Affairs Committee. One day several years ago, the Finance Committee was marking up the Crude Oil Equalization tax. It was a bill thought to have long-term effects on America's energy and economic future. On the same morning, one floor below, the Governmental Affairs Committee was holding hearings on alleged misdeeds of then Budget Director Bert Lance while he was a bank president in rural Georgia.

"The Lance hearing was covered by every TV network and by the national wire services. The Finance Committee meeting was covered by petroleum monthlies and by the *Wall Street Journal.* The Finance Committee was dealing with important issues. The Governmental Affairs Committee was engaged in political theater.

"I was at the Governmental Affairs Committee."[14]

WEINBERGER WAITING

In 1987 American warplanes attacked Iranian oil platforms in the Persian Gulf, and all three networks carried live a Pentagon briefing by Secretary of Defense Caspar Weinberger. Before Weinberger could begin talking, he had to wait for the network correspondents in the room to finish their on-air predictions of what he was about to say.[15]

SPOKESMAN

Before Bernard Kalb became the Reagan State Department spokesman, he once defined a government spokesman as a man who, when asked the time, looks at his watch and says "What time do *you* have?"[16]

THE PRESS ON POLITICIANS

"Every government is run by liars and nothing they say should be believed."

—I. F. Stone, editor of *I. F. Stone's Weekly* newsletter[17]

"The only way for a newspaperman to look at a politician is down."

—Attributed to Mark Sullivan, *New York Herald Tribune* columnist; Frank R. Kent, *Baltimore Sun* columnist; and Mark Twain[18]

"[T]he reporter and the man in government are natural allies. . . ."

—Joseph and Stewart Alsop, syndicated columnists[19]

"We were here before you got here, Ted, and we will be here when you are gone."

—James Reston, *New York Times* columnist, to President Kennedy's adviser Theodore Sorensen[20]

POLITICIANS ON THE PRESS

"[I]ts editor has done everything mean and contemptible except stealing. He would have done that had he had the moral courage and had the nights been long enough to conceal his thefts."

—Senator Sam Houston of Texas on *Galveston News* editor Willard Richardson[21]

"He sits there in senile dementia, with gangrened heart and rotting brain, grimacing at every reform, chattering impotently at all things that are decent, frothing, fuming, violently gibbering, going down to his grave in snarling infamy . . . disgraceful, depraved, corrupt, crooked and putrescent—that is Harrison Gray Otis."

—Governor Hiram Johnson of California on the founder of the *Los Angeles Times*[22]

"A newspaper is the lowest thing there is!"

—Chicago Mayor Richard J. Daley[23]

"They're just a bunch of goddamn animals. Why the hell should I have to put up with all of their shenanigans, anyway? I'm the Mayor and if I want them out of my office, out they go."

—New York City Mayor John Lindsay, telling an aide to keep reporters away from him[24]

"If this country ever fails—if this country ever becomes history—some future historian will blame it mostly on the media."

—Senator Barry Goldwater[25]

REMARKS

"Young man, if you're going to be a political writer, there's one thing you'd better remember. Never let the facts get in your way."

—Edward T. Folliard, *Washington Post* reporter, to Tom Wicker of *The New York Times*[26]

"Politics and media are inseparable. It is only the politicians and the media that are incompatible."

—Walter Cronkite, CBS anchor[27]

"Government is order. Journalism is disorder. Life imitates journalism."

—James Deakin, *St. Louis Post-Dispatch* reporter[28]

6

THE WHITE HOUSE

FIRSTS

First president to grant an exclusive interview: Martin Van Buren (1837–1841).

First to meet with reporters in groups: Grover Cleveland (1885–1889, 1893–1897).

First to distribute press releases: William McKinley (1897–1901).

First to provide a White House pressroom: Theodore Roosevelt (1901–1909).

First to speak off the record: Woodrow Wilson (1913–1921).

First to speak on radio: Wilson.

First to provide lengthy background information that could be published but not attributed to the White House: Franklin Roosevelt (1933–1945).

First to appear on television: Roosevelt.

First to receive a standing ovation from reporters: Roosevelt (at his first news conference).

First to open a news conference with a prepared statement: Harry Truman (1945–1953).

First to allow TV cameras to film news conferences: Dwight Eisenhower (1953–1961).

First to allow the live broadcast of news conferences: John Kennedy (1961–1963).[1]

PLANTING QUESTIONS

- Franklin Roosevelt's aides sometimes took reporters aside to suggest questions that would get particularly good answers. Although Roosevelt once grumbled that some questions were "planted" by anti-administration publishers, he never complained about his staff's plants.

- Many reporters covering the Eisenhower White House believed that Jack Horner of the *Washington Star* routinely asked White House–produced questions. When Eisenhower once prefaced an answer with "Mr. Horner, I'm glad you asked that question," the room erupted in laughter.

- President Kennedy's staff often planted a question or two. Press secretary Pierre Salinger later wrote that he would "simply call a reporter into my office and tell him that if he were to ask a certain question that day 'you will receive a most interesting answer.' "

- The Johnson White House frequently planted questions. The first occasion came early in the administration, at the suggestion of press secretary Bill Moyers. Johnson was so pleased with the result that, fifteen minutes before the next news conference, he handed an aide a list of ten questions to be planted (the aide didn't succeed). The practice grew so obvious that Moyers opened one briefing by saying "I'll take the planted questions first."

- Sometimes the information exchanges have been initiated by reporters. Edward Folliard of the *Washington Post*, Clark Mollenhoff of the *Des Moines Register-Tribune*, and

David Beckwith of *Time* have on occasion revealed their questions to the White House press office, so that the President would be prepared and, perhaps, so that their odds of being called on would increase. Before one Nixon news conference, the *Washington Star*'s Jack Horner—the ready conduit for planted questions during the Eisenhower years—asked press secretary Ron Ziegler, "Is there any fertile ground we should plow tonight?"[2]

THE EARLY YEARS

....

WYKOFF'S SCOOP

Portions of President Lincoln's first message to Congress appeared in the *New York Herald* before the text had even reached Capitol Hill. To find out who was responsible, the House Judiciary Committee called in the *Herald*'s reporter, Chevalier Henry Wykoff, for questioning.

Wykoff refused to name his source because, he said, he had entered into "an obligation of secrecy." The committee ordered that he be imprisoned until he was willing to cooperate. Then a White House gardener tried to take the blame, claiming that he had seen and memorized the message while arranging flowers, and that he had later repeated it, word for word, to Wykoff. The congressmen considered the story implausible.

The true culprit, the congressmen suspected, was probably the First Lady, Mary Todd Lincoln. Mrs. Lincoln had given information to reporters in the past, and she and Wykoff had been particularly friendly to each other. The accusations mounted. Finally President Lincoln appeared, unannounced, and declared under oath that his wife was innocent. After that the committee dropped its investigation and released Wykoff from prison. The *Herald* removed him from the White House beat.[3]

NO SECRETS

During the Civil War, General George B. McClellan told a friend that he hesitated to talk to President Lincoln about military matters. "If I tell him my plans," McClellan said, "they will be in the *New York Herald* tomorrow morning. He can't keep a secret."[4]

"BOGUS PRESIDENT"

After the hotly contested 1876 election, the *Washington Post* insisted that the Democratic nominee, Samuel J. Tilden, was the winner. A congressional committee determined that the new president was Republican Rutherford B. Hayes, but the *Post* refused to accept the verdict. For the next four years the newspaper churlishly referred to President Hayes as "the bogus President," "the acting President," and "his fraudulency."[5]

WILSON'S DAUGHTER

President Wilson grew furious when newspapers speculated that his daughter was about to get married. "My daughter has no brother to defend her," he told reporters, "but she has me, and I want to say to you that if these stories ever appear again I will leave the White House and thrash the man who dares utter them."[6]

WRITTEN QUESTIONS

President Hoover instructed reporters to submit their questions in writing. "The President of the United States," he said, "will not be questioned like a chicken thief by men whose names he does not even know."[7]

LOW BLOW

Aides in the Roosevelt White House were initially cool to Arthur Krock of *The New York Times,* whom they considered a "Hoover agent." Years later Krock told Hoover of the reputation. "I knew that Roosevelt made some evil remarks about you," Hoover replied, "but none so low as you mention. . . ."[8]

INSCRIPTION

President Franklin Roosevelt inscribed a photo of himself for the White House press room: "From their victim."[9]

PUNISHMENTS

When he was angry at reporters, President Roosevelt sometimes punished them directly. Once he ordered Robert Post of *The New York Times* to wear a dunce cap and stand in the corner. Another time he "awarded" a Nazi Iron Cross to John O'Donnell of the *New York Daily News.*[10]

COVERING ELEANOR

As First Lady, Eleanor Roosevelt decreed that only women could attend her news conferences. In order to get details of the First Lady's newsworthy activities, each Washington bureau was forced to hire at least one woman.[11]

FDR'S HEALTH

The press studiously avoided mention of President Roosevelt's polio-crippled legs. At the 1936 Democratic convention, the President slipped and fell in the mud. As Roosevelt struggled to his feet, CBS radio announcer Robert Trout told listeners that the President was steadily progressing toward the podium. On another occasion, the President fell on the floor in front of several photographers. None of them took a picture.

In 1944 Henry Luce helped choose photos of Roosevelt for *Life.* "In about half of them," Luce said, "he was a dead man!" Luce carefully selected pictures that made Roosevelt look healthy. Later Luce viewed the cover-up as a mistake. He said that the press, trying to be kind, had "infringed our contract with readers to tell them the truth."[12]

TRUMAN AND THE CRITIC

When Paul Hume of the *Washington Post* wrote a harsh review of Margaret Truman's singing debut, her father fought back. In a letter to Hume, President Truman wrote: "I have just read your lousy review buried in the back pages. You sound like a frustrated old man who never made a success, an eight-ulcer man on a four-ulcer job and all four ulcers working. I never met you, but if I do you'll need a new nose and a supporter below." Truman stamped the letter and dropped it in the mailbox himself.

When he received it, Hume couldn't believe the note was authentic. In Truman's telling, Hume showed it to a colleague from the *Washington Star,* who assured Hume it must be somebody's idea of a joke. Then the *Star* man, who had recognized the handwriting as Truman's, hurried back to write the story for his own newspaper.[13]

SELECTIVE READER

To avoid the *Washington Post*'s political coverage, President Eisenhower told aides to bring him the *Post*'s sports section only, snipping out other stories if necessary.[14]

MEDICAL DETAIL

After Eisenhower's 1955 heart attack, his doctor told reporters that the President's steady recuperation was shown by his normal bowel movements. The doctor presented the detail as important, and most editors included it in their coverage.

Afterward, one reporter composed a commemorative quatrain:

> O'er this rude pan that arched the bed,
> His ass to autumn's breeze unfurled,
> Our embattled prexy sat,
> And fired the shit heard round the world.[15]

BORED AT THE TOP

Russell Baker turned down a job with *The New York Times* because the *Baltimore Sun* would let him cover the White House and the *Times* wouldn't. He quickly came to regret the decision. He found that covering the Eisenhower White House (which he termed "The Tomb of the Well-Known Soldier") consisted mostly of "sitting in the lobby and listening to the older reporters breathe." When the *Times* later repeated its offer, Baker accepted the job on one condition: that he never be assigned to the White House beat.[16]

KENNEDY

....

THE CAMERA'S EFFECT

A study examined the effect of live television on reporters' behavior at presidential news conferences. At FDR's pre-TV news conferences, reporters' questions had averaged fourteen words in length. In the Kennedy administration—the first administration to air the news conferences live on TV—the average length was fifty words.[17]

EDITOR KENNEDY

On at least two occasions, President Kennedy reviewed articles about himself before publication.

The first came in 1961. Kennedy agreed to tell the full story of the Cuban missile crisis to two reporters, Stewart Alsop and Charles Bartlett, if they would let him check their article before it appeared in the *Saturday Evening Post.* Alsop and Bartlett agreed. Kennedy read, edited ("rather badly," according to Alsop), and approved the manuscript. After the article proved to be controversial, Kennedy and his aides strenuously denied any White House involvement.

The second incident came in the fall of 1962. Several far-right organizations were spreading a rumor that Kennedy had been married before, a story with potentially devastating consequences for the first Catholic president. Preparing an article about the organizations behind the rumor, *Newsweek*'s Ben Bradlee asked the White House for help. Press secretary Pierre Salinger told Bradlee that he could borrow the relevant FBI files if he would let the President see the article in advance. Bradlee and his editor, Osborn Elliott, agreed to the terms. Kennedy reviewed and approved the story. In an Oval Office meeting later, the President complimented Elliott on the article. "Well," Elliott replied, "we had to keep a tight asshole on that one, Mr. President."[18]

NO MUCKRAKING

Other news organizations also investigated the rumor of Kennedy's prior marriage. At *The New York Times,* though, the investigation was abruptly halted by James Reston, the Washington bureau chief. Reston decreed: "I won't have the *New York Times* muckraking the President of the United States."[19]

COVER SPY

On several occasions when *Newsweek*'s editors desperately wanted to know what *Time* planned to use on its next cover, *Newsweek*'s Ben Bradlee asked his friend John Kennedy. The President found out, presumably by sounding out a *Time* editor, and reported back to Bradlee.[20]

NEGOTIATIONS

In early 1962 the *Boston Globe* and the White House negotiated at length over a story that, President Kennedy feared, might doom his brother Ted's Senate candidacy in Massachusetts. Robert Healy, a *Globe* reporter, was trying to confirm the rumor that Harvard had expelled Ted Kennedy for cheating. Harvard refused to release the records without Kennedy's permission, and *Globe* editors didn't want to run the story without the official records as confirmation. ("In those days," Healy said later, "you didn't just float rumors.")

White House aide Kenneth O'Donnell asked Healy to come to Washington to meet with the President. In the Oval Office, Kennedy first suggested that the *Globe* might use the cheating incident as a small detail in a long profile of his brother, rather than devoting a separate story to it. Healy said no, and he was ushered out.

In a second meeting a few days later, Kennedy again urged a low-key, incidental placement for the information, and Healy again refused. Healy said that the *Globe* wouldn't use the story without the Harvard records. But, he continued, the story was bound to come out sooner or later, and it would be better for Ted Kennedy's sake to get it out before the election campaign. The President and several of his advisers—O'Donnell, Theodore Sorensen, and McGeorge Bundy—debated the issue while Healy listened. At one point the President complained, "We are having more trouble with this than we did with the Bay of Pigs." Bundy replied, "Yes, and with about the same result." The meeting broke up with no decision.

Healy was called to the Oval Office again a few days later. The President said he had decided to have Harvard release the records. He asked Healy, "Do you think you will play the story above the fold?" Healy said he didn't know.

The story ended up running under a subdued two-column headline, "Ted Kennedy Tells about Harvard Examination Incident," on the front page just at the fold. The lead said that Kennedy had "explained the circumstances surrounding his withdrawal from Harvard" because "he wanted to set the record straight." While a freshman he had arranged for a friend to take a final exam for him. A dean had discovered the incident and expelled both men. (Kennedy was allowed to reapply and was readmitted two years later.) "It was," Kennedy told Healy, "a bitter experience but it has also been a very valuable lesson."

After Kennedy won the Senate race, his brother Robert expressed his appreciation to *Globe* publisher Davis Taylor. "Both the President and I thank you for being fair and factual in the story on Ted's incident," he said at a White House reception, "and, incidentally, we think it went over very well."[21]

KENNEDY'S OFFER

In 1962 Arthur Krock of *The New York Times* urged President Kennedy to invite an African leader to visit the United States. At a Gridiron Club dinner, Kennedy mentioned the issue and referred to Krock's membership in an all-white club: "Krock criticized me for not letting President Tshombe of Katanga come here, so I told him we would work out a deal. I'll give Tshombe a visa and Arthur can give him a dinner at the Metropolitan Club."[22]

NEWS MANAGEMENT

In 1963 the Kennedy White House's so-called news management was the subject of a song at the Washington press corps' Gridiron Club dinner (sung to the tune of "Consider Yourself" from the musical *Oliver!*):

> Consider yourself our own,
> Consider yourself one of the Kennedys.
> We've taken you in so long,
> It's clear we never have been wrong.
> Consider yourself well snowed,
> Consider yourself part of the scenery.
> There's no other part you play.
> Who cares? We say all there is to say.
> Consider yourself our meat.
> We don't want to have no fuss,
> For after some consideration you are beat
> Unless you are one of us.

When it was his turn to speak, President Kennedy opened by saying: "Fellow managing editors."[23]

PRESIDENT'S DOG

Reporters covering the Kennedys once submitted a detailed questionnaire inquiring about the family's new dog. The First Lady filled it out. When she reached the question, "What do you feed the dog?" she wrote: "Reporters."[24]

JOHNSON

....

ON THE RUN

President Johnson sometimes invited reporters to join him on fast walks around the White House grounds. On one eighty-nine-degree August day, LBJ and a straggling band of reporters did fifteen brisk laps, a distance of nearly four miles. Reporters took to calling the mobile news conferences "Bataan death marches."[25]

LUNCHING WITH LBJ

In 1965 Bill Moyers, Johnson's press secretary, phoned CBS's Robert Pierpoint and invited him to have lunch with the President. Pierpoint assumed that Johnson had invited a group of White House correspondents, but when he got to the Oval Office he and the President were alone.

Johnson suggested a "little walk" before lunch. During two laps around the White House grounds, Johnson talked about his family and his Texas ranch. Whenever Pierpoint asked about Vietnam, Johnson gave a noncommittal answer and changed the subject.

LBJ then took Pierpoint to the White House family quarters, where the First Lady joined them for lunch. After they had eaten, Mrs. Johnson left and the President told Pierpoint to stay for coffee. By about 3:00 P.M. the conversation had become an LBJ monologue. Pierpoint tried again to leave. Johnson stood up and said it was time to cross the hall.

Pierpoint followed Johnson into a bedroom. The President started undressing, handing each piece of clothing to a valet. LBJ stripped naked, continuing his monologue the whole time. He put on a pajama top and walked into a bathroom, "speaking loudly," Pierpoint wrote, "over the sound of passing water." Then LBJ put on the pajama bottoms and got into the bed. He talked for another fifteen minutes and then said good-bye—nearly three hours after the conversation had begun.[26]

NICKNAME

When President Johnson was angry with the columnists Rowland Evans and Robert Novak, he would refer to them as "Errors and Nofacts."[27]

OSHKOSH RULE

Johnson once told Robert Pierpoint of CBS: "When you see on the ticker that Oshkosh says that Bob Pierpoint may be Chairman of the Joint Chiefs of Staff, you don't necessarily need to give much credence to it, because the very fact that it is on there is the best indication that it is not likely to happen." Under Johnson's Oshkosh Rule, premature publicity frequently undid presidential plans:

- *Newsweek* and the *Washington Post* reported that LBJ planned to make Lloyd Cutler, a prominent Washington lawyer, an under secretary of commerce, and also intended to move several other officials to different positions. The President blamed Cutler for leaking the story and dropped the plan.
- The *Baltimore Sun* reported on LBJ's plans for a program called Food for Peace. Johnson dropped the idea and ordered his aides to burn the news releases announcing it.
- Democratic officials in California told a number of reporters that Johnson planned to campaign there during the 1966 midterm elections. Tom Wicker of *The New York Times* saw bleachers under construction for one appearance. When newspapers predicted the trip, Johnson canceled it.
- In 1964 Johnson's press secretary, Bill Moyers, privately told Ben Bradlee of the *Washington Post* that the President was thinking of replacing FBI director J. Edgar

Hoover. When the story was published, LBJ called a news conference and announced Hoover's appointment for life. Afterward the President took Moyers aside and told him, "Now call up your friend Ben Bradlee and tell him I said, 'Fuck you.' "[28]

NEWS CRITIC

In the mid-1960s, when CBS's coverage grew more critical of the administration's Vietnam policy, President Johnson frequently telephoned the network with critiques of the news program. "Frank," LBJ once told network president Frank Stanton, "this is your President, and yesterday your boys shat on the American flag." On several occasions Dan Rather, then the CBS White House correspondent, answered his phone and heard LBJ's angry drawl: "Are you trying to fuck me?"[29]

LBJ ON KNOWING YOUR AUDIENCE

After his presidency, Lyndon Johnson told biographer Doris Kearns how he had dealt with different reporters:

"You learn that Stewart Alsop cares a lot about appearing to be an intellectual and a historian—he strives to match his brother's intellectual attainments—so whenever you talk to him, . . . emphasize your relationship with FDR and your roots in Texas, so much so that even when it doesn't fit the conversation you make sure to bring in maxims from your father and stories from the Old West. You learn that Evans and Novak love to traffic in backroom politics and political intrigue, so that when you're with them you make sure to bring in lots of details and colorful description of personality. You learn that Mary McGrory likes dominant personalities and Doris Fleeson cares only about issues, so that when you're with McGrory you come on strong and with Fleeson you make yourself sound like some impractical red-hot liberal."[30]

DISPLACED PATIENTS

While President Johnson was recuperating from gall bladder surgery, reporters took over a hospital wing that had formerly housed mental patients. LBJ asked his press secretary, Bill Moyers, what had happened to the mental patients. Moyers replied, "We gave them press badges."[31]

NIXON

....

NIXON ON THE PRESS

"[F]or sixteen years, ever since the Hiss case, you've had a lot of—a lot of fun. . . . [J]ust think how much you're going to be missing. You won't have Nixon to kick around anymore, because, gentlemen, this is my last press conference. . . ."

—News conference, 1962

"Don't take it that personally, but I'm not going to pay that much attention to you."

—To reporters, 1969

"The press is the enemy."

—To aides, 1969

"If we treat the press with a little more contempt we'll probably get better treatment."

—To aides, 1969

"Kicking the press is an art."

—To aides, 1972

"I have never heard or seen such outrageous, vicious, distorted reporting in twenty-seven years of public life. I am not blaming anybody for that."

—News conference, 1973

"Don't get the impression that you arouse my anger. . . . You see, one can only be angry with those he respects."

—News conference, 1973

"I have no enemies in the press whatsoever."

—To the American Society of Newspaper Editors, 1984[32]

MOON ROCKS

After the *Apollo 11* astronauts returned to earth, President Nixon arranged to send fragments of moon rocks to world leaders. He remarked privately that he hoped to find some "contaminated" pieces to send to reporters.[33]

GROUND RULE

In 1972 the White House granted Jack Horner of the *Washington Star* an exclusive interview with President Nixon. There was just one rule: In his written story, Horner could not quote his own questions. That meant Nixon could ignore Horner and talk about whatever he wanted to.[34]

MISTREATING TRICIA

After *Washington Post* reporter Judith Martin (who later wrote the *Post*'s "Miss Manners" column) described Tricia Nixon as "a 24-year-old woman dressed like an ice cream cone who can give neatness and cleanliness a bad name," the White House told Martin that she would not be permitted to cover Tricia's wedding.[35]

EHRLICHMAN VS. RATHER

In 1978 John Ehrlichman, Nixon adviser and Watergate convict, was released from prison. At a news conference to announce his forthcoming series of radio commentaries, Ehrlichman was asked about the rumor that, as one of Nixon's chief aides, he had told the president of CBS News to fire or reassign White House correspondent Dan Rather. Ehrlichman said he had never asked that Rather be removed; he had only complained that Rather was lazy and often inaccurate.

A few days later, according to Ehrlichman, he was told to report to the parole office in New Mexico (he would be on parole for two and a half years). His parole officer said that Dan Rather had filed oral complaints, first with the Parole Commission in Washington and later with the New Mexico office, accusing Ehrlichman of spreading lies about him. "As your parole officer," he said, "I would be very concerned if you became controversial." Ehrlichman, fuming, said that Rather was "using his clout" to try to silence criticism. The officer advised Ehrlichman to try to avoid such controversies in the future.[36]

ENEMIES LIST

During the Watergate hearings, John Dean testified that the Nixon administration had maintained an "enemies list." In response, the White House claimed that it was not an enemies list but merely a guide for helping to decide whom to invite to official dinners. No one believed the story, and the White House soon abandoned it.

Two versions of the list ultimately appeared. One version included twenty names, among them Daniel Schorr of CBS (termed a "real media enemy"), Ed Guthman of the *Los Angeles Times* ("highly sophisticated hatchetman against us in '68"), and Mary McGrory (who wrote "daily hate Nixon articles"). The other, longer version included more than fifty journalists, among them Jack Anderson, Rowland Evans, Joseph Kraft, James Reston, Tom Wicker, and Garry Wills.[37]

CALCULATED PRAISE

John Osborne, the White House columnist for the *New Republic,* once received a letter from a reader saying that "your scathing attacks on President Nixon have delighted me beyond belief." In a reflective column, Osborne wrote that the letter had forced him to recognize "a quality of sour and persistent disbelief" toward Nixon. The letter had in fact been written by White House aide Jeb Stuart Magruder, in hopes of making Osborne rethink his views. Osborne's mea culpa delighted Magruder and the rest of Nixon's staff.[38]

FINAL FLIGHT

On Richard Nixon's postresignation flight to San Clemente, he wandered back through Air Force One. The rear section had previously held reporters; now it held the Secret Service contingent. "Well," Nixon said. "It certainly smells better back here."[39]

FORD

....

FLATTERY

President Ford instructed his press secretary, Ron Nessen, to tell reporters that interviews with the President were over five minutes before the scheduled ending time. Then Ford could flatter the reporter by saying: "I'm really enjoying this. Let's let it go on for another five minutes."[40]

INTERRUPTION

At a briefing, Ron Nessen began an answer by saying "To tell you the truth—" Before he could continue, he was interrupted by loud, sardonic applause from the reporters.[41]

UNCLEAR RULES

Because of uncertainty about the rules, *The New York Times* didn't publish what would have been a major scoop:

that the CIA had, by President Ford's own admission, assassinated foreign leaders.

Ford made the remarks at a lunch with *Times* reporters and editors that hadn't formally been made off the record. Indeed, Ford had asked that one particular remark be kept off the record, which suggested that he believed the rest of the conversation was unrestricted.

But the *Times* writers couldn't agree. Columnist Tom Wicker and managing editor A. M. Rosenthal thought that Ford must have wanted to get the information out for publication. Three others believed it was off the record and could not be used—columnist James Reston, editorial page editor John Oakes, and Washington bureau chief Clifton Daniel. Finally Daniel asked White House press secretary Ron Nessen. Nessen adamantly said the remarks could not be published, and that ended the debate.

Some of the listeners sought to get the information out through other channels. Daniel and Rosenthal both tried, without breaking the ground rules of the lunch, to encourage *Times* investigative reporter Seymour Hersh to look into the foreign assassinations. At one point Rosenthal called Hersh and said, "Keep on working." On what? Hersh asked. "Never mind," said Rosenthal. "Keep working."

The story finally got out when Daniel Schorr reported the luncheon revelations on CBS, identifying Ford's listeners as "associates" of the President. Schorr apparently had heard the story elsewhere, and then had gotten at least one member of the *Times* lunch party to confirm it.[42]

CARTER

....

PIT

During a trip to India, President Carter was shown a pit filled with cow manure, which generated methane gas for energy. ABC's Sam Donaldson said, "If I fell in, you'd pull me out wouldn't you, Mr. President?" Carter replied, "Certainly—after a suitable interval."[43]

SOVIET LESSON

When the Soviet Union expelled an AP reporter in 1977, White House press secretary Jody Powell was asked if the United States planned to respond. "We did discuss something along those lines," Powell said. "It was our feeling that if the Russians got to kick an AP correspondent out of Moscow, we ought to get to kick an AP correspondent out of here."[44]

THE BLAIR HOUSE BUG

In the fall of 1981 "The Ear," Diana McLellan's gossip column in the *Washington Post,* reported that President Carter had bugged the guest mansion where President-elect Reagan and his wife had stayed prior to the inauguration. When he read the item, former President Carter announced plans to sue the *Post.* If he ignored the article, he said, the foreign leaders who had stayed at Blair House would believe that they had been bugged too.

The *Post* responded with several voices. Executive editor Ben Bradlee said he knew the columnist's source and believed the item to be accurate. But an editorial declared that the bugging story was probably inaccurate. The point of the "Ear" item, the editorial said, was "that *a story was circulating*"—circulating but false: "Based on everything we know of the Carter instinct and record on this subject, we find that rumor utterly impossible to believe."

Bradlee, meanwhile, appeared at the New Jersey home of Dotson Rader, a free-lance writer who was apparently the original source for the item. Rader, it seemed, had told Nancy Reagan a story, which she had told a friend, and which the friend had told the *Post*'s McLellan (though McLellan claimed to have "ten different sources"). Rader's story: Carter's wife, Rosalynn, and his sister, Jean Carter Stapleton, had listened to a tape of Nancy Reagan saying she wished the Carters would leave the White House before the inauguration so that she could get started redecorating. Rader claimed to have heard the story directly from Stapleton and Rosalynn Carter, though the women denied any knowledge of the tape.

Bradlee ordered Rader to sign sworn affidavits as to the facts, including the identities of his sources. Rader refused. Bradlee insisted, and issued a threat: If Carter sued for libel, the *Post* would subpoena Rader and force him to reveal his sources on the stand. Rader held firm. "I told him," Rader recalled, "I didn't see how the newspaper that used a 'Deep Throat' source in Watergate could haul a freelance journalist into court to try to force him to reveal a source."

The *Post* subsequently backed down. In a letter to Carter, publisher Donald E. Graham retracted the story and, somewhat gratuitously, the editorial as well (the editorial "did not intend to suggest that the paper prints rumors which it knows to be false, because that is not the policy"). The former President pronounced himself satisfied.

Afterward, the gossip column in the *Los Angeles Examiner* twitted the *Post* editorial's strained argument. The column reported a rumor that *Post* reporter Sally Quinn (wife of Ben Bradlee) was pregnant, "though, uh, we find that rumor utterly impossible to believe."[45]

REAGAN

....

REAGAN'S SEX LIFE

President Reagan told a group of teenagers at a drug clinic, "When you get to be my age, taking care of that machinery really pays off. You can tie your shoes . . . pull on your socks without sitting down, and get along doing things that are much more enjoyable than that." The audience laughed.

Later, George Skelton of the *Los Angeles Times* asked the President what "more enjoyable" things he had had in mind. Horseback riding, Reagan said. Skelton replied that people in the audience had assumed he was talking about sex. What, Skelton asked, was Reagan's sex life like at the age of seventy-two? White House aide Michael Deaver, sitting in on the interview, "damn near fell of his chair," according to Skelton. Reagan chuckled and refused to answer because, he said, of the trouble Jimmy Carter had gotten into when he talked about lust in a *Playboy* interview.

Skelton's article didn't mention the exchange. "My asking about sex," he explained, "told more about me than his answer told about him."[46]

TRAP

To prove that reporters were snooping around, press secretary Larry Speakes left two fake memos lying on an aide's desk. One suggested moving the pressroom next door, out of the White House and into the spacious but remote Old Executive Office Building; the other indicated that the President might announce his candidacy for reelection during halftime of a football game. The memos, Speakes said, were "facetious on their face," but two reporters who saw them "bit like snakes" and started phoning White House aides for confirmation. One of the reporters, Jim Hildreth of *U.S. News & World Report,* was ready to file a story about the pressroom move when Speakes confessed.[47]

BOYCOTTS

- In 1982 Reagan aide Michael Deaver decreed that reporters could no longer question the President at photo opportunities with foreign dignitaries. If reporters disobeyed the rule, Deaver said, then they would be excluded entirely, and only film crews and technicians would be admitted to the sessions. The networks' White House correspondents replied that they *and* their cameras would boycott the photo opportunities until the no-questions rule was rescinded. The boycott plan collapsed when NBC opted out of it, and the other networks, worried about missing out on pictures that a rival had, followed suit. With time the rule was forgotten.
- A similar incident occurred in 1985. The press office announced that President Reagan and the visiting Soviet For-

eign Minister, Eduard Shevardnadze, would walk alongside the Rose Garden. Still photographers and a network camera crew could film the men, Larry Speakes said, but no reporters could be present. The networks decided to boycott the event. As it happened, the decision came after the pool camera crew from ABC had already set up. At the request of the other networks, ABC erased the videotape without airing it.

- In 1983 White House photographers stood with folded arms and no cameras while the President honored two Costa Rican conservationists. The photographers were angry because the press office had refused to let them take pictures the previous day, when Henry Kissinger had visited President Reagan. Under pressure the White House released an official photo of the President with Kissinger.[48]

GUIDING PHILOSOPHY

On his desk, Larry Speakes posted a sign: "You don't tell us how to stage the news, and we don't tell you how to cover it."[49]

FREEDOM'S LIMITS

During his 1983 visit to Japan, President Reagan gave a speech praising freedom of the press. At his request, the speech was off the record.[50]

PRESIDENTS ON THE PRESS

....

"The newspapers of our country by their abandoned spirit of falsehood have more effectually destroyed the utility of the press than all the shackles devised by Bonaparte."

—Thomas Jefferson

"I don't think there ever was a time when newspaper lying was so general and so mean as at present, and there never

was a country under the sun where it flourished as it does in this."

—Grover Cleveland

"There is filth on the floor, and it must be scraped up with the muckrake; and there are times and places where this service is the most needed of all services that can be performed. But the man who never does anything else, who never thinks or speaks or writes save of his feats with the muckrake, speedily becomes, not a help to society, not an incitement to good, but one of the most potent forces of evil."

—Theodore Roosevelt

"I prepared for [news] conferences as carefully as for any lecture, and I talked freely and fully on all large questions of the moment. Some men of brilliant ability were in the group, but I soon discovered that the interest of the majority was in the personal and trivial rather than in principles and policies."

—Woodrow Wilson

"I really look with commiseration over the great body of my fellow citizens who, reading newspapers, live and die in the belief that they have known something of what has been passing in the world in their time."

—Harry Truman

"Well, when you come down to it, I don't see what a reporter could do to a president, do you?"

—Dwight Eisenhower

"Our most tragic error may have been our inability to establish a rapport and a confidence with the communications media."

—Lyndon Johnson

"I probably follow the press more closely and am less affected by it than any other President. I have a very cool detachment about it."

—Richard Nixon

"The White House press corps, in the main, are a bunch of prima donnas. I thought that kids in high schools asked better questions. . . ."

—Jimmy Carter

"Sons of bitches."

—Ronald Reagan, after reporters had persistently asked questions during a no-questions-allowed photo session; the remark was picked up by an open microphone[51]

7

POLITICAL CAMPAIGNS

PRESIDENT-MAKING NEWS

A few days before the 1884 election, Joseph Pulitzer's *New York World* published a front-page story headlined "The Royal Feast of Belshazzar Blaine and the Money Kings." The article told how James G. Blaine, the Republican presidential candidate, had hosted a fund-raising dinner for such "robber barons" as Jay Gould, John Jacob Astor, William Vanderbilt, and Andrew Carnegie. Alongside the article was a cartoon showing Blaine and his rich cronies eating "monopoly soup" and "lobby pudding," and ignoring a bedraggled couple and child who stood in front of the table. A few pages later an editorial termed the dinner "a Feast of Fraud" that threatened "death to the liberties of the people."

Cleveland won New York by 1,149 votes, and the state's electoral votes gave him the presidency. The outcome, he later said, might well have been different if not for the *World*'s "forceful and potent advocacy of Democratic principles."[1]

ROOSEVELT SHOOTING

When former president Theodore Roosevelt was in Milwaukee during his 1912 campaign to return to the White House, he was shot in the chest by a man named John Schranck. The bullet was slowed by items in Roosevelt's pocket—his glasses case and a rolled-up manuscript—and it penetrated only an inch into his body. After changing his shirt, Roosevelt delivered the scheduled speech. He told the audience that, though he still had a bullet lodged in his chest, "you can't stop a bull moose." After the speech he entered Mercy Hospital in Chicago to have the bullet removed.

Roosevelt's opponents claimed the shooting was a hoax to generate publicity and sympathy. To find out the truth, the *Chicago Examiner*'s Kent Hunter slipped into Mercy Hospital and stole an X-ray plate. The next day the *Examiner* splashed across the front page a copy of Roosevelt's X ray, showing what seemed to be a bullet lodged just under the skin.

Shortly after the election (which Roosevelt lost), a doctor told an *Examiner* editor that the X ray hadn't been Roosevelt at all. "It wasn't too clear, of course," he said, "but I'd swear that the thing you printed in your paper was a picture of a six-month-old fetus."[2]

PRESIDENT DEWEY

The best-known miscall of 1948—the *Chicago Tribune*'s headline "DEWEY DEFEATS TRUMAN"—wasn't the only one. *Life* had sent its President Dewey cover to press. The magazine paid a half-million dollars to change it. Rube Goldberg had sent out a President Dewey cartoon. In its place the *New York Sun* ran a blank space with the dual-meaning caption "RUBE GOLDBERG REGRETS." Stewart and Joseph Alsop had sent out a column advising President-elect Dewey to restructure the State Department. A Drew Pearson column predicted who would attend Dewey's inaugural. And former Cabinet member Harold L. Ickes's column authoritatively explained why Truman had lost.[3]

HEADSETS

At the 1952 Republican convention, television correspondents shouted questions at General Dwight Eisenhower's newly named running mate, Senator Richard Nixon. From the anchor booth, CBS producer Don Hewitt spoke by radio to the CBS reporter on the scene. At Hewitt's instruction, the reporter took off his earphones and put them on Nixon, explaining that "Walter Cronkite and Ed Murrow want to talk to you." Nixon answered the CBS men's radioed questions. The ploy turned the news conference into a virtual exclusive for CBS, because the other networks could pick up only half of the conversation.[4]

ABOARD THE BUS

The press corps covering the 1960 campaign included more women than ever before, and, according to *Washington Post* reporter Maxine Cheshire, jealous male colleagues accused nearly all of them of getting exclusives by sleeping with John Kennedy.[5]

WARN GOLDWATER

During the 1964 campaign, a supporter of Republican nominee Barry Goldwater once saw a group of journalists taking notes during the candidate's speech. The Goldwater booster hurried up to a Goldwater aide and said: "You've got to warn the Senator, right away. There are men out there taking down every word he says!"[6]

POLICE PROBLEMS: 1964

At the 1964 Republican convention, NBC reporter John Chancellor was arrested on camera for wandering where he wasn't welcome. As he was being led away, he signed off: "This is John Chancellor, somewhere in custody." In the anchor booth, Chet Huntley and David Brinkley chuckled. "John," Brinkley said, "call us when you can."[7]

POLICE PROBLEMS: 1968

At the Democrats' Chicago convention in 1968, two CBS correspondents ran into trouble with the police. The first incident came when Dan Rather was pursuing several security officers who appeared to be hauling a delegate away. When Rather stood in their path and asked what was going on, one of the men punched him hard in the stomach. Watching from the anchor booth, the usually unflappable Walter Cronkite said on the air, "It looks like we've got a bunch of thugs in here, Dan." A moment later Cronkite added: "If this sort of thing continues, it makes us, in our anger, want to just turn off our cameras and pack up our microphones and our typewriters and get the devil out of this town and leave the Democrats to their agony."

The next night Mike Wallace found himself in a tense confrontation with a policeman. Wallace smiled and, trying to be one of the boys, gently tapped the cop on the chin. The policeman slugged Wallace on the jaw. Another cop briefly arrested Wallace for assaulting an officer.

Later, some reporters reread a brochure the Chicago police had distributed at the convention. It said in part: "Welcome Newsmen! Welcome to Chicago, the City of 'The Front Page,' with an outstanding tradition of competitive journalism. Another tradition has been the excellent rapport between the Chicago police and working newsmen."[8]

LESSON LEARNED

Sixteen years before his own antipress presidential campaign, Gary Hart managed the 1972 George McGovern campaign. After the election, one reporter remarked that McGovern had had "the most garrulous staff that I've ever seen." Replied Hart: "Wait until next time."[9]

THE SHEEP PRANK

Covering Ford's 1976 campaign in Illinois, James Naughton of *The New York Times* arranged to play a prank on Thomas DeFrank of *Newsweek.* DeFrank was an "Aggie," a graduate of the farm school Texas A&M. Naughton decided to help him feel at home.

Ford's press secretary, Ron Nessen, kept DeFrank occupied in the hotel bar while Naughton and his co-conspirators rented a sheep and brought it to DeFrank's hotel room. When DeFrank walked in, he saw the sheep wandering around, periodically defecating on the rug. Naughton's gang quickly exited, saying that they knew DeFrank would want to be alone with his new friend. The next morning President Ford called DeFrank aside and said, "I understand you had a visitor last night."

Naughton included a five-dollar charge on his expense report for his share of "ewe rental." The *Times,* he later said, paid it without any questions.[10]

THE LEAK THAT WOULDN'T TAKE

In June 1979, as Senator Ted Kennedy was toying with the idea of running for president, the White House tried to send the message that President Carter planned to put up a fight. "If Teddy runs," the President told a group of visiting Georgians, "I'll whip his ass." White House aides waited for the press to pick up the no-nonsense remark, but the visitors kept it to themselves. "Frankly," one of them later said, "I just forgot about it."

The following week Carter tried again. At a dinner with three congressmen, he said, "If Kennedy runs, I'll whip his ass."

"Excuse me, Mr. President," said one congressman. "What did you say?"

"I don't think the President wants to repeat what he said," another congressman interjected.

"Yes, I do," Carter said. "If Kennedy runs, I'll whip his ass."

An aide to one congressman obligingly leaked the remark to the press. The White House asked another of the congressmen, Thomas Downey, to confirm the story if any reporters called him. Carter aides then gave Downey's unlisted home phone number to reporters. Disgruntled, Downey not only confirmed the quotation; he also revealed that the White House had asked him to do so—machinations that got more attention than the remark.

"I think what he meant to say," Kennedy said afterward, "was that he was going to whip inflation."[11]

THE REAGAN PRESS PLANE

In a feature about the Reagan press plane in 1980, Ira Allen of UPI wrote, "Lustful innuendo between passengers and the three stewardesses fly faster than the plane itself, and safety regulations are unheard of." Bruised by the publicity, United Airlines, which owned the chartered plane, replaced the stewardesses with men.

Reporters were indignant. The women "helped us relax," one said. Allen found himself the press plane's pariah, frequently insulted, occasionally threatened. At the beginning of every flight came a new, precautionary announcement over the plane's PA system: "From the office of the press secretary, this flight is off the record."

Campaign officials (and supposedly Reagan himself) called United to plead for the women's return. After a few days they reappeared, not as flight attendants but as "public relations representatives."[12]

NEWS ANALYSIS

During the 1980 campaign, a reporter snatched a sample of Reagan's hair from a barbershop floor and had it chemically analyzed. The analysis detected no dye.[13]

AUTHORITATIVE SOURCE

At the 1980 Republican convention, a governor told the *Wall Street Journal*'s Albert Hunt that Reagan had definitely chosen Gerald Ford to be his running mate. Hunt asked how the man knew. The governor said he had heard it from Dan Rather.[14]

THE JACKSON PRESS BUS

The press corps covering Jesse Jackson's 1984 presidential campaign was predominantly black. Minority status made some whites uncomfortable. A newsmagazine reporter approached the only other white reporter on the press bus and said nervously: "Do you think we are going to be okay?"[15]

TIMES REQUESTS

In 1987 *The New York Times* asked each presidential candidate for copies of medical and psychiatric records, school records (including high school grades), birth certificates, marriage and driver's licenses, employment records, financial statements, tax returns, and lists of closest friends. Most controversially, it asked the candidates to waive their rights of privacy to any confidential files the FBI and CIA kept on them.

Among the candidates, the initial responses were mixed. Bruce Babbitt, Paul Simon, and Richard Gephardt at first said they would cooperate. Michael Dukakis, Jack Kemp, and Joseph Biden indicated that they would provide everything except the waivers for confidential files. Pat Robertson flatly refused, saying: "I am not applying for employment at the *New York Times.*"

Media responses were mostly negative. Columnist Ellen Goodman wrote that, though she couldn't perfectly define "invasion of privacy," "I know it when I see it. This is it." Mike Royko of the *Chicago Tribune* called a *Times* spokeswoman and asked for the same information about the newspaper's editors. The *Times* woman hung up on him.

The *Times* finally backed off. Executive editor Max Frankel said in a memo to the staff that the requests "reach a bit too far." The newspaper would not, he said, press the candidates for FBI or CIA files, or for medical records unrelated to "fitness for the Presidency."[16]

HART BOWS OUT

On May 8, 1987, Gary Hart, at the time the front-runner for the Democratic presidential nomination, dropped out of the race, giving a feisty farewell speech that placed much of the blame on the press. Hart's quick downfall had begun five days earlier, when the *Miami Herald* reported that its stake-out team had seen Hart and a Miami model enter Hart's Washington town house together. Nobody had left the town house, according to the reporters, until the next day. Hart insisted that the woman, Donna Rice, had in fact exited through a back door. But the incident dogged him on the campaign trail, and finally he shut down his campaign (seven months later he briefly reentered the race).

Some sidelights:

- The day after Hart's candidacy ended, the *Miami Herald* published an editorial defending its reporting, which included a serious typo: "Let us not forget that the American press spares no one in pubic life, which is as it should be."
- A few days after leaving the race, Hart got a letter from another sometime press critic, Richard Nixon. "What you said about the media," the former president wrote, "needed to be said."
- Two of the *Herald* reporters donated their stake-out shoes to charity. At auction, one pair fetched forty-nine dollars; the others were held up in the mail.
- Don Johnson, costar of *Miami Vice,* told a reporter that he had moved out of Miami because "I didn't want to live in a town where there was a newspaper that was that irresponsible."[17]

TURNABOUT

At the final press conference before Hart dropped out of the race in 1987, Paul Taylor of the *Washington Post* asked whether Hart believed adultery was immoral. Hart said he did. Had Hart himself ever committed adultery? Hart stammered for a moment and then said, "I don't have to answer that."

A few weeks later, *People* magazine turned the tables, asking those same questions of several journalists:

Paul Taylor, *Washington Post* reporter: "Yes, I do consider adultery immoral. . . . The answer to the second question is 'None of your business,' which is the answer to that question except in the most extraordinary circumstances."

Mike Wallace, CBS *60 Minutes* correspondent: "Oh, Jesus,

I'll get back to you." Later: "I just turned 69, and I'm very flattered by the question."

Ted Koppel, ABC *Nightline* anchor: "Not only will I not answer that question, I won't even tell you how I vote."

Connie Chung, NBC News reporter: "If this is a shoe on the other foot question, I think I have a run in my stocking."

Linda Ellerbee, former *NBC News Overnight* coanchor: "To question No. 1, I'm a reporter. I don't make judgments. I just do my job. To question No. 2, as soon as I run for president, I'll let you know."

Columnist George Will's secretary: "I'm sure he wouldn't dream of answering! Anyone who knows Mr. Will knows the answer to that question."[18]

SHOUTING MATCH

"I'm at my relaxed and effective best when I'm reporting stories," CBS anchor Dan Rather told *Newsweek* in January 1988. On the day the magazine appeared on newsstands, Rather looked less than relaxed while reporting one story, a live interview with Vice President George Bush.

The interview was preceded by a filmed report showing apparent contradictions in Bush's statements about the Iran-contra affair. When he appeared on camera, Bush was visibly angry. "It's not fair to judge my whole career by a rehash of Iran," Bush said. "How would you like it if I judged your career by those seven minutes when you walked off the set in New York?"—a reference to the September 1987 day that CBS had gone black because Rather had left the *Evening News* set.

Rather began to act testy too. He repeatedly interrupted the Vice President. At one point Rather misstated a fact, prompting Bush to correct him and to admonish him to be careful. Rather snapped back: "I want *you* to be careful, Mr. Vice President." Later the anchor charged, "You made us hypocrites in the face of the world." Still later Rather asked if Bush would be willing to hold a news conference to answer questions about Iran. Bush started to reply that he had held eighty-six news conferences over the past few months, but Rather interrupted: "I gather the answer is no. Thank you very much for being with us, Mr. Vice President." Cut to commercial.

Rather received some good marks for questions but poor marks for manners. He "lost his cool," said Mike Wallace of *60 Minutes.* ABC correspondent Sam Donaldson thought Rather displayed "arrogance." In a *USA Today*/CNN poll, 64 percent of people said Rather had been out of line.

"Well," Rather told *Time,* "I am not a Buddha. I am not a robot. On my best days, I am a thinking reporter."[19]

REMARKS

"Well, those are my views, and if I said anything on the subject I must have said substantially that, but not nearly so well as that is said."

—Abraham Lincoln, asked by a *Chicago Tribune* reporter whether his article had accurately summarized a campaign speech[20]

"We're all going to have to seriously question the system for selecting our national leaders, for it reduces the press of this nation to hunters and presidential candidates to being hunted."

—Gary Hart, announcing his withdrawal from the race for the 1988 Democratic presidential nomination[21]

"Keep the press off the plane."

—Senator Bob Dole, asked what he would do differently after his unsuccessful campaign for the 1988 Republican presidential nomination[22]

FOREIGN ASSIGNMENTS AND WARS

REVOLUTIONARY PRAGMATIST

During the Revolutionary War, the editorial stance of the *New York Mercury* underwent a dizzying series of changes. At first the *Mercury*'s printer, Hugh Gaine, vowed to remain neutral. Tories and Yankees alike immediately assailed him for fence-sitting, so Gaine put his newspaper behind the Yankee cause.

The Yankees soon lost New York. Gaine, worried for his safety, slipped across the Hudson River to Newark and began publishing the *Mercury* there, once again adopting a strictly neutral editorial stance. The British, meanwhile, continued publishing a *Mercury* on Gaine's New York press. The British-produced version took on a decidedly anti-Yankee tone.

After a month, Gaine wanted to return to New York. The British offered to let him take over the original *Mercury* if he would maintain its pro-British stance. Gaine agreed. Where a few weeks earlier he had written of the patriots as "our army," now he referred to them as "the Rebels."

Then the Yankees retook New York. Gaine abandoned journalism.[1]

ATTACK AND COUNTERATTACK

During the Civil War, Union General George Meade was outraged when Edward Crapsey's *Philadelphia Inquirer* articles implied that Meade was overcautious and perhaps cowardly. At Meade's order, Crapsey was forced to wear a sign "Libeller of the Press" while he was hauled, sitting backward on a horse, through the encampment. It was to be, a Meade aide said, "a warning to his tribe."

Crapsey's colleagues responded with a punishment of their own: They banned Meade's name from their articles, a blackout that helped forestall the general's planned political career.[2]

NEWS HUNGER

Coverage of the Civil War sharply boosted newspapers' circulation. Wilbur F. Storey of the *Chicago Times* instructed one war correspondent: "Telegraph fully all news you can get and when there is no news send rumours."[3]

SHERMAN'S LAMENT

Union General William Tecumseh Sherman believed that reporters were dooming the war effort. "[N]o matter how rapidly we move," he wrote, "our enemy has notice in advance. To them more than to any other cause do I trace the many failures that attend our army. . . . Never had an enemy a better corps of spies than our army carries along, paid, transported, and fed by the United States." Sherman concluded that he would rather be ruled by Confederate President Jefferson Davis than continue to be "abused by a set of dirty newspaper scribblers who have the impudence of Satan."[4]

CIVIL WAR CENSORS

- When the *Sunday Chronicle* in Washington published an article about military movements, the army took over the newspaper's office, destroyed all copies of the issue, and arrested the editors responsible.

- A military commander closed down the *Chicago Times.* President Lincoln overrode the order three days later.
- Pro-South articles in the *New York Journal of Commerce* prompted the postmaster general to order the newspaper barred from the mails.
- Confederate sympathies in Missouri's *Boone County Standard* led the government to confiscate and sell the newspaper's presses.
- Although he had enjoyed mostly positive press coverage, the newly commissioned General Benjamin F. Butler prohibited reporters from, among other things, expressing "censure or praise" of any military movements. The *New York Tribune* responded: "Why, dear Major General! The newspapers have made you, epaulettes and all! Without the newspapers you would, at this moment, have been a petty attorney in a petty country town."[5]

BYLINES

A government decree caused newspapers to start routinely publishing reporters' names with their stories, rather than pseudonyms like "Agate" and "Shadow." Anonymous and "injudicious" articles, General Joseph Hooker announced in 1863, made it necessary to require newspaper correspondents either to use their full names or to register their pen names at military headquarters. Some reporters complained that the requirement inhibited "freedom and boldness in newspaper correspondence," and others said that they were ashamed to have their names attached to articles written hastily against deadlines, but most of them complied.[6]

PURITY

One Civil War general, Irvin McDowell, held reporters in particularly high esteem. "I have made arrangements for the correspondents of our papers to take the field," he wrote, "and

I have suggested to them that they should wear a white uniform to indicate the purity of their character."[7]

HEARST CLOUT

In 1898 William Randolph Hearst assigned the artist Frederic Remington to sketch the war in Cuba for Hearst's newspapers. Remington arrived before the sinking of the *Maine,* and he could find no signs of war. Bored, according to legend, he cabled Hearst: "EVERYTHING IS QUIET. THERE IS NO TROUBLE HERE. THERE WILL BE NO WAR. I WISH TO RETURN." Hearst replied: "PLEASE REMAIN. YOU FURNISH THE PICTURES AND I'LL FURNISH THE WAR."

The exchange is one of the best-known tales of American journalism, but some historians doubt whether it actually occurred. The story was first published in the memoirs of a Hearst reporter, James Creelman. Creelman never offered any evidence in support, and Hearst, according to one biographer, privately denied it. True or false, the cables entered the Hearst lore. The exchange even appeared in slightly altered form in *Citizen Kane.*[8]

HEARST IN THE FIELD

In one Spanish-American War battle, Hearst reporter James Creelman was wounded in the arm and back. Someone moved him to the rear, and he lay in pain, his eyes tightly shut. He felt a hand on his brow and looked up. There knelt William Randolph Hearst, wearing a straw hat festooned with a ribbon. "The man who had provoked the war," Creelman later wrote, "had come to see the result with his own eyes. . . ." Creelman couldn't write, so he dictated his story to Hearst.

"I'm sorry you're hurt," Hearst said when the story was written, "but wasn't it a splendid fight? We must beat every paper in the world!"[9]

EARLY SOVIET COVERAGE

In a lengthy *New Republic* article in 1920, Walter Lippmann and Charles Merz reviewed the past three years of *The New*

York Times' coverage of the Soviet Union. They found that the newspaper had reported the Soviet government's collapse ninety-one times. It had also reported Petrograd's capture six times, its near capture three times, and its destruction by fire twice. "From the point of view of professional journalism," they wrote, "the reporting of the Russian Revolution is nothing short of a disaster."[10]

BEHAVIOR BOND

During World War I any reporter who wanted to travel with the American Expeditionary Force had to post a $10,000 bond. If he behaved as "a gentleman of the Press," the money would be given back when he returned to the United States. If he violated any rules, it would be donated to charity.[11]

THIN-SKINNED FÜHRER

On several occasions in the early '30s, columnist Walter Winchell wrote that Hitler was homosexual. Winchell called Hitler "an out-and-out fairy," one of the "yoo-hoo boys of the swishy set," and "Adele Hitler." In one column Winchell quoted a cable that, he said, he had just received: "What are you doing over the weekend? Would you like to spend it with me? I think you're cute. Love, Adolf Hitler." In Germany, the official Nazi newspaper called Winchell "A New Hater of the New Germany" and said that his readers were "morons." Hitler himself was so troubled by the columns that he sent for a film of Winchell in order to get a look at his attacker.[12]

WORLD WAR II CENSORS

- In order to avoid reinforcing Axis propaganda about racial strife in the United States, censors instructed reporters not to publicize race riots at army camps.
- In 1942 people in Palm Beach heard explosions and saw in the distance a ship on fire. Clearly an enemy submarine had attacked an American ship, but censors told newspapers not to publish anything about the incident. After a number of readers phoned the *Palm Beach Post* to ask

why the newspaper was hiding a story that everyone knew about anyway, the *Post* published a succinct editorial: "If it's anything WE can't print, YOU shouldn't be talking about it."

- Army censors cut some articles out of newspapers being sent to overseas subscribers. From copies of the *Los Angeles Times* the censors once snipped out an article about Carole Lombard's funeral.
- Censorship rules limited news coverage of the weather in order to keep national weather forecasts out of enemies' hands. In an article about Washington's heaviest snowfall in twenty years, *The New York Times* explained: "Because of censorship restrictions which allow mention of storms in only one area of the country in any one issue of a newspaper, the *New York Times* does not print this morning a report of weather conditions which obtained in New York yesterday afternoon and last night." Coverage of the severe snowstorm that had hit New York City had to wait.[13]

FREEDOM FOR SOME

During World War II the newspaper trade magazine *Editor and Publisher* urged the government to close down all Japanese-language newspapers in the United States.[14]

ON-SCENE CENSOR

As Edward R. Murrow delivered his live radio broadcasts from the rooftops of London, a British censor stood next to him. Whenever Murrow would start to talk about a sensitive subject, the censor would tap him on the wrist, and Murrow would switch topics.[15]

UNWRITTEN STORIES: WAR

- During World War II the Japanese sent bomb-laden balloons across the Pacific. Some of them started forest fires in the Northwest. At the government's request, editors downplayed the fires and published nothing about the bombs, to keep the Japanese from learning that the tactic had succeeded.

- In 1945 General Leslie Groves told *The New York Times* that the United States was about to use an "atomic bomb" against Japan. Groves instructed a *Times* editor to begin preparing articles to be published when the bomb was dropped, but not to reveal anything beforehand. The editor complied. A week later Hiroshima was bombed.
- Many reporters knew that President-elect Eisenhower was visiting Korea a few weeks after the 1952 election. To protect his safety, nothing was published until he was en route back to Washington.[16]

REPORTER KENNEDY

In 1945 John F. Kennedy covered the British elections for William Randolph Hearst's International News Service. In one article Kennedy predicted that Winston Churchill's Conservatives would lose the elections to the Labor Party. "No sooner did that story hit New York," Kennedy later said, "than I got a rocket from Hearst, practically charging me with being out of my mind." Kennedy dutifully produced a story predicting an easy victory for Churchill.

On election day, the Conservatives lost. "If I had stuck with my original story," Kennedy said, "I'd have been a red-hot prophet. As it was, I was just another reporter—wrong."[17]

A WOMAN'S PLACE

During the Korean War the *New York Herald Tribune*'s Marguerite Higgins, one of the first women to cover a war, complained that she wasn't treated like one of the boys. Jimmy Cannon of the *New York Post* replied, "If the *Racing Form* sent a race horse to cover the war, he wouldn't be any more of an oddity than you are."[18]

CONGO COMPETITORS

In the early '60s Peter Younghusband covered the Congo for the *London Daily Mail.* After a charter flight to observe a battle, Younghusband noticed a small bullet hole on the plane's wing. He made it the centerpiece of an article, which the *Mail* ran under the dramatic headline "I Was Shot At By Baluba Rebels." The next day the correspondent for the competing *London Daily Express* received a cable: "YOUNGHUSBAND SHOT AT. WHY NOT YOU?"[19]

SOUVENIR

Malcolm Browne, an AP correspondent in Vietnam in the early '60s, hung on the wall of his Saigon office a souvenir that a Vietnamese photographer had found at the scene of an ambush: a dismembered, withered hand.[20]

EQUIVALENCIES

President Johnson supposedly said that the *Washington Post*'s hawkish editor, Russell Wiggins, was worth two divisions to the United States' effort against the Viet Cong. When he heard the remark, Philip Geyelin, the newspaper's sharply antiwar editorial writer, said, "I must be worth a battalion of V.C."[21]

EVITA'S RETURN

When the Argentinian military took power from Juan Peron in 1955, the new government secretly disinterred the body of Peron's wife Eva and shipped it to Italy. "Evita," as she was called, had attracted an enormous following prior to her death from cancer three years earlier, and the new government didn't want supporters of her ousted husband flocking to her grave.

In 1973 the Peronists returned to power, and Juan Peron ordered that his wife's remains be brought back to her homeland. An American television stringer phoned her editor and said, "They're bringing back Eva Peron." The editor responded, "See if you can get an interview with her in English."[22]

INTERVIEWING THE AYATOLLAH

In 1979, during the Iran hostage crisis, the three commercial TV networks came under strong criticism for their interviews with the Ayatollah Khomeini.

First was the matter of ground rules. "No question," as Mike Wallace later explained on *60 Minutes,* "could be asked unless it was approved ahead of time. No questions about Iran's internal politics. No questions about a lack of freedom under the Ayatollah." Senator S. I. Hayakawa charged that the networks had ceded the Ayatollah "complete control over the interview," a privilege, Hayakawa noted, that would never be granted to any American official.

The reporters were also denounced for undue deference. Before quoting a criticism of the Ayatollah, Mike Wallace put his hand on his heart and said: "Forgive me, Imam."

Some officials resented the networks' questions too. "In one damn set of interviews," State Department spokesman Hodding Carter said, "a rigid statement was set down on the inevitability of trials for our people. It put into concrete what could have been dismissed as a muttering behind closed doors."

Despite such sentiments, American officials sought to use the interviews for their own purposes. Before PBS's Robert MacNeil left for Iran (where his interview was ultimately canceled), a State Department official asked him to carry a message to the Ayatollah; he refused. After CBS had taped its interview, Hodding Carter phoned *60 Minutes* executive producer Don Hewitt and asked what the Ayatollah had said. Although the interview hadn't yet aired, Hewitt summarized it over the phone for Carter and Secretary of State Cyrus Vance. "I don't know what value it was to Vance," Hewitt later wrote. "It couldn't have been much, but it sure made me feel better to do it."[23]

COMPETITION TO MAKE NEWS

In 1986 the KGB arrested an American reporter in Moscow, Nicholas Daniloff of *U.S. News & World Report,* and charged him with spying. Before the Soviets released him, the story dominated front pages for weeks. Daniloff became a national hero. The magazine's owner, Mort Zuckerman, and its editor, David Gergen, became evening-news regulars. At a rival newsmagazine, jealous employees posted a sign: "KGB! Next time, take one of ours."[24]

CIRCUMVENTING CENSORS

- In 1916 Wythe Williams gave *The New York Times* a major scoop via cables that seemed to concern job negotiations. First Williams urged his managing editor, Carr Van Anda, to read a *Collier's Weekly* profile of General Henri Pétain written by Alden Brooks. Van Anda did so and responded by asking if Pétain was a candidate to replace a retiring commander: "DOES BROOKS MAN WANT JOB WITH US?" "YES," Williams replied, "WE DICKERING WITH HIM NOW." Later Williams cabled, "BROOKS MAN WANTS TOO MUCH THINK IT BEST CONSIDER HIS ASSISTANT," and then, a few hours later, "ASSISTANT ACCEPTS." Van Anda published the news: Pétain had been considered to replace the retiring commander, but he had asked for more power than the Allies would permit; instead, General Robert Nivelle, Pétain's "assistant," would get the post.

- In 1936 the United Press bureau in London received a mysterious message from its Madrid correspondent, Lester Ziffren. The long message began: "MOTHERS EVERLASTINGLY LINGERING ILLNESS LIKELY LARYNGITIS. AUNT FLORA OUGHT RETURN EVEN IF GOES NORTH LATER." After staring at the cable for a while, someone tried stringing together the initial letter of each word. The resulting message was the first news of the Spanish Civil War's outbreak to get past censors: "MELILLA FOREIGN LEGION REVOLTED MARTIAL LAW DECLARED."

- In 1939 James Reston of *The New York Times* used a simple code (the last words from each sentence formed the message) to report that a Nazi submarine had damaged a British ship. After the *Times* published the scoop, Scotland Yard spent eight weeks breaking the code.

- South Vietnamese censors kept back reports about Buddhist self-immolations and other protests during the Vietnam War. In order to test its equipment, the AP bureau in Saigon routinely transmitted a particular photo of a woman in a swimsuit. The bureau began putting information about the protests in place of the photo's usual caption. The censors never noticed.[25]

REMARKS

"We were just leeches, reporters trying to suck headlines out of all this death and suffering."

—Robert St. John, AP correspondent in World War II[26]

"No sensible reporter deludes himself that he is being heroic in this war. The heroics are reserved for the troops who do not enjoy the supreme privilege that any reporter can exercise at any time. That is the chance to say, 'I'd love to stay, fellas, but I've got to get back to Saigon and file.'"

—Charles Mohr, *New York Times* correspondent in Vietnam[27]

"This is not . . . a contest between the government and the editor; it is a contest where the government and the editor are on the same team. . . . Either you are going to help win, or you are not."

—Byron Price, director of censorship, to editors during World War II[28]

"There gets to be a point when the question is, whose side are you on? I'm the Secretary of State, and I'm on our side."

—Dean Rusk to reporters during the Vietnam War[29]

III

CONFLICTS

convicted on the
had been impli-
Jefferies, the for-
okerage firm that
r. Jefferies agreed
securities law viola-
ate with the Govern-
ation of crime on Wall
was implicated by Mr.

ment charged that Mr.
de millions of dollars by
g stock in takeover tar-
his ownership in those
by using secret accounts
s & Company, a West Coast
e, and later selling his hold-
r the stock price had risen.

Tax Losses

Bilzerian is also ch
raud for engagin
s in two securities t
losses. The charge
ve Mr. Bilzerian's
ger.

The charges inv
luett, Peabody & Comp
Robertson & Company, and the ha
mermill Paper Company, as well as a
stock transaction involving securities
of Armco Inc

n prison and $2.25 mil-
The case was the first
l of illegal stock parking,
wnership of securities is
to avoid disclosure or other
laws.

ilzerian was charged with two
s of securities fraud, five counts
ling false statements with the
vernment and two counts of con-
piracy.

Net Worth Put at $81 Million

Yesterday's sentence capped the
undoing of the career of a man who
appeared seemingly from nowhere to
engineer some of the most lucrative
that should
failing to cooperate.

Week

icials are scheduled to
ek and are expected to
by the subcommittee
Administration's views
wing Canadian problem.
of National Drug Control
h is directed by William
expected to announce the
ommittee next month
and domestic

in Jersey City when a Superior Court
en Auto Body's lawyer to have the
ue a restraining order from
om entering into an agreement
en Towing. Judge James Dow-
he request, but scheduled
ve the matter

ASHINGT
Federal
approv
ver Tr
New Y
acc
ne of

a maxi-
form the basis for policy
regulatory recommenda

ted States, banks m
r currency transac
re than $10,00
uch law.
st year Car
t permit
assets
or convi
The new law
ering a crime
Canada, though
believe the
as effective as those in
United States.

Several recent investigations have
disclosed significant ties between
money laundering operations by drug
dealers in the United States and Latin
America who have made use of Cana
dian banks, many of which ha
branches throughout Latin Amer
Federal authorities say that C
tion Polar Cap, the largest
laundering investigation in A
history, uncovered more th
lion that was laundered
month period, some of
through banks in Toror

Panama Bank Conv

In that case, Ca
thorities

contract specifications.
The city's response to the alle
that when it rejected Hoboken
sole bid on the contract
because it though
favorable offe
tised, an
bid

The Goldome offices that Man
turers Hanover is acquiring in
York, Nassau, Orange and
counties hold total deposits o
billion.

In approving the purchase,
rejected arguments that Man
ers Hanover had failed to
credit needs of low- and mod
come communities, prim
Brooklyn. The complaint wa
ted Mine Workers o
Association of C
tions for Reform

The Fed sa
reed
ment of drug profit
nizations."
risk of detection
of the enormou
ross the generall
border.

Fears of Publicizing Report

The report, which officials of the
drug agency said they had hoped to
keep confidential out of
publicity would further
drug traffickers to use
banks, came to light at
the Senate Foreign Rel
mittee's subcommittee o
narcotics and internat
tions. John F. Kerry, a M
Democrat who is chai
committee, obtained a c
port and cited it as
friendly country whose
thumbing their noses a

Continued

he wrote, "I wish I
the clock of time an
ever mistakes I may
a statement to the co
rian said his letter was
declined to say anything
However, Judge Ward
lieved Mr. Bilzerian had
guided by the desire for
had begun to misrepresent
to obtain it.

'In Short, He Lies'

"I have no doubt that in
years, he has done good thing
other people, but there is another
to the defendant," Judge Ward s
"The allure of money has caused h
to lose what I believe to be prop
perspective. In short, he lies."
Judge Ward added that the case
was "replete with false documents"
that supported his opinion.
While Mr. Bilzerian was not
charged with perjury, a Federal
judge can be permitted to consider
such a possibility when announcin
sentence.

During his testimo
spoke as thou
about

9

PRIVACY, SECRECY, AND LAW

PRIVACY

FIRST INVASION?

The first American newspaper to bump up against issues of privacy was the first newspaper to appear in the American colonies. On September 25, 1690, *Publick Occurrences Both Forreign and Domestick* told of a "very tragical accident" that had occurred in Watertown. The victim was an elderly man of "somewhat a silent and morose temper" whose wife had recently died. "The Devil took advantage of the melancholy," the newspaper reported, and the man grew so distressed that friends "kept a strict eye upon him, lest he should do himself any harm." But one evening he slipped away unnoticed. The friends found him in the cowhouse, "hanging by a rope, which they had used to tie their calves with, he was dead with his feet near touching the ground."[1]

EXECUTIVE'S PAST

In 1959 Frank Prince donated a half-million dollars to a St. Louis university. The *St. Louis Post-Dispatch* assigned reporters to write a feature about Prince, who was a major stockholder in the Universal Match company. The reporters soon discovered that Prince had served three prison terms, totaling almost ten years, for forgery, larceny, and issuing fraudulent checks. In the thirty-five years since he had left prison, his record had remained spotless. In fact the FBI had cleared him for defense-related work.

What had begun as a puff piece ended up under the headline "FRANK J. PRINCE, MAIN UNIVERSAL MATCH OWNER, IS EX-CONVICT." Prince, whose wife and twenty-four-year-old son hadn't previously known of his record, called the story "vicious," and many *Post-Dispatch* readers agreed. Managing editor Raymond L. Crowley was unrepentant. "I think," he said, "the stories simply speak for themselves."[2]

HEROISM'S PRICE

On September 22, 1975, in San Francisco's Union Square, Sara Jane Moore aimed a revolver at President Ford. Just as she pulled the trigger, a thirty-three-year-old man saw the gun, jumped Moore, and deflected her aim. The bullet missed Ford by a few feet. Whether ex-marine Oliver Sipple had in fact saved the President's life was unknowable, but San Francisco and the nation celebrated Sipple as a hero.

When reporters mobbed him for personal details, Sipple begged them not to publish "anything about me." His reason soon became apparent. In the *San Francisco Chronicle* two days after the shooting, columnist Herb Caen quoted local gay leaders as saying they were "proud—maybe this will help break the stereotype." The following day Daryl Lembke of the *Los Angeles Times* interviewed Sipple at length. Sipple confirmed that he had been active in gay causes, but he refused to say whether he was gay. Lembke suggested that Sipple's homosexuality might be the reason that Ford hadn't yet thanked him, but Sipple said he didn't care whether the President ever thanked him. After Lembke's front-page story appeared ("Hero in Ford Shooting Active Among S.F. Gays"), Sipple called a news conference and insisted: "My sexual orientation has nothing at all to do with saving the president's life."

In Sipple's hometown, the *Detroit News* disagreed. A *News* reporter told Sipple's mother about her son's apparent homosexuality. Mrs. Sipple was shocked. "No wonder the president didn't send him a note," she said. (In fact, the day before the *News* article appeared, the White House had released the text of a note from Ford to Sipple.) Although Sipple had been straightforwardly active in San Francisco's gay community, word had never reached his family.

Five days after he jumped Sara Jane Moore, Sipple filed a $15 million invasion-of-privacy suit against more than fifty reporters and news organizations. The suit meandered through the courts for nine years and finally was dismissed. By trying to save Ford's life, the judges ruled, Sipple had in essence waived his right to privacy.

In the years that followed the shooting, Sipple's life deteriorated. His mother refused to speak to him and, when she died in 1979, Sipple's father told him that he was not welcome at the funeral. Sipple's health declined and he began drinking heavily. In January 1989 he was found dead, apparently of natural causes, in his apartment. Former President Ford sent a condolence letter to a San Francisco bar where Sipple had passed the time. Ford would, he wrote, be "forever grateful" for Sipple's heroic act, and he "strongly regretted the problems that developed for him following this incident." Regrets were also voiced by one of the reporters who had publicized Sipple's homosexuality, Daryl Lembke of the *Los Angeles Times*. "If I had it to do over again," Lembke said after Sipple's death, "I wouldn't."[3]

HYPOTHETICAL SUICIDE

This hypothetical was presented to a group of newspaper publishers, editors, and writers:

"A prominent citizen is vacationing alone in Key West, and his hotel burns down. The wire service story lists him among those who escaped uninjured and identifies the hotel as a popular gathering place for affluent gays. The citizen says he'll commit suicide if you publish his name in the story."

Nine percent of respondents said the newspaper should omit the man's name. A plurality, 49 percent, said the story should omit the gay angle but include the man's name. Nearly as many respondents, 42 percent, said the entire story—gay angle *and* name—should be published.[4]

PERSONAL HISTORIES

- In 1976 the *Detroit News* revealed that Senate candidate Donald Riegle had had a "torrid" extramarital affair seven years earlier. Sexual behavior, in the view of Seth Kantor, the reporter who wrote the story, "tells you a lot about a man's judgment as well as his stability." Voters seemed to disagree: Riegle's one-point lead in the polls widened to six points on election day, and his campaign staff considered sending the *News* a telegram of thanks.

- In 1987, following the Donna Rice revelations that destroyed Gary Hart's presidential campaign, the *Cleveland Plain Dealer* reported allegations that Ohio Governor Richard Celeste had had three extramarital affairs. Two supposedly had occurred in the '70s; the third was said to have taken place in 1985. Editors at the *Plain Dealer* claimed to have known the information for some time. They decided to publish it, they said, because Celeste had indicated he might seek the Democratic presidential nomination and because he had falsely declared that he had no skeletons in his closet. Celeste and his wife responded that the episodes were no one else's business.

- In 1988 three presidential candidates faced press scrutiny over sexual matters. During the primaries the *Wall Street Journal* revealed that Pat Robertson had lied about his 1954 marriage date in order to mask the fact that his son was conceived out of wedlock, and the *Atlanta Journal-Constitution* reported that Jesse Jackson's wife had been pregnant when they married in 1962. Three weeks before the November election, the stock market fell 43 points because of a rumor that George Bush, the market's chosen candidate, was about to be exposed as an adulterer by the *Washington Post.* The stock market activity prompted the *Post* to take the unusual step of denying that it had any such story in the works. Many reporters had investigated rumors of Bush's infidelity but, *Los Angeles Times* editor William Thomas said, "This is one where nobody's ever pinned anything down."[5]

CHASING JACKIE O.

Ron Galella, a free-lance photographer and self-described paparazzo, made a career out of pursuing Jacqueline Kennedy Onassis. Among other tactics, he maneuvered a power boat next to Onassis while she was swimming and followed her children into their schools.

Onassis finally had Galella arrested for harassment. Galella responded by suing her for $1.3 million. Onassis countersued for $6 million. After a trial, in which the claims for money damages were dropped, a judge ordered Galella to stay fifty yards away from Onassis. On appeal the distance was reduced to about twenty-five feet.

In 1982 Onassis brought Galella back to court. He was found guilty of twelve violations of the twenty-five-foot rule and fined $120,000. The judge suspended the fine if Galella paid Onassis's legal costs ($10,000) and agreed never again to photograph her. The judge warned Galella that if he ever broke the agreement, each photo would cost him six months in prison.[6]

UNTOLD STORIES: JFK'S PRIVATE LIFE

Many reporters say that they knew about President Kennedy's extramarital affairs, though no articles about them were published during his lifetime. "Social and journalistic customs were different then," in the view of *Washington Post* columnist Maxine Cheshire. "That simply was not the way one covered the presidency at that time."

- According to a popular story among reporters, when Jacqueline Kennedy was showing a French reporter around the White House, the First Lady pointed to a woman and said in French, "There is the girl my husband is said to be sleeping with."

- During a trip to Palm Springs, Douglas Cornell of AP and Robert Pierpoint of CBS saw Kennedy leave a party with a woman other than his wife. The two got into a car, embraced, and disappeared from view. Several minutes later, when someone else approached the car, Kennedy and the woman got out and kissed good-bye.

- According to Maxine Cheshire, late one night during a presidential visit to California, reporters heard a woman's voice coming from the President's suite: "I don't give a goddamn if you are the President of the United States." Another time a young woman told Cheshire that she had lost her shot at a high bureaucratic post because she had refused to sleep with the President.

- A *New York Times* reporter saw a prominent actress (not identified) rendezvous with Kennedy at New York's Carlyle Hotel.

- A Washington woman named Mary Pinchot Meyer told James Truitt of *Newsweek* that she had had an affair with Kennedy and that the two of them had smoked marijuana in the White House.[7]

OTHER UNTOLD STORIES

- From FBI agents trying to discredit Martin Luther King, reporters learned of his extramarital affairs. Although the subject was widely talked about, no stories about it were published until after King's death.

- Philadelphia Mayor Frank Rizzo, who was married, asked reporters not to write about his compulsive flirtations. They complied.

- Eileen Shanahan of *The New York Times* and other reporters knew about the drinking and carousing of Congressman Wilbur Mills long before he made headlines by driving into the Tidal Basin with stripper Fanne Fox. "As long as it appeared that this was just a purely private sexual escapade that didn't affect his work," Shanahan said, "it was not considered news."

- Shanahan also observed drunkenness that did seem to affect public service: Senator Russell Long "visibly drunk on the Senate floor," which impeded the progress of a major tax bill during the Johnson administration; and Senator Harrison Williams, seemingly intoxicated at a committee hearing, asking nonsensical, rambling questions. She tried to get the Long story into print but *Times* editors rejected it. Because of that experience she didn't try printing the Williams story.

- One night during the 1964 campaign, Air Force One landed at a small town for a presidential visit. President Johnson stumbled off the plane, supported by Secret Service men at both elbows, and gave an incoherent speech to the assembled crowd. When CBS reporter George Herman asked how to deal with the apparent drunkenness in his story, his editor told him to leave it out. The editor suggested that the information might be aired later, but it never was.

- "At least half a dozen" reporters knew that Congressman Wayne Hays was keeping his mistress, Elizabeth Ray, on his official payroll, according to gossip writer Rudy Maxa, but the reporters believed that they might lose their access to other politicians if they published the story. The story emerged in 1976 when Ray obligingly submitted to a *Washington Post* interview ("I can't type, I can't file, I can't even answer the phone").

- During the 1980 presidential campaign, *Washington Post* executive editor Ben Bradlee learned from a reliable source in Congress that some of Ronald Reagan's closest advisers were gay. The source expressed the fear that the gay men might be subject to blackmail as White House aides. By talking with some of the Reagan advisers, a *Post* reporter, Ted Gup, confirmed that the tip was at least partly accurate. But Gup and his editors concluded that the blackmail threat was "purely speculative," and nothing appeared in the newspaper.

- In 1983 people at about a dozen news organizations in Mississippi saw affidavits stating that four male prostitutes had had sex with the Democratic nominee for governor, Bill Allain. The investigator who distributed the documents was being paid by prominent Republicans in the state, but reporters had to promise to protect the man's identity before they could see the affidavits. Although many reporters believed the allegations were true (the prostitutes had supposedly passed polygraph tests), no news organization would use the story without identifying the Republican-linked source. To get the information out, the investigator finally had to hold a public news conference, which produced coverage that focused on the dirty-tricks aspect nearly as much as on the allegations. Allain won the election, and three of the prostitutes later said they had been lying all along.

- In 1984 the *Charlotte Observer* interviewed a former church secretary, Jessica Hahn, who said she had been raped by televangelist Jim Bakker. The newspaper chose not to publish the allegation. Three years later Hahn's story found its way into print via other reporters.

- Not all untold stories concern sex or drinking. During his twelve years of life, David, a boy born with an immune deficiency—popularly known as "the boy in the bubble"—was the subject of thousands of newspaper articles and television reports. At the family's request, no one ever revealed his last name or the town where his family lived.[8]

WALLACE'S RESPONSE

On a special *60 Minutes* that examined the program's own methods, media critic Jeff Greenfield asked Mike Wallace, "How would you like somebody to point a camera at you that you didn't know was there, confront you with embarrassing material, perhaps about a life you once led or something you once did?"

"I wouldn't like it," Wallace replied, "which is why I lead a life beyond reproach."[9]

REMARKS

"Keep shooting, vultures!"

—Marilyn Monroe's press aide to photographers on the day of Monroe's death[10]

"I think I might take up being an astronaut, so I can get a little more privacy."

—Paul Newman to reporters[11]

"I never really understood until now why celebrities hate the press. . . . They never leave you alone."

—Carl Bernstein to his date, as photographers approached them[12]

"Journalists are as disruptive a menace to the public body as stones in the gall bladder are to the private body. They are the scavengers of society who, possessing no guts of their own, tear out the guts of celebrities."

—Caitlin Thomas, widow of Dylan Thomas[13]

"I want the drug abusers and adulterers to remain in your seats. The homosexuals and lesbians are fine where you are, and the AIDS carriers can stay scattered in the crowd. Let's have the alcoholics, liars and cheats sit in every other seat. Those of you without sin, stain, or stigma, please raise your hands, unless, of course, there's

something you want to tell me about your neighbor—see me afterward and I promise your name will be protected."

—Julian Bond, former Georgia state senator who had been accused of using cocaine, in a speech to reporters[14]

"I don't believe any politician in the United States ought to have a private life."

—Howard Simons, former *Washington Post* managing editor[15]

"Damn it, what do they want me to do? Go down to the press room and drop my pants and say, 'Here it is'?"

—President Reagan to press aides who wanted to announce that he had a urinary tract infection[16]

SECRECY

....

CONSTITUTIONAL NEWS MANAGEMENT

From the outset, George Washington was determined to prevent news leaks from the Constitutional Convention. When a delegate accidentally left a page of notes behind, convention president Washington held the paper up before the group. "I must entreat gentlemen to be more careful," he said, "lest our transactions get into the newspapers, and disturb the public repose by premature speculations. I know not whose paper it is, but there it is; let him who owns it take it." With that, Washington dropped the notes on the table, bowed, and strutted out. The paper went unclaimed.

After the convention's work was completed, Washington ensured a sympathetic first airing for the new Constitution by releasing only one copy to the press. At Washington's request, the cooperative *Pennsylvania Packet and Daily Advertiser* published the document in full.[17]

JAPANESE CODE

In 1942 Stanley Johnston of the *Chicago Tribune* learned that the Japanese had attacked Midway Island. Johnston had expected the Japanese to strike Midway as part of their Pacific strategy, and he believed that American military planners had shared the view. Using sketchy official navy reports, *Jane's Fighting Ships,* and informed speculation, Johnston and a colleague, Wayne Thomis, wrote a richly detailed account of the battle, including the fact that navy planners had anticipated the attack.

As soon as the *Tribune* published the story, Johnston and Thomis were called to Washington to meet with navy officials. The officials demanded to know the sources of their information. The reporters answered fully. Then the matter went before a federal grand jury. The jurors decided not to indict the men for espionage, but their names were publicly tarnished. The *Tribune* men were mystified by the heavy-handed response to an article that had, after all, described a major American victory.

The mystery was solved after the war's end. The key to the Midway victory, it developed, had been the navy's advance knowledge of the composition of the Japanese force, thanks to American codebreakers. Johnston and Thomis had no idea that the Japanese code had been broken, but their article had been so accurate that war planners feared that Japan would catch on. In fact, the Japanese never noticed the story.[18]

TESTING SECURITY

In 1951 radio commentator Paul Harvey decided to investigate what he understood to be lax security at the Argonne National Laboratory in Illinois, which conducted defense-related research. Late one night Harvey and two associates crept up to the lab grounds and climbed the fence. Harvey's coat caught on a wire and, while he was working to free it, several guards ran over and arrested the intruders. In Harvey's car the guards found a radio script, written in advance, that described Harvey's successful infiltration and decried the inadequate security.

A federal grand jury investigated the attempted break-in but didn't issue any indictments. Afterward Harvey tried to cast a positive light on the episode. "If our national security has been improved by the fact that national attention was focused on this situation," he said, "I am extremely grateful."[19]

UNWRITTEN STORIES: NATIONAL SECURITY

- Three *New York Times* writers, James Reston, Arthur Krock, and Hanson Baldwin, knew about America's secret spy-plane flights over the Soviet Union in the '50s. They published nothing until after the Soviets shot down one of the U-2 planes in 1960.
- The *New York Herald Tribune* postponed a story about the release of two American fliers who had been held in the Soviet Union. President Kennedy's press secretary, Pierre Salinger, insisted that premature publicity might cause the Soviets to cancel the planned release. Some reporters believed the true purpose was to give the President a major piece of good news to announce at his first White House news conference.
- President Kennedy urged *The New York Times* to kill a comprehensive article about the planned Bay of Pigs invasion. After a heated internal debate, the *Times* compromised. The paper published the article, omitting some information that seemed especially sensitive; and it changed the story's placement from a four-column, front-page lead, to a less obtrusive one-column headline near the middle of the front page. The President was furious anyway. "Castro doesn't need agents over here," he grumbled. "All he has to do is read our papers."

- During the Cuban missile crisis, President Kennedy convinced *The New York Times* and the *Washington Post* to hold back some information about the Soviet missiles in Cuba until he had delivered a TV speech on the subject. The cooperation, Kennedy later said, "made far more effective our later actions and thereby contributed greatly to our national safety."[20]

BAY OF PIGS AFTERTHOUGHTS

After the Bay of Pigs, President Kennedy expressed several contradictory views about the press's role in the debacle:

- First he chastised the press for having published too much. "[T]his nation's foes," he said in a speech to newspaper publishers less than two weeks after the landing, "have openly boasted of acquiring through our newspapers information they would otherwise hire agents to acquire through theft, bribery or espionage." Kennedy urged reporters to think twice before publishing sensitive information. "Every newspaper now asks itself, with respect to every story: 'Is it news?' All I suggest is that you add the question: 'Is it in the interest of national security?' " A few days after the speech, Kennedy proposed a more specific solution to several journalists: The government would give high-level security clearances to a group of reporters, who would then examine other reporters' articles in advance of publication and determine whether they threatened national security. The idea was never pursued.
- Later Kennedy chided two editors for having printed too *little* before the invasion—the viewpoint that reporters have most frequently cited in the years since. Meeting with editors to discuss his voluntary censorship notion, President Kennedy told Turner Catledge, managing editor of the *Times,* "Maybe if you had printed more about the operation, you would have saved us from a colossal mistake." More than a year after that, he made the same point to *Times* publisher Orvil Dryfoos: "I wish you had run everything on Cuba."

- A month after talking with Dryfoos, Kennedy reversed course again and thanked the *Times* for its cautious handling of the Bay of Pigs story. "[A]n important service to the national interest," the President wrote Dryfoos, "was performed by your agreement to withhold information that was available to you on Sunday afternoon."[21]

SECRECY AND THE PRESS: PRE-PENTAGON PAPERS

"The concept of a return to secrecy in peacetime demonstrates a profound misunderstanding of the role of a free press as opposed to that of a controlled press. The plea for secrecy could become a cloak for errors, misjudgments and other failings of government."

—Richard Nixon on President Kennedy's call for press self-restraint after the Bay of Pigs

"The secrecy of one of the highest organs of the United States has been seriously breached. What kind of advice can the President expect to get under such circumstances? How can there be any real freedom of discussion or of dissent; how can anyone be expected to advance positions that may be politically unpopular or unprofitable?"

—*New York Times* editorial concerning a *Saturday Evening Post* article that revealed details of the administration's debates over the Cuban missile crisis[22]

WHOSE VICTORY?

When the Supreme Court ruled that *The New York Times* and the *Washington Post* could resume publishing the Pentagon Papers, two weeks after courts had first ordered the newspapers to stop, journalists celebrated. At the *Times,* publisher

Arthur O. Sulzberger said he felt "complete joy and delight." *Post* publisher Katharine Graham said she was "completely gratified."

Outside the press, though, some people viewed the results as mixed. The *Times'* lawyer, Yale law professor Alexander Bickel, wrote that until the Pentagon Papers litigation, "there had never been an effort by the Federal Government to censor a newspaper by attempting to impose a restraint prior to publication. . . . The *New York Times* won its case over the Pentagon papers, but that spell was broken, and in a sense freedom was thus diminished."

The government's partial victory may have extended beyond the law. Erwin Griswold, the U.S. solicitor general who had argued against Bickel in the Supreme Court, said that "we won the case" in terms of national security. Of the eleven items he had insisted were especially sensitive, Griswold wrote, only one or two were published in newspapers (several others later appeared in the book version of the Pentagon Papers). "[T]here was one item," according to Griswold, "probably the most important, that has never been printed anywhere."[23]

STOPPING THE GLOMAR STORY

In 1974 and 1975 the Central Intelligence Agency tried to raise a sunken Soviet submarine northwest of Hawaii in order to learn about codes and technology. On its first try the CIA's costly minisub, the *Glomar Explorer,* brought up about a third of the Soviet vessel. Agency officials wanted to retrieve the other two-thirds, but they believed that they would lose the opportunity if the Soviets learned about the mission and sent a naval squadron to the area.

CIA officials particularly feared *The New York Times* and its reporter Seymour Hersh, who was investigating *Glomar.* While Hersh researched his article, CIA director William Colby worked to keep it from being published. He phoned several *Times* editors and writers, some of whom had never heard of the secret submarine, and asked that the newspaper postpone the story until *Glomar* could complete its second try.

In a letter to Colby, the *Times* formally agreed to postpone its story until the CIA had completed or abandoned the effort to raise the sub, or until some other news outlet was prepared to go with the story. In exchange, the CIA agreed to notify the *Times* as soon as any of these events occurred.

When Hersh turned in his manuscript, *Times* executive editor A. M. Rosenthal said the story was on hold because it concerned an "on-going intelligence operation." Hersh, miffed, asked how the *Glomar* story differed from the Pentagon Papers story, which had concerned the "on-going war" in Vietnam. Rosenthal said there was no comparison.

Colby, meanwhile, managed to get no-publication commitments from the *Los Angeles Times, Washington Post, Washington Star, Newsweek, Time,* AP, UPI, *Parade,* National Public Radio, and the three commercial networks. In his appeals Colby had placed great weight on the fact that *The New York Times* had agreed to hold back the story.

Several weeks later the *Times* got word that columnist Jack Anderson, ignoring Colby's requests, planned to tell the *Glomar* story on his radio program. Rosenthal instructed Hersh to update his article for the next morning's newspaper. Hersh, tongue in cheek, asked Rosenthal why the paper's plans had suddenly changed. "It still involves national security," the reporter said. "We didn't run it before—why should we do it now just because Anderson does it?" Rosenthal told him to shut up.

The *Glomar* episode, Charles Seib of the *Washington Post* concluded, proved one thing: Prominent, powerful media people are "easy to con."[24]

PREPUBLICATION REVIEW: THE PELTON SECRETS

In September 1985 *Washington Post* reporter Robert Woodward came to the paper's executive editor, Ben Bradlee, with what seemed like (as Bradlee later said) "the highest national security secret any of us had ever heard." Woodward described top-secret details of American "communications intercept capabilities"—technical methods of gathering intelligence, such as by using submarines to eavesdrop on Soviet military communications. The information was so sensitive, Bradlee said, that "[t]here was never a thought given to publishing" it.

In November the situation changed. Ronald Pelton, a National Security Agency employee, was arrested for selling secrets to the Soviets, apparently including the intercept information. If the Soviets already knew it, then why not publish it? On December 5 Bradlee and another *Post* editor presented that question to the head of the National Security Agency, Lieutenant General William Odom. Odom disputed their premise. The government, he said, was still uncertain exactly how much Pelton had told the Soviets, and publishing the material would "gravely threaten the security of the United States."

Over the next six months *Post* editors met repeatedly with Odom and other government officials. At the meetings the officials reviewed different versions of the *Post*'s article. Each time the officials said the article violated national security. Each time the *Post* editors disagreed but lacked the certitude to publish.

In May 1986, the officials raised the possibility of criminal prosecution. "I'm not threatening you," CIA director William Casey told Bradlee and another editor, "but you've got to know that, if you publish this, I would recommend that you be prosecuted under the intelligence statute." Ten days later President Reagan reiterated the warning in a call to Katharine Graham, chairman of the board of the Washington Post Company (though Graham characterized the call as "low-key" and "civilized"). The *Post* continued to hold the story.

On May 19, as Pelton's trial was beginning, the *Post* lost its scoop. NBC News reported that Pelton had revealed "a top-secret eavesdropping program by American submarines inside Soviet harbors." Bradlee, frustrated and resentful, called Casey. Later that day the CIA announced that it was referring the NBC matter to the Justice Department for possible prosecution.

The *Post* worked on its last revision. This one omitted all technical details, which seemed most likely to violate the espionage statute. The newspaper published the final version, unreviewed by any official, on May 28. Casey said the CIA was considering prosecution, but, as with the threat against NBC, nothing came of it.

Bradlee later questioned the process. The problem was not holding back secrets—he said the *Post* had withheld information from more than a dozen stories in the first six months of 1986—but in letting officials review the stories before publication. In the future, he said, "I'm not sure I'm going to show all these things to anyone."[25]

ATOMIC SECRETS

In the 1950s *Newsweek*'s Henry M. Paynter wrote detailed articles about American atomic weapons. Although the stories were based on nonclassified materials and Paynter's informed speculation, military officials were troubled. They asked Paynter to meet with intelligence officers.

On the appointed day Paynter met two officers at the National Press Club bar. As the men talked, an announcement came over the public address system asking Paynter to call the Polish embassy. Paynter, recognizing his friends' prank, remained seated. A few minutes later a second announcement was made, asking Paynter to phone the Soviet embassy. Again Paynter ignored it and continued talking. Then a man wearing a turned-up coat collar, dark glasses, and hat hurried over, handed Paynter an envelope, and said in a pseudo-Russian accent, "Mr. Paynter, you robber, here is your check. But this is the last five thousand dollars you get from us." After the "spy" had scurried away, one officer said with some exasperation, "Mr. Paynter, you don't seem to be taking this meeting seriously."[26]

REMARKS

"[B]y the villainous and mischievous newspapers, everything we do or design to do, not only our friends but also our enemies all over the world know of it, and are

thus advertised and cautioned to prepare to defeat everything we undertake."

—John Thomlinson, a British official stationed in the American colonies, complaining about press reports that Britain planned to send ships and troops to quell the colonists' uprising[27]

"Anything you don't want to see on the front page of The New York Times *tomorrow you should classify."*

—Advice given to James C. Thomson, Jr., by a State Department colleague[28]

"Our primary obligation is to our readers. I wouldn't know how to interpret our obligation to the government."

—Turner Catledge, *New York Times* managing editor[29]

"It's their job to keep secrets. It's our job to find out about them."

—Walter Mears, AP executive editor[30]

LIBEL AND OTHER LAWSUITS

....

PUNISHING THE LIBEL

In the early 1700s British authorities in America not only prosecuted printers responsible for published libels, they also sentenced libelous newspapers and pamphlets to be whipped and burned.[31]

Joseph Pulitzer, owner of the *New York World*, hid out at sea when President Theodore Roosevelt tried to prosecute him for "a string of infamous libels"—articles accusing Roosevelt of lying about the Panama Canal purchase. *Library of Congress*

Pulitzer's major rival was William Randolph Hearst, owner of the *New York Journal.* In Cuba during the Spanish-American War, Hearst said to a wounded *Journal* reporter: "I'm sorry you're hurt, but wasn't it a splendid fight?" *Library of Congress*

Frank Munsey, convinced that the newspaper business needed "organization and combination," bought and closed down six New York City newspapers. "He and his kind," William Allen White wrote, "have about succeeded in transforming a once noble profession into an eight percent security." *Library of Congress*

Henry Luce, the founder of *Time*, was the subject of a *New Yorker* profile that parodied *Time*'s writing style: "Certainly to be taken with seriousness is Luce. . . . Where it will all end, knows God!" *National Archives*

When losses at his new *USA Today* were escalating, Al Neuharth wore a crown of thorns to a dinner meeting. "I am the crucified one," he told his executives, and unless they reduced the newspaper's losses, it could turn out to be their "last supper." USA Today

John F. Kennedy was the first president to allow his news conferences to be televised live. The cameras had one clearcut effect: The length of the average question more than tripled. *John F. Kennedy Library*

Dan Rather covered fellow Texan Lyndon B. Johnson. When he was angry over a CBS story, President Johnson would phone Rather and say: "Are you trying to fuck me?" *Lyndon B. Johnson Library*

Barbara Walters got her start writing for the *Today* show. A few years after moving to the other side of the camera, she was interviewing presidents and other celebrities. *National Archives*

Walter Cronkite anchored the *CBS Evening News* for nearly twenty years. When some people talked of a political career for Cronkite, one of his colleagues asked, "Why in the world would Cronkite want to be President of the United States and give up all that power?" *Gerald R. Ford Library*

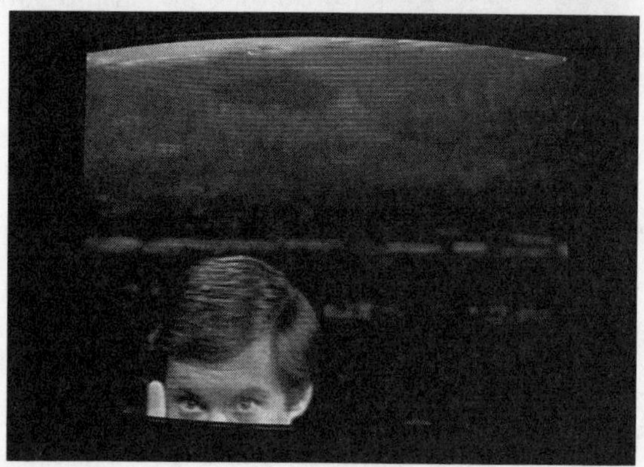

When an earthquake struck during Los Angeles's KNBC morning news, anchor Kent Shocknek disappeared under his desk. He said afterward: "If I disappointed those gore fans who wanted to see a klieg light come crashing down and split my skull open, I'm sorry." Washington Journalism Review

New York Herald publisher James Gordon Bennett, Jr., asked an editor to compile a list of the newspaper's indispensable reporters—and then fired everyone on it. *National Archives*

New York Tribune editor Horace Greeley initially refused to publish theater advertisements because "a large proportion of those connected with the stage are libertines or courtesans." His partners, worried about profits, convinced him to cancel the policy. *Library of Congress*

Margaret Fuller wrote reviews for Greeley's *Tribune* and lived in the Greeley household. Greeley criticized her philosophy, politics, and even diet. His nagging, he wrote, "did not tend to ripen our intimacy." *Library of Congress*

Charles Dana, managing editor of the *Tribune*, fired the newspaper's London correspondent, Karl Marx. The young *Communist Manifesto* author had been submitting invoices for articles he hadn't yet written. *Library of Congress*

Columnist Westbrook Pegler was ordered to pay nearly $200,000 to foreign correspondent Quentin Reynolds. Pegler had called Reynolds, among other things, a nudist, war profiteer, and coward. *Franklin D. Roosevelt Library*

The *Washington Post* publishes Jack Anderson's column on the comics page. *Post* editors once considered relocating the column, according to Anderson, but he urged that it be left where people had come to expect it. *Gerald R. Ford Library*

The identity of Carl Bernstein (left) and Bob Woodward's Watergate supersource, Deep Throat, is known by only a handful of people. Bernstein's ex-wife Nora Ephron isn't one of them, according to Bernstein: "She used to ask me a lot, and I had the good sense not to tell her." *AP/Wide World Photos*

Benjamin Franklin wrote the "Speech of Polly Baker"—a young woman being prosecuted for giving birth to her fifth illegitimate child—to make a point about women's rights. The speech was treated as genuine by many newspapers and history books. *Library of Congress*

Richard Adams Locke wrote in the *New York Sun* that astronomers had discovered a wide variety of plant and animal life on the moon. The *Sun*'s circulation increased dramatically before Locke admitted it was a hoax. *Library of Congress*

An artist drew this busy lunar scene from the *Sun*'s descriptions.
Library of Congress

In the *New York Evening Mail*, H.L. Mencken published a colorful, detailed history of the bathtub. Years later, after much of the information had entered reference books, Mencken said he had invented the whole "tissue of absurdities," because researching the true story would have been "a dreadful job." *Library of Congress*

FOREIGN ASSIGNMENTS AND WARS

For the *New York Herald*, Henry Morton Stanley set out for Africa to find missing missionary David Livingstone. Nearly two years after leaving New York, Stanley approached an elderly man in a red jacket and said: "Dr. Livingstone, I presume?" It was. *Library of Congress*

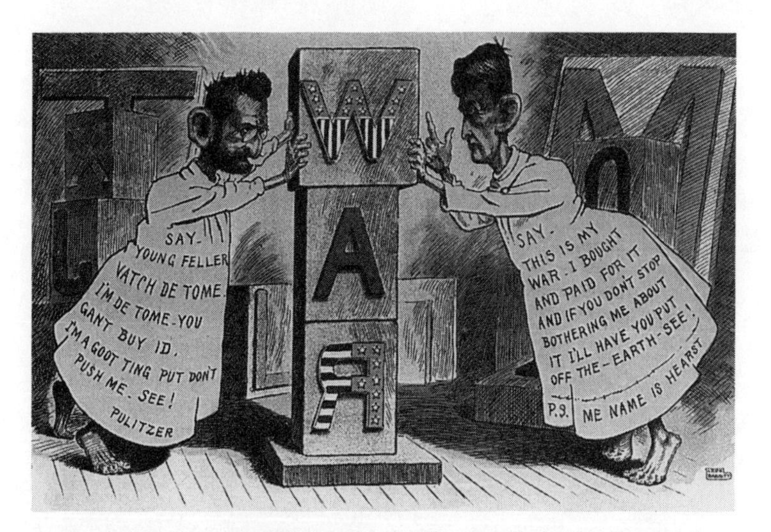

A cartoonist (borrowing from the "Yellow Kid" comic) depicts the newspaper war behind the Spanish-American War. Hearst's *New York Journal* published the obituary of Colonel Reflipe W. Thenuz. When, as expected, Pulitzer's *New York World* stole the story, the *Journal* revealed that the name was a rough anagram of "we pilfer the news." *Library of Congress*

Columnist Walter Winchell wrote that Adolf Hitler was "an out-and-out fairy." The official Nazi newspaper responded that only "morons" read Winchell, but Hitler himself was disturbed by the attack. *Franklin D. Roosevelt Library*

When Edward R. Murrow delivered his live radio broadcasts from the London rooftops, he would stand next to a British censor. The censor would tap Murrow on the wrist whenever he started to talk about a sensitive subject. *National Archives*

Marguerite Higgins of the *New York Herald Tribune* was virtually the only woman to cover the Korean War. When she complained that she was treated differently from the other reporters, Jimmy Cannon of the *New York Post* replied: "If the *Racing Form* sent a race horse to cover the war, he wouldn't be any more of an oddity than you are." *Brentano's*

On his trips abroad, Secretary of State Henry Kissinger spoke with reporters on the condition that they identify him only as a "senior U.S. official." One reporter wrote that "the senior U.S. official was last seen entering a long black limousine with Nancy Kissinger."
Gerald R. Ford Library

Thomas Nast's cartoons helped destroy New York City's corrupt Tweed ring. When Tweed (with beard at left) tried to hide out in Spain to avoid prosecution, he was turned in by someone who recognized him from a Nast cartoon. *Library of Congress*

President Johnson liked to talk to reporters as he walked briskly around the White House grounds. After fifteen laps one sweltering August day, reporters started calling the mobile news conferences "Bataan death marches." *Lyndon B. Johnson Library*

Reporters might find ways to get President Nixon's attention, but they couldn't get his respect. After the Apollo 11 astronauts returned with moon rocks, Nixon said he hoped there were some "contaminated" ones that he could send to the press. *National Archives*

In separate incidents during the 1968 Democratic convention, Chicago police arrested CBS's Mike Wallace (above) and Dan Rather. A few days earlier, the police department had boasted of its "excellent rapport" with the press. *AP/Wide World Photos*

CIRCULATION BOOSTERS

In his *New York Herald* in 1836, James Gordon Bennett, Sr., published a series of melodramatic articles about the murder of a prostitute. As part of the coverage, Bennett questioned the prostitute's madam—the first newspaper interview in the United States. *Library of Congress*

The *New York World* assigned Nellie Bly to find out if a person could travel around the world in eighty days, like Jules Verne's fictional hero. When Bly made it back in seventy-two days, the *World* published the triumphant headline FATHER TIME OUTDONE! *Library of Congress*

Daily Globe.

DAILY GLOBE:	
Sept. '92	200,143
Sept. '91	154,178
GAIN	45,965

OCTOBER 10, 1892—TEN PAGES. PRICE TWO CENTS.

LATEST!

For Other Evening News See Second, Fourth, Fifth and Eighth Pages.

ASTOUNDED.

All New England Read Story.

Globes Were Bought by Thousands.

Lizzie Borden Appears in New Light.

Belief in Her Innocence Sadly Shaken.

Excitement Runs High in Fall River.

Police Think the Scoop is a Corker.

Lawyer Jennings Says Lies Have Been Told.

Doesn't Believe There is Any Secret.

Opinions on That Spying by Detective McHenry.

[illegible]

LIZZIE HAD A SECRET.

Mr. Borden Discovered It. Then a Quarrel.

Startling Testimony of 25 New Witnesses.

Seen in Mother's Room With a Hood on Her Head.

Accused Sister of Treachery and Kicked Her in Anger.

Theft of a Watch—Money Offered to Bridget—Story of a Will.

[illegible]

The *Boston Globe*'s Lizzie Borden scoop—sensational evidence showing that Borden had murdered her parents—turned out to be a hoax. The *Globe* fervently apologized for adding to the young woman's "terrible burdens." *Louis M. Lyons*, Newspaper Story

Richard Outcault initially drew the "Yellow Kid," the first regularly appearing newspaper comic, for Pulitzer's *New York World*, and then accepted a better offer from Hearst's *New York Journal*. The battle for the popular comic produced the term "yellow journalism." *Library of Congress*

The *New York Graphic* produced this "composograph"—a photo created through staging and superimposing—showing a wealthy businessman, Edward "Daddy" Browning, bickering with his fifteen-year-old wife, Peaches, while their pet goose looks on. *Frank Mallen*, Sauce for the Gander

In another composograph, printed after film star Rudolph Valentino's unexpected death, tenor Enrico Caruso shows the newcomer the sights of Heaven. *Frank Mallen*, Sauce for the Gander

A *New York Daily News* photographer smuggled a camera into the execution chamber and produced this moment-of-death photo. The *News* published and sold a million extra copies of the issue. N.Y. Daily News *photo*

FRANKLIN'S SOLUTION

In a newspaper article published in 1789, Benjamin Franklin urged libel victims to rely on extrajudicial remedies. "My proposal, then," he wrote, "is to leave the liberty of the press untouched, to be exercised in its full extent, force and vigor, but to permit the liberty of the cudgel to go with it. . . . Thus, my fellow citizens, if an impudent writer attacks your reputation, dearer to you perhaps than your life, you may go to him as openly and break his head."[32]

FRONTIERSMAN PLAINTIFF

As a frequent libel plaintiff who often represented himself in court, James Fenimore Cooper became known as the nation's leading expert on libel law in the 1830s and 1840s. Cooper filed sixteen lawsuits, many of them over unfavorable reviews of his books, and he won most of them.

One jury ordered Horace Greeley of the *New York Tribune* to pay Cooper two hundred dollars. Greeley wrote a light-hearted account of the trial for the *Tribune,* and Cooper sued him again, this time for three thousand dollars. Greeley wrote an article proposing an out-of-court settlement: "Now, Fenimore, you push a very good quill of your own, except when you attempt to be funny—then you break down. . . . [W]hy not settle this difference at the point of the pen? We hereby tender you a column a day of the *Tribune,* for ten days, promising to publish *verbatim* whatever you may write. . . . We will further agree not to write over two columns in reply to the whole. . . . Be wise now! most chivalrous antagonist, and don't detract from the dignity of your profession!" Cooper, though he didn't accept Greeley's offer, dropped the suit.[33]

CHERRY SISTERS IN COURT

At the turn of the century the *Des Moines Register* won a landmark libel case. The *Register* had been sued by the Cherry Sisters, an Iowa singing group who had taken umbrage at a review in the paper: "Their long skinny arms, equipped with talons at the extremities, swung mechanically, and anon waved frantically at the suffering audience. The mouths of their rancid features opened like caverns, and sounds like the wailings of damned souls issued therefrom." At trial the judge listened to the sisters' act and then ruled in favor of the newspaper.[34]

LIBELPROOF

In the '50s the *Las Vegas Sun*'s editor-publisher, Hank Greenspun, found himself in an unusual position: He could write anything about Senator Joseph McCarthy without risking a libel suit. The situation came about because McCarthy had called Greenspun an "ex-Communist" in a 1952 Las Vegas speech. For once McCarthy's charge had been a slip of the tongue. He had meant to say "ex-convict," which was accurate. The baseless communism charge left McCarthy vulnerable to a defamation lawsuit, which Greenspun could initiate as soon as McCarthy returned to Nevada—and McCarthy couldn't sue Greenspun without entering the state.

The *Sun* used its license to publish rumors that other publications avoided. Several articles reported that McCarthy was homosexual, and a series of columns raised the question "Is McCarthy a Secret Communist?" McCarthy tried to stop the articles without entering Nevada, by convincing the postmaster general to have Greenspun indicted for mailing material that tended to "incite murder or assassination." A jury acquitted him.[35]

STOPPING THE PRESS

In 1960 *The New York Times* faced $6.2 million in libel actions in the state of Alabama. (The Supreme Court's landmark *New York Times vs. Sullivan* ruling, which insulated the press from many libel judgments, came four years later.) *Times* lawyers thought they could get the suits dismissed on the grounds that Alabama courts lacked jurisdiction. That defense, however, would collapse if a process server could find a *Times* employee, other than a lawyer on official business, in the state. So the *Times* ordered its reporters to stay outside Alabama—effectively stifling *Times* coverage of the state's civil rights movement for more than a year.[36]

REPORTERS AS PLAINTIFFS

- NBC's Chet Huntley won ten thousand dollars from a woman who had called him a Communist.
- In the early '60s an editorial in the *Fairbanks News-Miner* in Alaska told readers that the newspaper would no longer publish columns by "the garbage man of the fourth estate," Drew Pearson. Pearson claimed that the remark damaged his reputation, and he sued for $176,000. A judge threw out the suit, asking rhetorically: "How many garbage pails must a person empty to be called a garbage man?"
- In 1968 columnist William F. Buckley, Jr., sued writer Gore Vidal and *Esquire* over a Vidal article that implied that Buckley was homosexual and anti-Semitic. Three years later *Esquire* settled the suit for $15,000, an additional $100,000 in advertising for Buckley's magazine *National Review,* and a published recantation of the Vidal allegations.
- C. L. Sulzberger, a *New York Times* columnist (and cousin of *Times* publisher Arthur Ochs Sulzberger), wanted to sue former *Washington Post* reporter Carl Bernstein. Bernstein had written in *Rolling Stone* that Sulzberger had accepted a confidential briefing paper from the CIA and then published it "almost verbatim" in his column. Sulzberger denied the allegation, and he urged the *Times'* lawyers to sue Bernstein for libel and force him to reveal his sources. "The public," Sulzberger said, "is entitled to be in a position where it can judge whether the charges are true or false." The lawyers decided against a lawsuit.
- The most famous libel suit between journalists is *Reynolds vs. Pegler.* In 1939 Westbrook Pegler, an acerbic right-wing columnist, accused left-wing columnist Heywood Broun of dishonesty and compared him to Hitler and

Stalin. Broun, deeply troubled by Pegler's attack, died of pneumonia a few weeks later. In 1950 Broun's friend Quentin Reynolds, a respected foreign correspondent and best-selling author, wrote a book review implying that the Pegler column had hastened Broun's death. Pegler struck back wildly. He wrote in his column that Reynolds had been "an absentee war correspondent" and war profiteer, that he had belonged to a nudist group that included "a conspicuous Negro Communist," and that he had a "mangy hide," a "yellow streak," and a "protuberant belly filled with something other than guts." Reynolds hired attorney Louis Nizer and sued for libel. After an eight-week trial, at which Reynolds's good character was attested by fellow journalists Walter Kerr, John Gunther, and Edward R. Murrow, the jury awarded Reynolds $175,001. Including interest and other charges the total came to nearly $200,000, the largest amount collected in any libel case up to that time.[37]

THE COST OF A BROKEN PROMISE

News organizations have frequently faced legal threats for refusing to divulge a source's identity. In 1988 two newspapers ended up in court for *revealing* the name of a source.

The tale began a week before the 1982 election, when Dan Cohen, a Minneapolis advertising agency employee and part-time Republican party consultant, contacted four reporters separately. Cohen said that he had important information about the campaign and that he would reveal it only under a strict promise of confidentiality. All four reporters agreed to the terms. Cohen told them that the Democratic candidate for lieutenant governor had been convicted of shoplifting.

Two news organizations, the Associated Press and a TV station, kept their promises. AP published the information without revealing the source. The TV station, WCCO, decided not to use the story.

At the other two organizations, the *St. Paul Pioneer Press Dispatch* and the *Minneapolis Star Tribune,* editors believed that the source *was* the news. In their eyes the Republicans' last-minute smear campaign mattered at least as much as what turned out to be a twelve-year-old conviction for taking items worth six dollars. Both newspapers overruled their reporters and published Cohen's name. A few days later the *Star Tribune* also published a sharply critical column and an editorial cartoon showing Cohen wearing a trashcan.

Cohen lost his ad agency job as a result of the controversy, and he sued the two newspapers for breach of the oral contracts to keep his identity secret. The newspapers' lawyers argued that the First Amendment prohibited such lawsuits, but the judge disagreed. It was, he said, simply a case about "contracts and misrepresentation." After two weeks of testimony, the jury awarded Cohen $700,000. An appeals court reduced the award to $200,000.[38]

THE FORCE OF LAW

....

HARBOR DEFENSE

In 1908 the *New York World* and the *Indianapolis News* reported that the United States was paying forty million dollars for Panama Canal property worth only twelve million. The *World,* owned by Joseph Pulitzer, further accused President Theodore Roosevelt of lying about the deal.

President Roosevelt called the stories a "string of infamous libels." "It is idle," he said in a message to Congress, "to say that the known character of Mr. Pulitzer and his newspaper are such that the statements in that paper will be believed by nobody; unfortunately, thousands of persons are ill informed in this respect and believe the statements they see in print. . . ."

At Roosevelt's instruction the government started legal proceedings on several fronts. In Washington a judge issued warrants for the arrest of Pulitzer and others. Pulitzer, an invalid, hid out at sea on his yacht, the *Liberty.* In Indianapolis a federal attorney resigned rather than prosecute the *News,* and a judge dismissed the case. In New York government lawyers charged the *World* with an unlikely crime—violating a statute "to protect harbor defense from malicious injury."

The actions worked their way through the courts over the next few months. Ultimately all were dismissed. "If this is to be a government of the people," Pulitzer wrote afterward, "it is a crime to put into the hands of a President such powers."[39]

ADMINISTRATION LIMITS

When the People's Republic of China was ready to talk, the United States refused to let reporters listen. In the mid-1950s the government of China hinted that, for the first time since the Communist takeover, it was ready to admit reporters from *The New York Times.* But the American government at the time didn't recognize the People's Republic, and the Eisenhower administration didn't want to publicize the regime. After the administration threatened to prosecute the *Times* for "trading with the enemy," the newspaper dropped its plans.[40]

CONGRESSIONAL THREAT

In 1971 questions were raised about a CBS documentary, *The Selling of the Pentagon.* The filmmaker, Peter Davis, had spliced a few interview sentences out of their original order, in one case placing a subject's answer after an entirely different question. A congressional subcommittee decided to investigate.

The subcommittee subpoenaed all materials, including outtakes, related to the show. CBS said it would turn over the documentary but not the outtakes. Surrendering outtakes, a network official said, "would have a chilling effect on the ability of journalists . . . to report and interpret the news. . . ." The subcommittee sent out a new subpoena, this time demanding the outtakes and an appearance by CBS president Frank Stanton.

Stanton came empty-handed and reiterated the network's position. The subcommittee voted to cite Stanton for contempt of Congress, which could include a prison term. The full House decided to let the matter drop. Effective lobbying on CBS's behalf, it turned out, came from the Nixon White House, which was eager to put the network in its debt.[41]

BROKEN PROMISE

At the 1970 Gridiron dinner in Washington, Attorney General John Mitchell joked about his reputation for wiretapping. "[Y]our privacy tonight is absolutely guaranteed," he said. "Purely as a precaution, however, I do suggest that, if you have anything really confidential to say at the dinner table, don't speak too close to the salt shakers." He finished by saying "[I]n the spirit of reciprocity, may I close with this promise: 'If you'll stop bugging me, I'll stop bugging you.' "[42]

JOB INVESTIGATION

In 1971 several people told Daniel Schorr that FBI agents had been asking questions about him, supposedly because he was under consideration for a sensitive federal job. That was the first that Schorr, a CBS correspondent, had heard about any new job. He asked the FBI to halt the investigation. The bureau apparently did so, and Schorr heard nothing more. A few months later, in response to a *Washington Post* article about the incident, White House officials said that Schorr had been up for a job "in the area of the environment," that the investigation had been "clumsily handled," and that procedures had been overhauled.

During the Watergate hearings the truth emerged. On August 18, 1971, Schorr had reported on CBS that the White House had no plans to aid parochial schools and that Nixon's statement to the contrary appeared to be "for political or rhetorical effect." The next day Nixon learned about the segment and ordered aide H. R. Haldeman: "Get the FBI to pull the file on that son-of-a-bitch, Schorr." Haldeman told an assistant to phone J. Edgar Hoover with the instruction. Somewhere the message got garbled: Nixon wanted a quiet investigation, but Hoover understood that the request was for a full field investigation. After Schorr complained, the White House called everything off.[43]

DENIABILITY

A man who provided confidential documents to Jack Anderson's assistant Les Whitten anticipated that the leak would be investigated. So that the source could truthfully testify that he had never given anything to Whitten, Whitten brought his eighty-four-year-old mother to the rendezvous, and the man handed her the documents.[44]

PANAMANIAN EXCISION

In 1988 government officials in Panama tore an article out of each copy of the August *Penthouse,* twelve hundred in all, that entered the country. The article reported that General Manuel Noriega, Panama's leader, used Grecian Formula hair coloring and pimple medications.[45]

REMARKS

"And forasmuch as great inconvenience may arise by liberty of printing . . . you are to provide by all necessary orders that no person keep any printing-press for printing, nor that any book, pamphlet, or other matter whatsoever be printed without your especial leave and license first obtained."

—Instructions from the British government to its officials in the American colonies[46]

"The liberty of the press consists, in my idea, in publishing the truth, from good motives and for justifiable ends, though it reflect on the government, on magistrates, or individuals."

—Alexander Hamilton[47]

"Newspapers, if they are to be interesting, must not be molested."

—Frederick the Great[48]

ETHICS

NEWSGATHERING DECEPTIONS

....

HEIFETZ

Harry Romanoff, a police reporter on the *Chicago Herald-Examiner* (later renamed *Chicago Today*), was called "the Heifetz of the telephone" for his masquerades. Gathering information on the 1966 murders of eight student nurses, Romanoff first called a policeman and identified himself as the Cook County coroner, and then called the mother of the principal suspect, Richard Speck, and identified himself as Speck's attorney. Another time Romanoff pretended to be with the State Department and spoke to high officials in the Kremlin. On other occasions Romanoff pretended to be the chief of police, a reporter for another newspaper, a White House official, the governor of Illinois, and a bishop. "Once in a while," Romanoff said after his retirement in 1969, "you have to shade things to protect the public's right to know."[1]

WATERGATE

According to their book *All the President's Men,* Bob Woodward and Carl Bernstein employed several deceptions and other ethically arguable practices. The *Washington Post* reporters:

- Got confidential telephone toll records from phone company sources. Bernstein was troubled by the "ethical questions" and knew that he would be "outrage[d]" if he were the victim of such a disclosure.
- Exchanged information with law-enforcement authorities. At one point an investigator for a district attorney asked Bernstein to gather information about a man named Neal Sonnett for "a case we're working, not related to Watergate." Bernstein got the information from a Pentagon source, but by then the investigator said he didn't need it after all. Bernstein later found out that Sonnett was a candidate for DA, running against the investigator's boss. "Trading information with a source was a touchy business and a last resort. . . ."
- Misled potential sources from the Nixon reelection committee. "[T]he approach that seemed to work best was less than straightforward: A friend at the committee told us that you were disturbed by some of the things you saw going on there, that you would be a good person to talk to. . . ."
- Left a phone message that omitted mention of their employer. "Bernstein bent the rules a bit. The *Post* had a firm policy that its reporters were never to misrepresent themselves."
- Lied to their super-source. "Though it wasn't true, Woodward told Deep Throat that he and Bernstein had a story for the following week saying that . . ."

- Revealed the identity of a previously cooperative FBI source in order to punish him for refusing to cooperate further. "They had realized that confronting the agent's boss was unethical as soon as they had done it."
- Asked grand jurors to violate the law by telling what had gone on during secret grand jury proceedings. "They felt lousy. They had not broken the law. . . . But they had sailed around it and exposed others to danger. They had chosen expediency over principle. . . ."[2]

DECEPTIONS

- Nellie Bly (pseudonym of Elizabeth Cochran) of the *New York World* pretended to be insane in order to be committed to the asylum on Blackwell's Island. Her articles about the inhuman conditions brought about a grand jury investigation and important reforms. Later Bly worked in a sweatshop, got a job as a chorus girl, and had herself imprisoned, all in order to write exposés.
- When the press was barred from the New York City pier where the *Titanic* survivors landed, many reporters got through by dressing as doctors or priests.
- A reporter for the *San Francisco Chronicle,* Pierre Salinger, had himself arrested for vagrancy so he could investigate prison conditions. He chose the name Peter Flick (*flic* is French slang for policeman). Later, when the FBI investigated Salinger before he became White House press secretary, he had to explain his pseudonymous arrest record to President Kennedy.
- In the early '60s Gloria Steinem spent a month as a "bunny" in the New York City Playboy Club and then wrote about the experience for *Show* magazine. To get the job, Steinem (under the name Marie Catherine Ochs) had posed for photos in a bunny costume and signed a model's release. Later, when Steinem gained stature in the feminist movement, the photos periodically reap-

peared in *Playboy*. It was, Steinem said, "*Playboy*'s long-running revenge."

- When antibusing activists grew angry over what they considered a probusing slant in the *Boston Globe*, some *Globe* reporters covering the story said they worked for the *Christian Science Monitor*.
- The *Chicago Sun-Times* ran an undercover bar, the Mirage, for four months in 1977 to document corruption among city inspectors. The newspaper's twenty-five part series was initially in line for a Pulitzer Prize, but the Pulitzer board disapproved of the newspaper's deception and overruled the jury.
- A *National Journal* reporter offered an illegal contribution to several 1980 presidential campaigns. All of the campaigns explained that they couldn't accept the thirty thousand dollars. Four Republican campaigns—those of Ronald Reagan, George Bush, Howard Baker, and Philip Crane—suggested alternatives that at least raised questions of legality. *National Journal*'s editor decided not to publish the article because, he said, "people were quoted without knowing they were talking to a reporter."
- In 1981 a *Los Angeles Herald Examiner* reporter, Merle Linda Wollin, impersonated an illegal alien and got a garment factory job in order to report on working conditions. As with the *Chicago Sun-Times* Mirage investigation, the *Herald Examiner* report was recommended for a Pulitzer by the jury but overruled by the board. "In a day when we are spending thousands of man-hours uncovering deception," said one board member, Ben Bradlee of the *Washington Post*, "we simply cannot deceive."
- In 1983 Carla Cantor of New Jersey's *Morristown Daily Record* visited the family of a murder victim and, to get them to open up to her, identified herself as "from the morgue." The state prosecuted her for impersonating an official.[3]

REMARKS

"As the child of God-fearing parents I think I may say I had a strict sense of private property rights: I would not have pilfered ten cents or ten dollars. But my conscience was wholly untroubled about [stealing and opening a telegram to get a story], because I had done the conventional thing. I was living up to the standards of my fellows."

—Silas Bent, reporter for several New York newspapers between 1914 and 1920[4]

"The ethical difference between a reporter's accepting stolen information (for example, the Pentagon Papers) and actually stealing the information is so slight as to be of little consequence: it is simply the difference between being a thief and being a fence."

—Robert Sherrill, *Nation* reporter[5]

"I like to know personal things about the interviewee, if at all possible. I like to know who he or she's having an affair with. . . . If I can let it drop that I know of something the least bit questionable or illicit, I don't mind doing that because then they say, 'You're not really interested in that, are you?' You say, 'Not right now, no. . . .' It keeps them off balance."

—Wendell Rawls, Jr., *New York Times* reporter[6]

"No, I'm taking notes like crazy."

—Sandy Golden, a reporter working with the *Washington Post,* to a source who asked if Golden was recording the phone call; Golden's tape of the call was later played in court during a libel trial[7]

HOAXES AND EMBROIDERY

....

STIRRING SPEECH

In 1747 the *General Advertiser* in London published a story that was quickly picked up by newspapers in the American colonies. It told of Polly Baker, a New Englander who was being prosecuted for giving birth to an illegitimate child—her fifth such offense. She protested to the judges that she was simply obeying "the first and great command of nature, and of nature's God, 'increase and multiply.' " How, she wondered, could it be a crime "to add to the number of the King's subjects in a new country that really wants people?" For the "public disgrace" she had endured in the repeated prosecutions, Baker concluded, she should be honored with a statue, not punished with a whipping and a fine. Captivated by the speech, the judges acquitted her, and the next day one of them married her.

Thirty years later the truth came out: Benjamin Franklin admitted that he had invented Polly Baker and her 1,100-word speech, in an effort to show how society unjustly punished women in the name of morality. Franklin had not published the speech in his own *Pennsylvania Gazette;* instead he had sent the manuscript to London, where it had found its way into the *General Advertiser.* Although a number of writers (including Voltaire and Balzac) recounted the hoax and Franklin's responsibility for it, history books published as late as 1917 treated Polly Baker and the speech as genuine.[8]

MOON LIFE

In 1835 the *New York Sun* reported the existence of life on the moon. The story, supposedly reprinted from the respected *Edinburgh Journal of Science,* told of discoveries announced by a noted astronomer, Sir John Herschel. Herschel described trees "unlike any I have seen except the largest class of yews in the English churchyards," "continuous herds of brown quadrupeds, having all the external characteristics of the bison, but more diminutive," and "a strange amphibious creature of a spherical form." The story gave the *Sun*'s circulation a strong boost. Other newspapers reprinted it, claiming that they too had gotten it from the *Edinburgh Journal.* Finally the *Sun*'s Richard Adams Locke admitted it was a hoax.[9]

OCEAN VOYAGE

In 1844 the *Sun* mounted another hoax, reporting that a "great problem is at length solved! The air, as well as the earth and the ocean, has been subdued by science, and will become a common and convenient highway for mankind. *The Atlantic has been actually crossed in a Balloon!*" The story said that eight people, including the "well-known aeronaut" Monck Mason, had crossed the Atlantic in seventy-five hours. The hoax was revealed a short time later. Its author: Edgar Allan Poe.[10]

COLLABORATION

Some early hoaxes and exaggerations came about because reporters were paid by the column inch. After a minor streetcar crash in Chicago, for instance, the assigned reporters from the city's newspapers sat down together to stretch the story. Whereas three people had actually been injured, the reporters agreed to write that fifteen people had been hurt. The papers gave their stories more space, and the reporters made more money.[11]

BATHTUB HISTORY

In 1917 the *New York Evening Mail* published a colorful history of the bathtub. The first tub in the United States, H. L. Mencken wrote, had been installed in Cincinnati in 1842 by a cotton dealer, Adam Thompson, who had grown partial to tubs while visiting England. From Cincinnati the tub's progress was slow, because the American medical profession initially believed that baths caused illness. For a time several cities prohibited bathing except under medical supervision. In 1850 President Millard Fillmore ordered a bathtub for the White House, and that helped defuse the opposition.

Mencken's history quickly became the accepted wisdom. Chiropractors cited it to provc that traditional medicine often stood in the way of progress. Cincinnati advertised itself as the birthplace of the American bathtub. Reference works recounted the roles of Thompson and Fillmore in bathtub history.

In 1926 Mencken unrepentantly announced that the article had been "a tissue of absurdities, all of them deliberate and most of them obvious." He had, he said, no idea what the true history of the bathtub was; "digging it out would be a dreadful job, and the result, after all that labor, would probably be a string of banalities." Seeing his whimsical fictions taken so seriously, he added, had made him wonder about how many other guesses or inventions had entered history books. He concluded by quoting Henry Ford: "History, said a great American soothsayer, is bunk."[12]

METAHOAX

A. J. Liebling often told the story of his firing from the *New York Times'* sports department. Liebling's job was to compile comprehensive box scores. When reporters couldn't remember who had refereed a game, Liebling listed a referee named "Ignoto"—Italian for "unknown." Ignoto sometimes would be shown as refereeing several games in different parts of the city, according to Liebling, and when his editors caught on, they fired him.

Liebling's biographer, Raymond Sokolov, has provided a different version of the tale. "Ignoto" appeared not numerous times, as Liebling had said, but only twice. In fact, Liebling was fired for something else entirely. A *Times* boxing reporter, James Dawson, wrote a story about his own election to the board of the Boxing Writers Association. Whereas Dawson usually signed his articles "James P. Dawson," this one he proudly signed with his full name, "James Patrick Dawson." Copyreader Liebling thought that Dawson was putting on airs. To needle him, Liebling changed the byline to "James Parnell Dawson," a reference to a late Irish political leader, Charles Stewart Parnell. The "Ignoto" explanation for the firing, biographer Sokolov concluded, was itself a hoax.[13]

CRONKITE'S INVENTIONS

After his junior year at the University of Texas, Walter Cronkite left college to become a radio sportscaster. Cronkite, like other sportscasters of the time (including Ronald Reagan), broadcast live play-by-play descriptions of games based only on wire copy. To make the studio broadcasts sound realistic, Cronkite employed sound effects, described the appearance of players and cheerleaders, and spotted friends in the stands. On one occasion the wire machine broke down and Cronkite had to invent plays for twenty minutes. "I marched them up and down the field—with frequent and protracted time outs," he remembered. "When the wire finally came back, I discovered that Notre Dame had scored. I had them on their own twenty-yard line. I had to get them all the way back downfield to score in a hurry."[14]

THE LAST MAN ON EARTH

In the event of a nuclear war, the *San Francisco Chronicle* wondered in print in 1960, "Could an average city dweller exist in the wilderness tomorrow with little more than his bare hands?" To find out, the *Chronicle* sent its outdoor columnist Harvey Boyd, along with his wife and three children, to spend six weeks roughing it in the mountains above San Francisco. Day after day *Chronicle* readers learned of the Boyds' battle for survival in, Boyd wrote, "the most brutish, hellish, most miserable days of our lives." Boyd described making a fishhook from one of his daughter's rings and catching seven trout. Then he lost the ring—a mishap that he called "the greatest disaster of my lifetime." Their luck gradually changed. His son learned to capture frogs, and Boyd figured out a way to trap a deer. Boyd concluded that, ten days away from civilization, he was feeling "ahead of the game at last."

Editors at the rival *San Francisco Examiner* decided to check up on the Last Man and family. An *Examiner* reporter found the campsite, where "little more than bare hands" turned out to include kitchen matches, canned spaghetti, fresh eggs, watermelon rinds, and the current *Reader's Digest.* The Last Man on Earth had, the *Examiner* chided, seemingly "tramped off into the woods much better equipped for survival than Girl Scouts on a weekend cookout in the Waldorf-Astoria." The Last Man's campsite did lack one feature: the Boyds. As the saga of their travails was continuing in the *Chronicle,* they were unwinding at home.[15]

TOM WOLFE VS. THE NEW YORKER

In 1965 the *New York Herald Tribune*'s Sunday magazine section published a two-part article on the *New Yorker,* written by thirty-four-year-old Tom Wolfe. The headline exemplified Wolfe's frenetic style of the time: "TINY MUMMIES! THE TRUE STORY OF THE RULER OF 43D STREET'S LAND OF THE WALKING DEAD!" The article said that the "mummified" *New Yorker* had deteriorated into "the most successful suburban women's magazine in the country." Wolfe wrote that *New Yorker* editor William Shawn had "the perfect qualifications for a museum custodian, an undertaker, a mortuary scientist."

After Shawn saw an advance copy of the article, he tried to get the *Herald Tribune* to cancel it. He wrote a letter to *Herald Tribune* publisher John Hay Whitney, calling Wolfe's article "vicious, murderous," "false and libelous," "ruthless and reckless." Clay Felker, editor of the Sunday magazine, told reporters that he was "amazed that a man in the same business we are should ask that we not distribute a story." The article was published as scheduled.

A few months later *New Yorker* staff writers produced two long critiques that challenged Wolfe's facts. One was written by Dwight Macdonald for the *New York Review of Books,* and the other by Renata Adler and Gerald Jonas for the *Columbia Journalism Review.* Both critiques uncovered dozens of errors in Wolfe's article. Names, dates, titles, quotations, and even descriptions of wall hangings were wrong. Macdonald concluded that Wolfe "seems to be honestly unaware of the distinction between fact and fabrication."

In the *New Yorker* writers' eyes, Wolfe's most remarkable error was his assertion that Shawn's "retiring" nature stemmed from a major childhood trauma. According to Wolfe, "records show" that Shawn had been Nathan Leopold and Richard Loeb's first choice for their 1924 kidnapping-murder. They ultimately had settled on one of Shawn's classmates, Bobby Franks. Macdonald and Adler separately inspected the official files of the Leopold and Loeb trial. Nowhere in the 4,713-page record, they wrote, was there any evidence to support Wolfe's assertion.

Wolfe responded that his critics were screaming "like weenies over a wood fire." As for the challenges to his research, he said: "The only factual error in the pieces was a misplaced comma."[16]

THE COOKE AFFAIR

On September 28, 1980, the *Washington Post* published "Jimmy's World," the story of an eight-year-old heroin addict in Washington's black community. The story described a man injecting Jimmy with heroin ("the needle slides into the boy's soft skin like a straw pushed into the center of a freshly baked cake") while Jimmy's mother looked on. It quoted Jimmy as saying that at school he was interested only in math "because I know I got to keep up when I finally get me something to sell." The story was written by a twenty-six-year-old reporter named Janet Cooke.

The story produced a strong reaction, which initially focused on Jimmy's plight. Washingtonians, including Mayor Marion Barry, urged the newspaper to reveal Jimmy's name and location so he could be helped. *Post* editors refused. "I don't think of the journalist as a cop," said executive editor Ben Bradlee.

Questions about the story soon surfaced. When a citywide search failed to find any trace of Jimmy, Mayor Barry said he doubted Jimmy's existence. A Howard University therapist, who treated young drug users and who was quoted in the story, told a *Post* editor that the story seemed fishy. The editor accused the therapist of being jealous because the article hadn't devoted more attention to her. In the *Post* newsroom, quiet grumblings began, but they too were often dismissed as jealousy. "We stand by our story," metro editor Bob Woodward told a news conference. Over the weeks to come, the issue gradually faded.

"Jimmy's World" splashed back into public attention the following April, when Cooke won the Pulitzer Prize for features. After the prize was announced, reporters tried to confirm information on the bio sheet that Cooke had submitted with her Pulitzer entry, such as her degrees from Vassar and the University of Toledo and her graduate work at the Sorbonne. The statements turned out to be false.

Cooke at first insisted that, though her résumé contained falsehoods, Jimmy was genuine. *Post* editors scrutinized her notes and listened to her taped interviews. They could find no mention of a Jimmy. One editor ordered Cooke to take him to Jimmy's house. They drove in circles for a time, until Cooke said she couldn't find it. Finally she confessed that "I never encountered or interviewed an eight-year-old heroin addict."

Post ombudsman Bill Green wrote more or less steadily for twenty-four hours, turning out an eighteen-thousand-word analysis of the episode for publication in the *Post.* Green concluded that a "journalistic felony" had been committed and that it had gotten into print because of "a complete systems failure." Despite such indictments, Green's report ended on an upbeat note: "The *Post* is one of the very few great enterprises in journalism, and everyone associated with it ought to be proud of it." The National News Council later suggested that Green himself deserved some of the blame for the systems failure, for having failed to unravel the Jimmy story when it was first published.

Woodward's involvement in the Cooke debacle inspired a joke that circulated for a time around Washington: Jimmy does exist; he lives next door to Deep Throat.[17]

EMBROIDERY AND INVENTION

- Although he considered James Callender of the *Richmond Examiner* a friend, President Jefferson refused to make Callender the postmaster of Richmond. Callender, the President wrote privately, was "totally unfit" for the job. Callender responded with a series of vehement newspaper attacks on Jefferson, including stories alleging that Jefferson had fathered several children by a "black wench," a Monticello slave named Sally Hemings. The Hemings story had never before been published, and some scholars believe that Callender spitefully invented it from whole cloth.

- After several weeks' reporting for the *New York World* in the 1890s, Theodore Dreiser got his first front-page byline. Dreiser's article told how a composer, working on a new waltz late at night, had been disturbed by the sound of a neighbor's snoring. The composer had awakened the man, and a horrible fight had broken out. "Rather well done," Dreiser's editor said. Dreiser had invented the composer and the waltz to spice up a run-of-the-mill brawl. Shortly thereafter he left the *World* to pursue straight fiction.

- In 1911 a journalism teacher assigned a student, William Ferguson, to write an imaginary murder article. To make the assignment more interesting, Ferguson went to an abandoned mill, smeared chicken blood on the floor, dropped some of his sister's hair in the blood, and left a heavy club nearby. A watchman discovered the "evidence" and notified the police. Ferguson contacted the *St.*

Louis Post-Dispatch, the *Kansas City Star,* and other newspapers, which hired him as a stringer to cover the murder investigation.

- In the '20s Arthur Pegler of the *New York Daily News* was assigned to investigate a rooming-house death. The facts were mundane, so Pegler invented a more colorful story. The dead man, he wrote, was Nicola Coviello, an opera composer who had stopped in New York on his way to Saskatchewan. While seeing the sights of New York, he had ventured to Coney Island and heard, for the first time, the new music called jazz. The sound, Pegler wrote, had killed him instantly.

- In 1961 Alastair Reid invented several scenes in supposedly factual *New Yorker* articles. Reid's inventions came to light more than twenty years after the fact, when Reid explained his techniques to a Yale writing class. One of the students subsequently got a job on the *Wall Street Journal,* where she wrote about Reid's revelations. Accuracy, Reid said in his defense, sometimes requires reporters "to go much further than the strictly factual."

- In 1969 David Freeman wrote an article called "The Lifestyle of a Pimp" for *New York* magazine. When pressed on whether the characters in his articles, including that one, were composites, Freeman replied enigmatically: "It is often possible for the facts to get in the way of real truth." Freeman subsequently moved to Hollywood and wrote the script for a 1987 movie, *Street Smart,* in which a magazine reporter (Christopher Reeve) can't get the information for an assigned article, so he makes the whole thing up. *New York* movie critic David Denby called Freeman and asked if he, like his movie character, had invented any of "Lifestyle of a Pimp." "All of it," Freeman answered.

- In July 1971, during the Pentagon Papers litigation, many newspapers ran prominent articles about the "Buckley papers"—a set of secret documents about the Vietnam War that William F. Buckley, Jr., had published in his *National*

Review. The papers revealed, among other things, that military officials had wanted to use nuclear weapons in Vietnam. A few days later Buckley announced that the papers were a hoax. "The *New York Times* has instructed us that it is permissible to traffic in stolen documents," he said (referring to the Pentagon Papers), "but they have not yet instructed us on whether it is permissible to traffic in forged documents." Fourteen newspapers, teed-off about the hoax, canceled Buckley's column. "People," Buckley later said, "don't have much of a sense of humor when they themselves are victimized."

- In *The New York Times Magazine* in 1981, free-lance writer Christopher Jones described his visit to Cambodia. A few weeks later the *Village Voice* pointed out that the closing sentences of the article were remarkably similar to a passage in an André Malraux novel. Then the *Washington Post* reported that, according to officials in Cambodia, Jones had never visited some of the areas the article discussed. Jones admitted that he had invented the entire chronicle. It was, he said, "a gamble."

- A few weeks after the Janet Cooke episode, *New York Daily News* columnist Michael Daly resigned when a story in his column, about a British soldier shooting a youth in Belfast, was shown to be partly fictitious. In his defense, Daly said he had written three hundred other columns using the same techniques of pseudonyms and reconstruction.

- After Janet Cooke's disqualification, the Pulitzer for features went to Teresa Carpenter of the *Village Voice* for her article on the murder of former Congressman Allard Lowenstein. The article suggested that Lowenstein and the man who ultimately killed him, Dennis Sweeney, had maintained a homosexual relationship. Many of Lowenstein's friends considered the allegation outrageous, and they looked into Carpenter's methods and sources. A major source seemed to be Sweeney himself. The article said: "Now, from his cell at Rikers Island, Sweeney denies. . . ." The paragraph continued with references like "according to Sweeney" and "he claims." In fact, Lowenstein's friends discovered, Carpenter had never talked to Sweeney. Carpenter responded that the story didn't actually say she had interviewed him. "The reader," she said, "has got to trust me when he or she is reading the piece."[18]

SOURCES AND THEIR RULES

. . . .

NEWS PRICES

- In the nineteenth century a speaker of the House earned a hundred dollars a week by charging reporters for interviews.
- *The New York Times* footed the bills for Robert E. Peary's expedition to the North Pole in exchange for exclusive rights to his story. Later the *Times* paid Charles Lindbergh $5,000 for the story of his historic flight.
- *Life* bought the rights to the stories of the *Mercury* astronauts (about a half-million dollars), the rights to the Zapruder film of President Kennedy's assassination ($150,000), the rights to Lee Harvey Oswald's diaries ($20,000), and some family photos from the man who had murdered Washington physician Michael Halberstam ($8,000).
- For film footage of American prisoners held by North Vietnam, NBC paid Hanoi $12,000.
- For exclusive interviews, CBS paid two Watergate defendants: H. R. Haldeman received $100,000, and G. Gordon Liddy got $15,000. Later the network paid $10,000 for a look

at the body of disappeared Teamster Jimmy Hoffa, but the man who promised to take a *60 Minutes* crew to the body absconded with the money and the body was never found.[19]

WINCHELL'S CALCULUS

The gossip columnist Walter Winchell had a three-for-one rule for press agents. For every three items of usable gossip or humor that a press agent submitted, Winchell would run a plug for one of the agent's clients.[20]

EXCHANGE

Jack Anderson said that his muckraking column will hold back a story under certain circumstances: "We will give immunity to a very good source as long as the information he offers us is better than what we've got on him."[21]

SOURCES AND SECRETS

Occasionally news stories reveal the identity of a source, the content of an off-the-record remark, or other confidential information:

- In 1982 the *Boston Globe* published some colorful characterizations that President Carter had made just before leaving office. Carter had called Henry Kissinger a "liar" and former State Department spokesman Hodding Carter a "creep." The remarks were made at an off-the-record dinner with reporters, but the *Globe* reporter who had been present, Curtis Wilkie, said that Carter had implicitly lifted the restriction by covering some of the topics in his memoir, *Keeping Faith.*
- Testifying before the Iran-contra investigating committee in 1987, Oliver North claimed that Congress couldn't be trusted with secrets. As an example, he said that members of Congress had leaked information that "very seriously compromised our intelligence activities" after an American plane had intercepted a plane carrying Egyptian ter-

rorists. *Newsweek* challenged North's assertion by revealing that members of Congress had not provided the interception story to Washington reporters. The actual source, the magazine reported, had been "none other than North himself." The magazine's chief editor, Richard Smith, said it was proper to finger North as the source because he was falsely accusing Congress. Reporters in the magazine's Washington bureau had not been consulted, though, and some of them thought the magazine had made a mistake. A few *Newsweek* reporters said that in the future, they would keep sources' identities secret even from their New York bosses.

- Bob Woodward's *Washington Post* stories about intelligence matters often relied on unnamed "senior administration officials." In his 1987 book *Veil,* Woodward revealed that one confidential source had been the late CIA director William Casey. "Agreements of confidentiality," Woodward said, "cannot extend to or from the grave."[22]

COMPETING LOYALTIES

....

SECOND INCOMES

- To boost his press relations, President Andrew Jackson rewarded loyal reporters with government jobs, mostly as postmasters. In the early months of the administration, one in every ten job appointments went to a journalist.

- During the 1872 presidential campaign the GOP slipped money to an estimated three hundred reporters.

- In the early '20s the *Denver Post* got embroiled in the Teapot Dome scandal. An oilman, John Leo Stack, stood to make five million dollars if the government canceled its lease of the oil-rich Teapot Dome fields to the Mammoth

Oil Company. Stack approached the co-owner of the *Post,* Fred Bonfils, with a proposition: In exchange for Bonfils's help, Stack would sign over about half of his potential interest to Bonfils and his partner. Bonfils agreed, and the *Post* set to work. A series of editorials labeled the lease "arbitrary and autocratic," an "unpardonable and inexcusable blunder," and a news story revealed that the president of Mammoth Oil had secretly met with the Secretary of Interior, who was responsible for the lease decision. To quell the criticism, the president of Mammoth Oil offered to settle Stack's claim for about a million dollars, and Stack accepted. The *Post,* whose owners stood to receive half of the settlement, abruptly lost interest in the Teapot Dome lease. The scandal continued to unravel without the *Post*'s help, and a congressional probe publicized the newspaper's apparent conflict of interest.

- Jake Lingle, a *Chicago Tribune* reporter in the '20s, always seemed to be living beyond a reporter's means. In addition to the home he shared with his family, he had a summer house and he kept a large suite at a Chicago hotel. He frequented racetracks, betting heavily, and he wore a diamond-studded belt. He explained to friends that he had inherited fifty thousand dollars from his father. In 1930 Lingle was gunned down on a crowded street, and in the search for the killer, new facts emerged about the victim. Lingle had inherited only five hundred dollars; the other money had come from the Chicago mob. Lingle had been their liaison to the police, negotiating payoffs. The diamond belt, in fact, had been a gift from Al Capone in recognition of a job well done.
- To help ensure positive coverage, the mortuary handling Rudolph Valentino's burial in 1926 gave each reporter a silver plate that could be redeemed for a deluxe, $1,000 funeral.
- In 1952 Joseph Kennedy lent a half-million dollars to John Fox, owner of the *Boston Post,* on condition that the *Post* endorse Kennedy's son John for U.S. Senate.

- One Pulitzer Prize in 1950 honored reporters who had uncovered a press scandal. The *Chicago Daily News* and the *St. Louis Post-Dispatch* published stories showing how the Illinois state government was paying out nearly a half-million dollars annually to editors and publishers of more than fifty newspapers. Whereas a few of the press employees kept regular hours in the statehouse, most of them earned their paychecks solely by publishing canned editorials and articles praising the administration.

- One of Philadelphia's best-known investigative reporters, Harry J. Karafin of the *Philadelphia Inquirer,* was revealed in 1967 to be (in the newspaper's words) "a remarkably adept shakedown artist." One home-repair company had paid Karafin twelve thousand dollars to keep him from writing an exposé about the business. Dozens of others had also made payoffs to prevent harmful publicity. When Karafin's double-dealing was uncovered by *Philadelphia* magazine, the *Inquirer* fired him. He died in prison.

- R. Foster Winans, who wrote the influential column "Heard on the Street" for the *Wall Street Journal,* kept a wealthy broker apprised of what would appear in forthcoming columns. The broker invested accordingly and turned a profit of nearly a half-million dollars. One of his clients also used the information and made nearly $600,000. Winans received $31,000 for his efforts from the broker and, when the double-dealing came to light, eighteen months in prison from a federal judge.[23]

SECRET LIVES

- During World War II a number of *The New York Times* British-born reporters who worked overseas were agents for the British secret service. With their *Times* credentials they were able to gather information for the British government.

- In 1955 Winston M. Burdett, a CBS foreign correspondent, told a Senate subcommittee that he had belonged to the Communist party through the early '40s and that, while on assignment for CBS abroad, he had spied on behalf of the Soviet Union. He insisted that his Communist days were over, and CBS believed him. He remained with the network, and in 1967 he won an Emmy.

- Jacque Srouji, a reporter for the *Nashville Tennessean,* led two secret lives. She undertook some projects for the Soviet Union, such as visiting a sensitive nuclear plant. At the same time she reported on her activities, as a Soviet helper and as a journalist, to the FBI. When her triple-dealings came to light, the *Tennessean* fired her.[24]

CAMPAIGN LOYALTIES

- During the 1965 New York mayoral election, columnist Woody Klein endorsed John Lindsay in the *New York World-Telegram.* Klein wrote that he particularly admired Lindsay's white paper on housing. Klein, as a part-time volunteer in the Lindsay campaign, had written the white paper.

- The Nixon reelection campaign hired two journalists, Seymour K. Freidin and Lucianne Cummings Goldberg, to spy on the Democratic presidential candidates. Goldberg, who identified her employer as Women's News Service, was paid a thousand dollars a week, she later said, for information on "who was sleeping with who, what the Secret Service men were doing with the stewardesses, who was smoking pot on the plane—that sort of thing."

- At the request of campaign officials, columnist George Will helped Ronald Reagan prepare for a 1980 debate with President Carter. After the debate, Will appeared on ABC to evaluate the candidates' performances. He was full of praise for Reagan's "thoroughbred" effort, finding it "more confident, less nervous, and less defensive" than Carter's.

When his Reagan work came to light in 1983, Will insisted that as a columnist he wasn't bound by the usual hands-off rules of objective journalism. Editors at eight newspapers suspended his column anyway. Will later announced that, in light of the public's "intense" expectations for people in his place, "I shall not again come as close to a political campaign as I did in 1980."[25]

INTERMEDIARIES

- After President Woodrow Wilson's incapacitating stroke, the cabinet tried to keep the President's condition absolutely secret. Wilson didn't improve as the weeks passed, and some cabinet secretaries argued that the Vice President should take over. The men finally agreed that somebody should explain the situation to Vice President Thomas Marshall and get his thoughts. To convey the message, they wanted someone who knew the Vice President well (which none of them did), who would inform Marshall tactfully, and who would not reveal Wilson's illness to the public. They settled on Fred Essary, a *Baltimore Sun* reporter who was close to Marshall. Essary, fully briefed, told Marshall about Wilson's illness and asked whether the President should be removed from office. The Vice President said that the cabinet should "let things stay as they are." Wilson remained president, and Essary's involvement came to light only after his death.

- After a 1986 interview in Monte Carlo, Iranian arms merchant Manucher Ghorbanifar asked ABC's Barbara Walters to take a message to President Reagan. She agreed. Back in Washington, she dropped her notes off at the White House. The information was, it turned out, nothing new to the White House, but Walters's involvement agitated the Washington press corps. "We don't deliver messages," sniffed Judith Miller of *The New York Times.* Walters's bosses at ABC announced that she had violated "a literal interpretation" of company policy, which prohibits employees from "cooperating with government agencies unless threats to human life are involved." Walters herself said she "felt terrible" about what she had done.[26]

LAURA FOREMAN

In 1975 Laura Foreman, a reporter for the *Philadelphia Inquirer,* fell in love with a state senator named Buddy Cianfrani. They began seeing each other frequently, and Cianfrani gave her more than ten thousand dollars' worth of gifts. On seven occasions Foreman wrote articles about him. The relationship, she later wrote, was "common knowledge around the *Inquirer* newsroom," and no one said anything to her about it.

That changed two years later, when an FBI investigation of Cianfrani uncovered the gifts (Cianfrani later went to jail for dealings unrelated to the relationship). Foreman by then had moved from the *Inquirer* to *The New York Times*' Washington bureau, and she had stopped seeing Cianfrani. Even though her misbehavior hadn't occurred on its payroll, the *Times* demanded her resignation. "It's okay to fuck the elephants," *Times* executive editor A. M. Rosenthal said, "just don't cover the circus."[27]

REMARKS

"One answer to the problem of how to treat reporters is to treat them frequently."

—F. H. Brennan, *St. Louis Post-Dispatch* writer[28]

"You cannot hope to bribe or twist
Thank God! the British journalist.
But, seeing what the man will do
Unbribed, there's no occasion to."

—Humbert Wolfe, poet[29]

"Anybody who wouldn't screw a dame for a story is disloyal to the paper."

—Jay McMullen, *Chicago Daily News* reporter who was dating city hall official (and future mayor) Jane Byrne[30]

"A newspaper should have no friends."

—Joseph Pulitzer, responding to criticism that Pulitzer's *New York World* never stood by its friends[31]

11

THE PRESS AS A BUSINESS

THE MEDIA MARKET

SATURATED MARKET

In 1721 James Franklin of Boston announced plans to start a newspaper. Friends and relatives tried to talk him out of it. The *Boston News-Letter,* they said, was invincible, and, as James's younger brother Benjamin later wrote, "one newspaper [was] in their judgment enough for America." James Franklin went ahead anyway, and his *New-England Courant* lasted for five years.[1]

FOUNDING MONOPOLIST

Later, James Franklin's brother Benjamin, printer and postmaster, helped make his own *Pennsylvania Gazette* a success by barring competing newspapers from the mails.[2]

R.I.T.

At the turn of the century, the press mogul Frank Munsey was among the most vigorous advocates of newspaper mergers. "There is no business," he said, "that cries so loud for organization and combination as that of newspaper publishing." He thought that the number of separate newspapers was at least 60 percent too large, and he did his part to reduce it. In New York City alone, he bought and then killed or merged six newspapers.

When Munsey died, William Allen White eulogized him in the *Emporia Gazette:* "Frank Munsey, the great publisher, is dead. Munsey contributed to the journalism of his day the great talent of a meat packer, the morals of a money changer and the manners of an undertaker. He and his kind have about succeeded in transforming a once noble profession into an eight percent security. May he rest in trust."[3]

CLASSIFIED CONCERNS

In the early '80s newspaper publishers lobbied Congress to bar AT&T from the "information transmission business." Their concern, the publishers said, was that the phone company would send information over phone lines to subscribers' home computers or special terminals. The phone company could use its monopoly to squeeze out other information producers, which, the publishers argued, would jeopardize the diversity of information available to the public and threaten fundamental First Amendment values.

Although the publishers tried to downplay it, the information that particularly concerned them wasn't news—AT&T had promised not to produce traditional articles and features—but advertising. Computers would let the phone company create "living Yellow Pages." Readers could search specifically for the type of ad that interested them, and advertisers could update the ads at will. That, the publishers feared, would decimate classified advertising, which provides newspapers with about a third of their advertising revenues, and cut into supermarket and other display ads as well. The lobbying effort convinced Congress, which banned AT&T from undertaking such activities for at least seven years.[4]

REMARKS

"Freedom of the press is guaranteed only to those who own one."

—A. J. Liebling, *New Yorker* press critic[5]

"Monopoly is a terrible thing, till you have it."

—Rupert Murdoch[6]

ADVERTISERS AND THEIR IMPACTS

....

FRONT-PAGE ADS

In 1899 General Charles H. Taylor was asked why his *Boston Globe* continued to run front-page advertisements after most newspapers had stopped the practice. Taylor replied that there was rarely enough major news to fill page one. "The papers that do not print advertising on the first page," he said, "find it mighty hard to get enough good matter to make a good show window out of their front page. So they put matter on it that ought to go to the back of the store or down in the basement."[7]

PATENT MEDICINES

In the early 1900s, when state legislatures considered bills to regulate patent medicines (such as by requiring that ingredients be listed on the labels), newspapers usually fought the proposals. Ingeniously, patent medicine companies had included this clause in their standard contracts: "It is mutually agreed that this contract is void if any law is enacted by your State restricting or prohibiting the manufacture or sale of proprietary medicines." Newspapers wanted to keep the lucrative advertising, so they became lobbyists on behalf of the drug companies.[8]

ADVERTISING CAUTIONS

The New York Times was unusually fastidious about advertising at the turn of the century. At one point the city of New York decided to move all of its advertising, totaling about $150,000 a year, to the *Times.* The *Times* refused the offer, fearing that it might bias the paper's reporting about the city government. On another occasion an advertiser urged the *Times* to modify some of its policies. Adolph Ochs, the publisher, wrote in reply: "You must excuse me from discussing with you the policy of *The New York Times.* It is a subject we do not care to discuss with an advertiser. . . . You seem to wish that *The New York Times* should go about as a mendicant, begging for advertising patronage. We will never do anything of the kind. . . ."[9]

O. HENRY'S REJECTION

O. Henry submitted his "An Unfinished Story" to the *New York World,* which sometimes published fiction. The story concerns a department store saleswoman who is paid six dollars a week. It ends in Heaven, where an angel asks the narrator if he ever paid "working-girls" such miserly wages as her employer had. "Not on your immortality," the narrator replies. "I'm only a fellow that set fire to an orphan asylum, and murdered a blind man for his pennies." Worried that the sentiment might offend department store owners, *World* editors rejected the story.[10]

ADLESS EXPERIMENTS

Several publishers have started newspapers that accepted no advertising, a policy intended to foster editorial independence.

E. W. Scripps founded the adless *Chicago Day Book* in 1911 and the *Philadelphia News-Post* in 1913. The *Day Book,*

Scripps decreed, was to be "the poor man's advocate whether the poor man be right or wrong." Its chief political writer was the poet Carl Sandburg. The newspaper lasted six years and came close to breaking even before the war forced it to suspend publication. The less successful *News-Post* lasted only two years.

In New York in 1940, Marshall Field III and several other businessmen founded the best-known adless newspaper, *PM* (for "picture magazine"). The newspaper's goal, in Field's words, was "the scalpel dissection of the interested motives which certain power groups may have in propagandizing a given version of the news." *PM* accepted no advertising but, catering to readers' interests, did publish a news column listing noteworthy department-store sales. Edited by Ralph Ingersoll, a former publisher of *Time,* the newspaper almost broke even after six years. By that time Field had lost $4.3 million, though, and the experiment ended. The newspaper started accepting advertising in 1946, changed hands and became the *Star* in 1948, and closed down in 1949.[11]

NO CIGARS

The cigarette manufacturer that sponsored the *Camel News Caravan,* NBC's first television news program, ordered that no film be shown of anyone smoking a cigar. One exception was permitted: Winston Churchill.[12]

WEATHER AND ADVERTISERS

In the '50s and '60s, business considerations sometimes influenced newspapers' weather reports. Weather predictions in the *Sacramento Bee* never included the word "hot," which newspaper officials feared might dissuade businesses from relocating to Sacramento. Instead, even blistering weather was described as "unseasonably warm." On the East Coast, Boston newspapers downplayed major winter storms that threatened downtown shopping. After a 1956 blizzard brought city traffic nearly to a standstill, for example, the *Globe* reassured readers "SNOW CLEANUP CONTINUES; TRAVEL NORMAL."[13]

REJECTED ADS

- The *Los Angeles Municipal News,* which was published from 1911 to 1913, refused to advertise patent medicines, psychics, or attorneys.

- In the mid-1960s the *Los Angeles Times* and several other California newspapers refused to run ads for a company that threatened the livelihood of real-estate brokers. The Galar Corporation offered to put home buyers directly in touch with sellers for a fixed fee, eliminating the need for brokers. A *Times* representative told Galar that the ad couldn't run because it was offensive to a particular industry—an industry, though the *Times* didn't emphasize the point, that is responsible for much of a newspaper's classified advertising. Galar, unable to reach customers effectively, went bankrupt.

- The *Los Angeles Times* bars the word "smog" from its real-estate section. Ads may say "cleaner skies," but such phrases as "no smog here" are forbidden.

- During the Vietnam War *The New York Times* refused to sell space to groups that opposed war taxes or defense bonds. The policy reflected, a *Times* executive said, the "best interests of the country."

- In 1987 *The New York Times Magazine* refused an ad for the perfume Charlie. The ad showed a man and woman walking away from the camera. The woman's hand was reaching out to slap the man's derriere. Equality dictated the result, according to the *Times*—if the ad had shown a man slapping a woman, however playfully, it would be unacceptable. *Ms.* and ten other women's magazines found the reasoning unpersuasive; they ran the ad.

- The *Boston Globe* refuses ads for companies that write term papers for college students.

- The *Christian Science Monitor* refuses advertisements for, among other things, medicines and tombstones.

- The Mormon Church–owned *Deseret News* in Salt Lake City accepts "tasteful advertising" for all lawful services and products "except the following: Liquor, beer, tobacco, tea and coffee, and X-rated motion pictures."[14]

NO OMISSIONS

Some newspapers, at the urging of florists' trade associations, refuse to include the sentiment "please omit flowers" in obituaries. A spokesman for one such paper, the *Pittsburgh Press,* explained that the phrase "urges a boycott, just like 'don't buy grapes,' and we don't permit that."[15]

INTERRUPTIONS

In 1966 CBS chose not to cover the Senate Foreign Relations Committee's hearings on Vietnam. Instead it aired its regular reruns of *I Love Lucy* and *The Real McCoys,* among others, which so incensed CBS News president Fred Friendly that he resigned. A few months later CBS did interrupt its daytime programming for live coverage of the Pillsbury Bake-off prize ceremony. The Bake-off, unlike the Vietnam hearings, had a sponsor—Pillsbury.[16]

NEWS FOR THE MONEYED

Some newspapers have self-consciously tailored the news to the interests of affluent, advertiser-desired readers. *Detroit News* editors were told in a 1976 memo to run more stories about "the horrors that are discussed at suburban cocktail parties." The memo specifically recommended more front-page attention to "sex, comedy and tragedy." The ideal stories, the memo added, "won't have a damn thing to do with Detroit and its internal problems."

Otis Chandler, who became publisher of the *Los Angeles Times* in 1960, once boasted that the newspaper had "arbitrarily cut back on some of our low-income circulation." Devoting more space to minority issues, he said, "would not make sense financially," because "that audience does not have the purchasing power and is not responsive to the kind of advertising we carry." At any rate, Chandler said, "It's not their kind of newspaper. It's too big; . . . it's too complicated."[17]

MURDOCH'S READERS

Rupert Murdoch, according to a widely told story (denied by Murdoch), once asked a department store president why his store didn't advertise in Murdoch's *New York Post.* "Rupert," the president replied, "you don't understand. Your readers are our shoplifters."[18]

REMARKS

"The greatest cigarette vending machine ever devised."

—Ad promoting CBS to tobacco companies, 1962[19]

"What I am most interested in doing is labor reporting, possibly working up to political reporting later. . . . I detest beyond description advertising and circulation, and that is what a newspaper executive spends most of his time worrying about."

—Katharine Meyer (later Graham), 1937[20]

"The American press, with a very few exceptions, is a kept press. Kept by the big corporations the way a whore is kept by a rich man."

—Theodore Dreiser[21]

"Journalism consists in buying white paper at two cents a pound and selling it at ten cents a pound."

—Charles A. Dana, *New York Sun* editor[22]

12

OBSTACLES TO TRUTH

ATTAINING ACCURACY

PREDICTING 1916

In the 1916 presidential election, the *New York Evening Post*'s David Lawrence correctly predicted how every state would vote. The extraordinary prescience, it turned out, owed something to editorial pressure. Lawrence had originally written that Charles Evans Hughes would narrowly win the presidency. The *Post*'s editor, Oswald Garrison Villard, said that the article had to predict victory for the *Post*-endorsed candidate, Woodrow Wilson. So Lawrence switched California from Hughes to Wilson, and thereby achieved complete accuracy.[1]

CHECKING THE COMPETITION

As part of its opposition to President Franklin D. Roosevelt's Office of Price Administration, William Randolph Hearst's *New York Journal-American* ran photos of seven New York women under a banner headline: "OPA? NO! THESE NEW YORK WOMEN DENOUNCE AGENCY AS CAUSE OF BLACK MARKET."

One of the women called a competing newspaper, *PM,* and said the *Journal-American* had misquoted her—she had told the reporter she opposed black markets, not the OPA. A *PM* reporter phoned the other women, and the next day *PM* had a banner headline of its own: "OPA? YES! HOW HEARST LIED SEVEN TIMES."[2]

DUBIOUS NEWS

In wartime, newspapers often receive important but unverified information. During World War II the *Boston Globe* printed "Unconfirmed" over such reports. During the Civil War some newspapers used a more direct approach: "IMPORTANT IF TRUE."[3]

EARLY OBITUARIES

When Ernest Hemingway was injured in a 1953 plane crash, many newspapers reported that he had died. Hemingway read the obituaries closely. "There were certain inaccuracies," he said, "and many good things were said that were in no way deserved. Most of the obituaries I could never have written nearly as well myself."[4]

NUMBERS GAME

In October 1967 a major antiwar protest was held in Washington. Crowd estimates varied widely, in part reflecting the news organizations' editorial sentiments:

Washington Post: 50,000
Time: 35,000
Wall Street Journal: 2,500[5]

RULE 18

Cosmopolitan distributed a list of rules for writers to follow. According to Rick Ackerman, who briefly worked at the magazine in the early '80s, Rule #18 read: "Unless *you* are a recognized authority on a subject, profound statements must be attributed *to* somebody appropriate (even if the writer has to invent the authority)."[6]

CORRECTIONS

"An article in the April 5 editions of the Washington Post *presented an inaccurate depiction of Texas Tech University and the city in which the university is located, Lubbock. Texas Tech students do not carry guns to class, as the article stated. . . . There is no 'pistol-packing' tradition in Lubbock, as the article inaccurately implied."*

—Washington Post

"Ear writhed with anguish to learn that Dean Acheson, whom it had listed among Terrifics whooping it up at a divine party recently, is a teensy bit dead, and has been for ages. Ear happens to believe that he is at divine parties anyway, *but is glad to have plucked his Ear pin from the outgoing mail in time."*

—"The Ear" (Diana McLellan),
Washington Post

"The June 28 issue of People *contained a story on a new diet product called starch blockers. On rechecking his tapes, reporter David Sheff has found that he misquoted Dr. J. John Marshall. Dr. Marshall did not say that writer Cameron Stauth was 'a dirty rotten scum who got very greedy.' What he said was, 'He's an unscrupulous little [pause] gentleman.'"*

—People

"The band Raging Saint bases its music on born-again Christian principles. They are not 'unrepentant headbangers,' as reported in the 'Nightlife' column last Friday."

—*Austin American-Statesman*

"An article on Nov. 1 about Imelda Marcos's appearance at an arraignment hearing in Manhattan misstated her shoe size in alluding to her reputation for extravagance. The size is 8½."

—*New York Times*

"The phrase 'Dummy head,' which was accidentally printed beneath a photograph in Thursday's Virginian-Pilot, was intended as a typographical notation for use in the production process. It was not intended to describe in any way the subject of the photograph."

—*Norfolk Virginian-Pilot*[7]

REMARKS

"Here is a lie. I know it is a lie, but I must print it because it is spoken by a prominent public official. The public official's name and position make the lie news. Were the source some unknown person, I could and would gladly throw it in the wastebasket."

—Oliver K. Bovard, *St. Louis Post-Dispatch* managing editor[8]

"Accuracy is to a newspaper what virtue is to a woman."

—Joseph Pulitzer[9]

"Remember, son, many a good story has been ruined by oververification."

—James Gordon Bennett, *New York Herald* founder[10]

"The immunity journalists had in the early seventies no longer exists. If you call somebody a thieving pigfucker now, you'd better be ready to produce the pig."

—Hunter S. Thompson, *Rolling Stone* political writer[11]

THE PRESS, MISLED

....

AWARD HOAX

In the '60s an officer of the Organization of International Communicators (OIC) appeared on the *Today* show and presented an award to host Hugh Downs. Years later *Today* staff members admitted that they had invented the organization and hired someone to present the award. The point of the hoax was to commemorate Downs's constant on-air use of the phrase "Oh, I see."[12]

HITLER DIARIES

The headlines on two *Newsweek* covers in 1983 told the story: "Hitler's Secret Diaries" and "Forgery: Uncovering the Hitler Hoax." In light of their success, the fake diaries (the work of a German named Konrad Paul Kujau) were surprisingly unsophisticated. The paper, binding, glue, and thread all were manufactured long after Hitler's death. The stains on the pages were from tea, not age. The gothic initials stuck to the cover of one volume were postwar plastic, and on close inspection they turned out to be "FH," not "AH." The diaries contained errors, most notably entries supposedly written just after the assassination attempt that injured Hitler's right arm. But the forgery of Hitler's handwriting was excellent, and at first no one looked further.

The German magazine *Der Stern,* which had paid nearly $4 million for the diaries, hoped to recoup some of its investment by selling publication rights for Europe and the United States. For American rights the magazine accepted a $3-million bid from *Newsweek,* but then reopened the bidding when Rupert Murdoch offered to pay more.

Newsweek decided to publish without paying. "We are covering the story as news," the magazine's publicity director announced. The result was a thirteen-page cover story, consisting partly of sample diary entries that *Stern* had provided during the auction. *Newsweek* published seventeen diary quotations, more than even *Stern* initially ran, prompting a *Stern* official to issue a threat: "We were cheated and I guarantee *Newsweek* will regret what they did."

The Germans soon had more pressing problems. Hitler biographers insisted that he had never kept a diary. Hugh Trevor-Roper, the British historian and Hitler scholar who had initially endorsed the diaries as genuine, voiced growing doubts. Long-postponed chemical tests showed that the paper and ink had been manufactured after the war. Within a few days the hoax collapsed.

Newsweek's coverage, both before and after the diaries were shown to be fake, elicited sharp criticism from other journalists. The magazine's initial diaries article had said: "Genuine or not, it almost doesn't matter in the end." Anthony Lewis of *The New York Times* responded: "It matters a lot." After the forgery was revealed, *Newsweek*'s article laid all the blame on *Der Stern*—the German magazine had seemingly been guided, *Newsweek* charged, "more by commercial ambition than by journalistic ethics." *Washington Post* ombudsman Robert McCloskey chided *Newsweek* for failing to acknowledge that its own splashy coverage had been unwarranted and misleading.

Newsweek owner Katharine Graham said afterward that marketing Hitler had "bothered us." The magazine's editor,

William Broyles, disagreed. "I am very proud of what appeared in the magazine," he said. "I have no regrets."[13]

POPCORN

Faith Popcorn, a professional trend-spotter and 1987 media star, told reporters that her surname came about when immigration authorities misheard her Italian grandfather identify himself as "Papa Corne." *The New York Times,* among others, published her explanation. In fact, as *Newsweek* discovered, she had been born Faith Plotkin, and the Papa Corne story was pure invention. "Some people," she said of the fiction, "say it was my best piece of work."[14]

HOAX ARTISTS

Operating separately, two New Yorkers share an unorthodox hobby: providing amusing, plausible, and completely false human-interest stories to credulous reporters.

Alan Abel began misleading the media in the 1950s by campaigning to put pants on animals. In the '80s he appeared as Omar Rockford, proprietor of Omar's School for Beggars, on CNN's talk show *Sonya* (his fake mustache was slipping off). Stories about the school ran in the *Miami Herald, Newsday,* and *New York.* On another occasion Abel got on the *Morton Downey, Jr., Show* as the leader of "Females for Felons"—a group of public-spirited women who, he said, "want to provide heterosexual relations for those men who don't want to be homosexuals behind bars." In 1980 Abel got his own obituary published in *The New York Times.* The newspaper reported that he had died of a heart attack while scouting locations for a movie in Utah.

Joey Skaggs engineers similar hoaxes. In 1976 Skaggs announced a "cathouse for dogs," where pets could "get a little tail." A local news program interviewed him for a segment on cruelty to animals and won an Emmy for it. In 1986, under the name Joe Bones, Skaggs announced that his "Fat Squad" would, for three hundred dollars a day, help people keep to their diets by staying with them at all times and, if necessary, holding them back from the refrigerator door. This time Skaggs fooled the *Washington Post,* the *New York Daily News,* the *Philadelphia Inquirer,* and *Good Morning America.* Skaggs's other pranks included a gypsy who insisted that the gypsy moth be renamed, a doctor who claimed to have developed a healing serum from cockroaches, and the robbery of a celebrity sperm bank. Reporters, Skaggs said, are "always more interested in what makes a good story than they are in the truth."[15]

THE PRESS AND ITS CRITICS

....

MENCKEN RESPONSE

H. L. Mencken used a printed postcard to respond to reader complaints: "Dear Sir or Madam, You may be right."[16]

WASHINGTON BOYCOTT

In 1986 the *Washington Post* presented its revamped Sunday magazine section. The first issue featured a cover story on a black singer accused of murder and a column sympathetic to local merchants who, fearing robbery, were refusing to admit young blacks. In response to what struck her as an antiblack bias, Cathy Liggins Hughes, a local radio personality, organized a protest. The following Sunday, hundreds of people dumped thousands of copies of the magazine on the steps of the *Post* building. The protest continued every Sunday thereafter. Three months later more than a quarter-million copies had been dumped.

The *Post* admitted error. On the Op Ed page, executive editor Ben Bradlee formally apologized "for the offense that two articles in the first issue plainly—if inadvertently—gave to certain segments of our audience." Donald Graham, the publisher, appeared on Hughes's radio talk show for three consecutive days, where he pledged that the *Post* would cover the black community more sensitively. He also promised to come back to Hughes's show twice yearly for the next ten years. Hughes announced that the boycott was over.

At least for a while, *Post* coverage did seem to change. Upbeat stories about blacks became so prevalent that Hughes said the newspaper "looks just like *Ebony.*" According to reporters, more than a dozen critical articles about the city's black mayor, Marion Barry, got postponed, buried, watered down, or killed.[17]

WASHINGTON POST VS. DAVIS

After the *Washington Post*'s Ben Bradlee and Katharine Graham reacted vehemently to a 1977 Graham biography, *Katharine the Great,* the publisher recalled and shredded thousands of books. Deborah Davis, a free-lance writer, suggested in her book that the CIA was closely tied to the *Post* in general and to Bradlee in particular. Although Davis didn't directly state that Bradlee was a CIA agent, she did say, among other things, that he "may or may not" have been spying for the government when he worked in the American Civil Liberties Union in the mid-1950s and that his "Harvard chum" Richard Ober, a CIA agent, was Deep Throat.

Bradlee was incensed. "It will give many folks intense pleasure," he said, "to learn that when the shoe is on the other foot, when the cry of 'foul' comes from an editor's throat, things look a little different." In a letter to Davis's publisher, Harcourt Brace Jovanovich, Bradlee listed twenty-six factual errors. Whereas some were relatively trivial (his father had married a third cousin, not a fourth cousin), others related to the *Post*-CIA nexus (Bradlee insisted he had never met Ober). Harcourt Brace, Bradlee wrote, belonged "in that special little group of publishers who don't give a shit for the truth." Katharine Graham wrote a more restrained letter to the publisher, saying that she was "puzzled that such a book could have been published by a firm as distinguished as yours."

Harcourt Brace capitulated. All remaining copies of the book, nineteen-thousand out of twenty-five-thousand printed, were shredded. William Jovanovich, president of the company, wrote Graham, "I cannot tell you how pained I am by the circumstances which have caused you, quite unnecessarily, distress and concern."

Davis sued the publishing company for breach of contract and accepted a $100,000 out-of-court settlement. Her book was reissued in 1987 by National Press. It included a letter from Bradlee, insisting that *"all* of the allegations about my association with people in the CIA are as false today as they were when you wrote them."[18]

THE BINGHAMS VS. CHANDLER

The Bingham publishing family of Kentucky used copyright law to try to stop publication of a controversial biography, *The Binghams of Louisville: The Dark History Behind One of America's Great Fortunes.* The book, written by Pulitzer-winning reporter David L. Chandler, alleges that in 1917 Robert Worth Bingham drugged his wife in order to get her to sign an addition to her will that left him five million dollars.

The publisher, Macmillan, was about to release the book when Robert Bingham's son, Barry Bingham, Sr., read it in galleys. Bingham responded by copyrighting not only his father's letters, but also his own written answers to Chandler's questions (Bingham had refused to submit to a face-to-face interview). The copyrights meant that Chandler could not quote extensively from the letters or the answers. Bingham also sent Macmillan an eight-pound package of documents, which he said refuted Chandler's allegations.

Three weeks before bound copies were scheduled to be shipped to stores, Macmillan canceled the book. The decision, the publishing house said in a written statement, was based on "serious substantive disagreements" with Chandler, and "not upon legal considerations." When the decision came, thousands of copies had been printed and were awaiting binding. Ultimately another publisher, Crown, brought out the book.[19]

OTHER BOOK BATTLES

- In 1943 E. P. Dutton published *Under Cover,* an exposé of Fascist, Nazi, and "superpatriot" organizations in the United States written by John Roy Carlson (a pseudonym for reporter Arthur Derounian). One of the organizations criticized in the book, the Committee for Constitutional Government, had been created by Frank Gannett, founder of the Gannett newspaper chain. Gannett said that he wanted to "kill the book." To that end he sent threatening letters to bookstores and book wholesalers, saying that he was putting them on notice about the book's libelous nature so that they could "take whatever steps are required." Fearing a lawsuit, several of the companies initially refused to handle the book. Executives at Dutton publicly accused Gannett of "interference with the freedom of the press," and he backed off, never filing any lawsuits. The book became a best-seller.
- In 1971 *TV Guide*'s Edith Efron wrote *The News Twisters,* which purported to prove statistically that the network newscasts had been grossly biased against Richard Nixon during the 1968 presidential election. ABC and NBC took the accusations in stride, but CBS responded with what Efron characterized as a "smear campaign of astonishing virulence." In information passed to book reviewers and media critics, the network depicted the work as part of the Nixon-Agnew assault on the press and argued that Efron had manipulated the data to fit her thesis. The controversy gave Efron material for a second book, *How CBS Tried to Kill a Book.*
- In 1982 Don Kowet and Sally Bedell wrote a *TV Guide* article, "Anatomy of a Smear," that sharply criticized the CBS documentary *A Vietnam Deception: The Uncounted Enemy* (the same documentary that prompted General William Westmoreland to sue CBS). The program, Kowet and Bedell wrote, contained "massive distortions." When Kowet went on to expand his findings into a 1984 book, *A Matter of Honor,* the network exerted so much pressure

that the publisher, Macmillan, accused CBS of "an unprecedented and shocking attempt to chill" a book's publication. As the publication date approached, the network mailed written attacks on the book to fifty book reviewers. After publication, CBS arranged for the producer of the challenged documentary, George Crile, to appear on interview shows where Kowet was scheduled to appear.

- CBS and *Time* both went after Renata Adler's 1986 book *Reckless Disregard,* which chronicled General Westmoreland's libel suit against CBS and Ariel Sharon's libel suit against Time Inc. The book's publication was held up for several weeks while lawyers for the publisher, Knopf, reviewed lengthy complaints written by the news organizations. Adler and her publisher were particularly troubled by CBS's fifty-page rebuttal, a document whose "main purpose," Adler said, "was intimidation." The CBS offensive continued after the book's publication. Just as he had followed Kowet to talk shows, documentary producer George Crile showed up unannounced to debate Adler at a Yale forum.[20]

REMARKS

"You get a quart of sour milk at your local grocery store . . . take it back to the check-out counter and say the milk is sour and the guy will say to you either, 'Get a new quart' or 'Here's your money back.' The equivalent of taking a quart of sour milk back to a newspaper is you're lucky if they don't pour it on your head. . . ."

—Donald Jones, *Kansas City Star and Times* ombudsman[21]

"Bastards like us might check things more, were it not for our conviction that bastards like you would do it for us."

—Ben Bradlee, responding to a reader who had pointed out an apparent error in the *Washington Post*[22]

"Go fuck yourself."

—Tom Shales, *Washington Post* TV critic, responding to a letter that had found fault with a Shales column[23]

"The press does not have a thick skin, it has no skin."

—Edward R. Murrow, CBS reporter[24]

PROPOSALS FOR CHANGE

....

- The poet Johann Wolfgang von Goethe thought that, in order to avoid transitory affairs, one should let newspapers age a month before reading them.

- Thomas Jefferson suggested that editors divide their newspapers into four sections: Truths, Probabilities, Possibilities, and Lies.

- Étienne Cabet, a nineteenth-century French social theorist, believed editors should be elected by readers.

- The novelist Albert Camus suggested creating a "control newspaper," which would publish reviews of other newspapers' articles, estimating their accuracy and bias. "But," Camus wondered, "do people really want to know how much truth there is in what they read? Would they buy the control paper? That's the most difficult problem."

- In his book *The Brass Check,* Upton Sinclair recommended a law requiring that newspapers submit articles to the persons quoted and get their approval before publication.

- A. J. Liebling, the *New Yorker* press critic, proposed that the American Society of Newspaper Editors establish an annual award for lying. The prize would, Liebling said, "inspire far more interest than Pulitzer prizes, the latter having by now attained all the prestige of bean-bags tossed to good little newspapers by other papers that had them last year."[25]

IV

.....

MAKING NEWS, MAKING HISTORY

13

NEWSROOM RELATIONS

BENNETT'S EMPLOYEE RELATIONS

James Gordon Bennett, Jr., the publisher of the *New York Herald* during the latter half of the nineteenth century, was a notoriously difficult boss. When a music critic didn't get a haircut, as Bennett had instructed, Bennett gave him a new assignment—covering Russia. Another time Bennett asked his editors for a list of the paper's indispensable reporters. When he got the list he fired everyone on it, to demonstrate that nobody was truly indispensable.[1]

BYLINE: KARL MARX

In 1851, the *New York Tribune* invited Karl Marx to become its London correspondent. Although the thirty-three-year-old Marx was already famous as the author of the *Communist Manifesto,* he was also impoverished—his political writings had made little money and he had been unemployed for a year—so he gratefully accepted the newspaper's offer.

His gratitude was short-lived. To Friedrich Engels, his occasional collaborator on *Tribune* articles and other writings, Marx complained steadily about the job. When the *Tribune* cut back on its foreign coverage to make room for news of the 1856 presidential campaign, Marx grumbled that the newspaper "can be approached seriously only when the Presidential-dung is at an end." When the *Tribune* published some of his dispatches as editorials, without bylines, Marx was at first thrilled ("the editorial staff of the Tribune for the last eight weeks have been Marx-Engels") but soon turned resentful ("the dogs have succeeded in obscuring my name before the Yankee public"). Most of all Marx complained about his wages. The newspaper had spent a fortune sending a reporter to India, he told Engels, "and that rascal writes worse and less from there . . . than I write from here about the same subject." Marx said he had gradually realized that "I have given these fellows too much for their money."

In 1862 the *Tribune*'s managing editor, Charles A. Dana, told Marx that his services were no longer needed. The newspaper's owners, Dana explained, had decided to devote less space to foreign news. Tactfully, Dana didn't mention a contributing factor: his discovery a few months earlier that Marx had been billing the newspaper for articles he hadn't yet written. With his new free time, Marx resumed his political writings and activities.

A century later President Kennedy chided a group of newspaper publishers for Marx's dismissal. "If only this capitalistic New York newspaper had treated him more kindly," Kennedy said, "if only Marx had remained a foreign correspondent, history might have been different."[2]

PULITZER CRITERION

Joseph Pulitzer fretted that his *New York World* was turning stodgy. "I think," he told a member of his staff, Don C. Seitz, "it's because nobody on the staff gets drunk. . . . When I was there someone always got drunk, and we made a great paper. Take the next train back to the city, find a man who gets drunk and hire him at once."

In New York, Seitz voyaged through the saloons that were popular with newspapermen. In one, he found Esdaile Cohen, a talented reporter who had just been fired from the *New York American.* "I can't let the hard stuff alone," Cohen explained sadly. Seitz hired him on the spot.[3]

SHIFTING SCIENCE

Joseph Medill, the owner and editor of the *Chicago Tribune* in the late nineteenth century, made sure that *Tribune* articles conformed to his all-encompassing scientific theory of the moment. One reporter, hewing to Medill's policy, wrote that an Egyptian plague had been caused by sunspots. By the time he got the manuscript, though, Medill had adopted a new theory. He changed "sunspots" to "microbes" throughout the article.[4]

THE *WORLD*'S CHAPIN

In the early twentieth century, nearly every reporter in New York knew a story about Charles Chapin, the irascible city editor of the *Evening World.* Among the tales:

- Chapin sent a young reporter to interview a burly cowboy who had just eloped with his boss's daughter. The cowboy declined to answer questions; instead he hurled the reporter down a stairway and threatened to do worse if the man returned. The reporter phoned Chapin and told him what had happened. "Look here," Chapin said, "you go back and tell that bully he can't intimidate me."
- After Chapin was overheard complimenting a reporter for writing of the "melancholy waters" of the East River, all the reporters began writing about melancholy waters. Chapin quickly found the expression tiresome. When reporter Dwight Perrin used it in a story, Chapin fired him.

How, Chapin asked Perrin, could the waters of the Hudson be melancholy, anyway? "Perhaps," the reporter replied, "it was because they had just gone past Yonkers." "Not bad," Chapin said, and rehired him.

- Chapin told one reporter, Charlie Keegan, to follow another reporter in order to see if the man dawdled on his way to an assignment. Keegan headed straight to a bar, found the other reporter killing time, and explained his mission. The two drank for a while and then meandered uptown for the interview. Afterward Keegan informed Chapin that the reporter under suspicion had gone straight to the assignment, where he had been kept waiting by the news source. "Charlie," Chapin replied, "you take six weeks off without pay. I had someone following you."
- One morning a courthouse reporter missed the Staten Island ferry to get to work. The reporter phoned Chapin from the dock and said he was at the courthouse. "Cover the flood," Chapin told him. "What flood?" "There must be a terrible flood at the Criminal Courts building," Chapin said. "I can hear the boats whistling."
- When a reporter used in a story the word "questionnaire," which was not yet in dictionaries, Chapin fired him.
- A reporter came to work late and explained to Chapin that he had scalded his foot in the bath. Several days later Chapin told the man he was fired. "I would have fired you earlier," Chapin said, "but I wanted to see how long you could keep on faking that limp."
- *World* owner Joseph Pulitzer put his son to work as a reporter on the newspaper. Pulitzer, Sr., instructed Chapin: "Treat him exactly as you would any other beginner." Chapin agreed. After about a month, he fired Joseph Pulitzer, Jr., for tardiness.

Chapin's temper finally got the better of him. In 1918 he murdered his wife. He was sent to Sing Sing prison, where he died in 1930.[5]

PATTERSON VS. WINCHELL

At a 1942 dinner party, Cissy Patterson, owner of the *Washington Times-Herald,* told columnist Walter Winchell to stop writing so much about the Nazi threat. The column, she said, "is becoming a bore." Winchell snapped that Patterson should get herself "another boy." Patterson rushed away in tears.

The exchange set off a heated feud. Patterson used her *Times-Herald* to call Winchell a "cockroach" in an inch-tall headline. The *Times-Herald* continued to carry the Winchell column, but with sizable chunks omitted. Winchell fired back with a paid advertisement in another Washington newspaper, implying that the *Times-Herald* was trying to protect the Nazis from Winchell. That prompted Patterson to remark, in reference to Winchell's volunteer duty in the navy, "There isn't a night goes by that I don't get down on my knees and pray that they take the bastard off shore duty and put him on a destroyer that will sink." Winchell called Patterson "the craziest woman in Washington, D.C." Patterson filed suit for libel, and declared: "He is forever boasting that he is the American Hitler would most like to hang. In what respect does that make Hitler different from anybody else?"[6]

HELPING HAND

One night Stanley Woodward, sports editor of the *New York Herald Tribune,* and sports writer Red Smith were out drinking. Woodward challenged a man to a wrestling match. Within a few seconds Woodward was pinned to the floor. "Smith," he said, "help me up."

As Smith recounted it: "I handed him a scotch and soda where he lay. He knew I went into newspapering because I disliked lifting things."[7]

COMMUNISTS ON THE *TIMES*

In the mid-1950s *The New York Times* fired several copy readers and low-level editors who, when subpoenaed by a Senate subcommittee, had invoked the Fifth Amendment. In a letter to one of them, publisher Arthur Hays Sulzberger said that journalists had a professional duty to answer the questions. "Even though he may have the legal right to do so," Sulzberger wrote, "a reporter who refuses to answer questions on the ground that the answers may incriminate him, immediately destroys the confidence in his objectivity that is essential for his work." Sulzberger later modified his views and kept a copy editor on the payroll who, though he had answered questions about his own involvement in the party, had taken the Fifth when asked about other party members.[8]

INTERVIEWING SARNOFF

On NBC's *Today* show, Dave Garroway occasionally interviewed David Sarnoff, the founder of the network. Sarnoff's staff would script the interview in advance and transcribe it on cue cards. Sarnoff demanded that everything be written out, even such asides as "Good question, Dave."[9]

THIN-SKINNED ANCHOR

During the 1968 Democratic convention, executives grimaced as CBS anchor Walter Cronkite used the word "erosion" over and over to describe the shift in delegate support away from Hubert Humphrey. Robert Wussler, director of the network's special-events unit, spoke by intercom to Jeff Gralnick, an associate producer who shared the small anchor booth with Cronkite: "Jeff, try to get Walter not to use the word 'erosion' away from Humphrey. We're getting a lot of heat from on high about this."

"I'll write him a gentle note," said Gralnick.

"Jeff, it's only the *word* 'erosion' they're objecting to."

A few moments later Gralnick came back on the intercom: "Mr. Cronkite just answered the note with 'I quit!' "

Wussler turned to the monitor (not then going out over the air) and saw Cronkite sitting back in his chair, looking incensed. By the time a director cued him, Cronkite had regained his composure. He carried on.[10]

INTEGRATING POOLS

In 1949 Ben Bradlee, a young *Washington Post* reporter, covered a racial confrontation at a whites-only city swimming pool. The confrontation soon escalated into a four hundred–person riot. Bradlee interviewed participants and police and wrote a comprehensive story.

The next day Bradlee discovered that his story had gotten buried in the *Post*'s second section, with some details omitted and the word "riot" changed to "incident." Bradlee was protesting to his editor when the publisher, Philip Graham, told Bradlee to follow him. In Graham's office Bradlee found Clark Clifford and other federal officials who held ultimate control over Washington city services. Graham told the men that the race riot would remain buried in the paper *if* the government would immediately close all city pools for the season and reopen them, fully integrated, the next year. The officials agreed.

Bradlee later voiced doubts about the resolution. "[I]f we'd put this on page one and called it what it was, you might have had the 1968 riot in 1949," he said. "It might have been better if we had."[11]

REPORTERS AND RACE

"All the rules of journalism calling for objectivity, balance and fairness are white people's rules that have been used in the past by the white media to distort black news. While the black reporter should feel free to criticize movement leaders and their programs, he should never forget that his primary loyalty is to other blacks and the movement."

—Tony Brown, dean of Howard University's School of Communications[12]

"You can be a black or you can be a journalist. Being a reporter pays a lot better than being a nigger."

—William Raspberry, black *Washington Post* columnist[13]

"Along with the country as a whole, the press has too long basked in a white world, looking out of it, if at all, with white men's eyes and a white perspective. That is no longer good enough."

—Kerner Commission on Civil Disorders, 1968[14]

"For a long time, newspapers in this town talked wistfully about how hard it was to find competent Negro reporters. Then the disturbances began; the black nationalists refused to talk to white reporters, and there was a spectacular rise in respect for the talent of the Negro journalist."

—Murray Kempton, *New York Post* columnist[15]

NEAR MISS

Washington Post reporter Carl Bernstein nearly wasn't around to cover the Watergate scandal. Bernstein had asked executive editor Ben Bradlee to make him the full-time rock critic. Bradlee had agreed, but the job had ended up going to someone else.

Resentful, Bernstein decided to leave the *Post.* He wrote to *Rolling Stone* and asked if he could replace the departing Hunter S. Thompson as political writer. Bernstein was waiting for a reply when he was assigned to cover the break-in at the Democratic National Committee's Watergate offices.[16]

PRESSROOM TOXICITY

When occupational health researchers suspected that newspaper pressrooms might be highly toxic work environments, they set out to investigate. In order to conduct tests, they proceeded to the *New York Times, New York Daily News, New York Post, Chicago Daily News,* and *Chicago Tribune.* Every newspaper refused to cooperate.[17]

SCHORR LEAVES

In 1976 CBS correspondent Daniel Schorr passed a secret government report to the *Village Voice,* denied having done so, seemingly tried to finger another CBS reporter, and in the end left the network. The episode began when Schorr managed to get a copy of the 338-page House Intelligence Committee Report on the CIA several days before its scheduled release. Schorr revealed details of the report on CBS, scooping most of the rest of the press. Then, for reasons of national security, the House of Representatives voted not to release the report publicly after all.

Schorr decided to try to get the secret report published as a book, for which he would write the introduction. First he asked if any of CBS's publishing subsidiaries would be interested, but he got no response. After several intermediaries had entered the picture, the *Village Voice* agreed to publish excerpts of the report. For payment Schorr asked the *Voice* to make a "substantial contribution" to one intermediary, the Reporters Committee for Freedom of the Press. Schorr no longer wanted his name attached to the report, because the *Voice* had published an unfavorable article about him and CBS (by this point, Schorr later said, he would have been happy to get the report published in *Pravda* so long as it appeared somewhere). Instead, the introduction was written by writer Aaron Latham.

When the *Voice* appeared with "The CIA Report the President Doesn't Want You to Read," a *Washington Post* reporter asked Schorr if he was the source. Schorr denied it. "I thought I had the only copy," he told the reporter, "but someone must have stolen it from under me." The *Post* reporter concluded that Schorr was trying to blame a CBS colleague, Lesley Stahl, who was dating Aaron Latham. In initial conversations at CBS, Schorr also implied (or, according to some listeners, outright stated) that Stahl must be the source. When she heard about the allegations, Stahl consulted a lawyer about suing Schorr.

CBS officials were angry about Schorr's unauthorized use of what they regarded as network property, and angrier still about his attempt to implicate Stahl. Network executives made him sign an undated letter of resignation. They cooled off before activating the letter, but Schorr left anyway.

If he had it to do over again, Schorr said, he would just photocopy the report and throw the copies off the CBS building.[18]

NAUGHTON'S FAREWELL

A few days before James Naughton was scheduled to leave *The New York Times* for the *Philadelphia Inquirer,* he told his editors that he wanted to write about astronomers' new theories concerning Uranus. The editors scheduled the piece. The deadline came and went with no sign of the reporter or the article. Finally a message arrived from Naughton: "Please scratch Uranus."[19]

ANONYMITY

David Shaw, media critic of the *Los Angeles Times,* examined the issues raised by newspapers' reliance on unnamed sources. In interviews, several reporters said that unnamed sources constitute a serious problem—and asked Shaw not to publish their names.[20]

CHANGING A QUOTE

For an article about the making of the movie *All the President's Men, Washington Post* reporters interviewed other *Post* reporters and editors. An editor, Harry Rosenfeld, said of the film: "We usually dish it out; now we may have to take it." Later Rosenfeld phoned the reporter who had interviewed him and asked to change the remark. When the reporter resisted, Rosenfeld said, "If that shows up I'm not going to be like these tolerant guys around here. I'll personally throw your desk out the window. Your career is at stake, friend." As published, the story included Rosenfeld's original quotation as well as the threat.[21]

LAST SUPPER

In the fall of 1984 the new newspaper *USA Today* was losing considerably more money than management at its parent company, Gannett, had projected. Al Neuharth, the newspaper's founder, convened a special meeting of the newspaper's executives to discuss austerity measures.

After the meeting, the group went out to dinner. They waited in the restaurant for a private dining room, and Neuharth disappeared. Half an hour later the door swung open, revealing Neuharth standing in front of a wooden cross and wearing a crown of thorns. "I am the crucified one," he announced. Unless the newspaper's losses were cut, they would all be "passed-over," he said, and this might turn out to be their "last supper."

Neuharth later said that the group needed to be "jarred into reality," and that the drama had succeeded. One executive called it "the most offensive thing I have seen in my adult life."[22]

COUNTDOWN

After *The New York Times* announced that executive editor A. M. Rosenthal would retire at age sixty-five, one antagonistic reporter programmed his personal computer to tell him, each time he logged on, how many Rosenthal days remained.[23]

MEDIA LEAKS

- In 1974 CBS executives contemplated reassigning White House correspondent Dan Rather, who was still controversial from his battles with the just-departed Nixon administration. Someone leaked the top-secret option, and several television critics wrote columns accusing the network of spinelessness. CBS News president Richard Salant told colleagues that his network bosses were so outraged about the leaks, they were talking about creating a special investigative unit to track down the leakers—CBS's own version of Nixon's "Plumbers."

- CBS subsequently installed equipment that recorded every phone number dialed from network phones, enabling executives to find out who was responsible for leaks to *The New York Times* and *Newsday*.

- In 1974 new reporters on the *Washington Post* were given a memo that instructed: "Be completely loyal to the newspaper, especially in private conversation with news sources, fellow staff members and other friends, never grousing or complaining."

- Later the *Washington Star*'s gossip column, "The Ear," began running derogatory items about "O.P." (the Other Paper). *Post* executive editor Ben Bradlee announced that anyone caught passing information to "The Ear" would be fired.

- When *USA Today* reported on job changes at *The New York Times, Times* executive editor A. M. Rosenthal concluded that a Washington bureau reporter named Ben Franklin was the probable source. Rosenthal instructed editors that Franklin's name was not to appear in the paper. It was some ten weeks before Franklin got his next byline.[24]

REMARKS

"Unless I am put in absolute control of the property and of all who are employed therewith, I would not undertake the management at any price, for I am certain I could not succeed as manager with any abridgement of almost autocratic power."

—Adolph Ochs before buying
The New York Times, 1890s[25]

"Because I say so."

—Arthur Ochs Sulzberger, *New York Times* publisher (and Adolph Ochs's grandson), on why executive editor A. M. Rosenthal had to retire at sixty-five[26]

"The pattern of a newspaperman's life is like the plot of Black Beauty. *Sometimes he finds a kind master who gives him a dry stall and an occasional bran mash in the form of a Christmas bonus, sometimes he falls into the hands of a mean owner who drives him in spite of spavins and expects him to live on banana peelings."*

—A. J. Liebling, *New Yorker* press critic[27]

"Every reporter is a hope; every editor is a disappointment."

—Joseph Pulitzer[28]

14

.....

COMPETITORS

FIRST WITH THE NEWS

Starting in the 1830s David H. Craig built a successful news service by getting European news ahead of his competition. Craig would intercept ships from Europe at sea a few hours before they docked, or board them at Nova Scotia before they reached the United States. From the ships he would send brief news bulletins by carrier pigeon (on occasion other reporters tried to shoot down the birds), to be followed by fuller accounts by Pony Express. Craig's fervor stemmed partly from a financial incentive: James Gordon Bennett paid a bonus of five hundred dollars for each hour that his *New York Herald* received the news ahead of other New York newspapers.[1]

ARCTIC SCOOP

In 1854 the steamer *Arctic* missed its scheduled arrival in New York, and rumors began to circulate that the ship had sunk in the North Atlantic. A *New York Times* editor, riding home on a city horsecar, overheard a man telling the conductor that he had been aboard the *Arctic* when it had sunk. The editor tried to get details from him, but the man was drunk and incoherent. All the editor could make out was that the passenger had already talked to reporters from the *New York Herald* and that they had given him a bottle of wine.

The editor returned to the *Times,* ordered the presses stopped, and sent a pressman out to get an early copy of the *Herald.* The pressman came back and reported that it couldn't be done: The *Herald* wasn't distributing any papers until other newspapers were out on the streets, in order to protect its *Arctic* scoop. The editor told the pressman to try again, and offered a $50 reward. This time the pressman succeeded. The *Herald* he brought back contained a complete chronicle of the disaster as told by the first survivor to return to the city, the drunk on the horsecar. The editor had the *Herald* story set in type and put it on the *Times'* front page, presenting it as a *Times* exclusive.

Despite the late change, the *Times* reached the street close to its usual hour. The *Herald,* because of its secrecy, was an hour late. As a result, many readers assumed disdainfully that the *Herald* had stolen the *Times'* story.[2]

MEDIA CRITICS: NINETEENTH CENTURY

"The decline of The New York Times *in everything that entitles a newspaper to respect and confidence has been rapid and complete."*

—*New York Sun*

"Old Satanic."

—New York Times *on New York Tribune* editor Horace Greeley

"The Little Villain."

—*New York Tribune* on *New York Times* editor Henry Raymond

"A life-like portrait of the sensitive editor of the [Rocky Mountain] Herald. *Copyright secured."*

—*Rocky Mountain News,* under a picture of a donkey's hind end[3]

CIRCULATION DISPUTE

During the Civil War *The New York Times* insisted that its circulation had exceeded that of the *New York Herald.* If the *Herald* could prove otherwise, the *Times* promised to give $2,500 to the families of volunteer soldiers. James Gordon Bennett of the *Herald* declined the offer, replying that "betting is immoral; we cannot approve of it."[4]

TRACKING NEWS THEFTS

- In the late nineteenth century, editors at the *Chicago Daily News* were convinced that *News* stories were being lifted by the *Chicago Post & Mail,* which was owned by the McMullen family. The *News* ran a story about a Serbian famine, which reported that the provincial mayor had issued a statement "ending with the ominous words: 'Er us siht la Etsll iws nel lum cmeht' (the municipality cannot aid)." As expected, the *Post & Mail* lifted the article. *Daily News* editors then pointed out that the phrase backward read, "The McMullens will steal this sure."

- In 1919 the *New York Daily News* and *New York Evening Mail* shared an office, including a wire-service teletype. *Mail* editors believed that the *News* was publishing some wire material that arrived during the *Mail*'s exclusive hours. On teletype paper the *Mail* men typed a one-sentence story: "Ekafasti, Greece—Burglars today broke into the village bank and stole one million drachma, about $7.38." The editors left the item in the *Mail* slot, and the next day the story appeared in the *News.* That afternoon the *Mail* published on its front page: "Our esteemed contemporary, the *Daily News,* has printed a news item with a date-line, 'Ekafasti.' It's astounding that when this word is spelled backwards, it says, 'It's a fake.' "

- The best-known hidden message appeared in William Randolph Hearst's *New York Journal* during the Spanish-American War. From Cuba the *Journal* reported the death of "Colonel Reflipe W. Thenuz, an Austrian artillerist of European renown." Joseph Pulitzer's *New York World* lifted the item, datelining it "On board the *World* dispatch boat." The *Journal* delightedly announced that the colonel's name was an anagram, more or less, of "we pilfer the news." The *Journal* subsequently published a frivolous cartoon of the colonel ("specially taken by the *World*"), a poem honoring the colonel's wartime exploits, and illustrations of proposed monuments to Thenuz's memory. To help build the monument, *Journal* readers sent in contributions—all in Confederate currency and other worthless paper.[5]

FRAUDULENT FEATURE

Walter Howey, the managing editor of the *Chicago Herald & Examiner* in the 1920s, liked to deceive his former employers at the *Chicago Tribune.* Once he had an actress tell *Tribune* reporters that she was a terminally ill heiress and that, in order to go out with a bang, she planned to spend ten million dollars before she died. After the *Tribune* splashed its feature across the front page, Howey announced that the *Herald* was about to publish a serialized novel called "The Ten Million Dollar Heiress." He thanked the *Tribune* for the publicity.[6]

NO DISTRACTIONS

During his 1929 visit to the United States, British Prime Minister Ramsay MacDonald delivered an exclusive address over NBC radio. At CBS William Paley, concerned that the public might choose CBS entertainment over the important NBC speech, ordered his network to leave the air until MacDonald was finished.[7]

TIME VS. *NEW YORKER*

The *New Yorker*'s famous parody of *Time*'s writing style grew out of longstanding antagonisms. In 1925 *Time* started the feud with a snide review of the *New Yorker*'s debut issue. Then in 1934 *Time*'s sister magazine, *Fortune,* revealed the salaries of *New Yorker* editors and top staff members. The *New Yorker* responded with an item in its "Talk of the Town" section: "The Editor of *Fortune* gets $30 a week and carfare."

Two years later the *New Yorker* assigned Wolcott Gibbs to write a profile of *Time* founder Henry Luce. Gibbs wrote in a sharp imitation of *Time* style. He described Luce as an "ambitious, gimlet-eyed Baby Tycoon." Several sentences lived up to the profile's description of *Time* writing ("Backward ran sentences until reeled the mind"), including the article's close: "Certainly to be taken with seriousness is Luce at 38. . . . Where it will all end, knows God!"

Luce complained to Harold Ross, editor of the *New Yorker,* that the article contained not "a single favorable word." Ross responded that the article portrayed Luce as "practically heroic," that Luce's own magazines were notorious for "cruelty and scandal-mongering and insult," and that Gibbs had omitted some of the most damning material. Luce replied that "my only regret is that Mr. Gibbs did not publish all he knew so that I might learn at once exactly how mean and poisonous a person I am."

Two years later *Time* retaliated mildly, adding to its masthead the name "Eustace Tilley"—the foppish character with top hat and monocle who appears periodically on *New Yorker* covers. *Time* planned to carry the name for a few issues and then announce that Tilley had been fired. But Tilley's creator threatened to sue, and the prank was called off.

Years later Luce appeared unannounced at a college class called "Contemporary Biography" and found the students discussing the *New Yorker* profile of him. "So now," Luce said, "my question is: *Is* this thing going to be engraved on my tombstone?"[8]

NEWSMAGAZINE ATTACK

Bill Emerson of *Newsweek* did what he could to undercut *Time.* On a whistlestop tour through the South during the 1960 presidential campaign, Emerson would sometimes slip a *Time* ID badge off a dozing reporter and, brandishing the badge, shout at Southerners: "Henry Luce wants to know what you white trash are thinking about!"[9]

TUGBOAT EXCLUSIVE

In 1962, when a plane crashed in New York's East River, only one tugboat was operating. The boat helped pull bodies and survivors from the wreckage. When it returned to the dock, a horde of reporters rushed aboard and the captain started to tell his story. CBS producer Don Hewitt interrupted to ask, "Who owns this tug?" The other reporters groaned at the irrelevant question. "New Haven Tug," the captain answered.

Hewitt walked to a pay phone, called his editor, and returned to the tug. A few minutes later the phone in the boat's wheelhouse rang. The captain stepped away from the reporters to answer it. When he returned he asked, "Which one of you guys is Hewitt?" Hewitt identified himself. "Okay," the captain said, "the boat is under charter to you. What do you want to do?"

"First thing I want to do is get these guys off my boat."

The captain cleared everyone else off, and Hewitt and his camera crew sailed out to get the first pictures of the crash.[10]

AP VS. UPI

- United Press (before it became United Press International) won its first Pulitzer Prize the year that Kent Cooper of the Associated Press left the Pulitzer board. During the twenty-five years that Cooper had been on the board, AP had won fourteen prizes to UP's zero.

- After a *Wall Street Journal* article accused UPI of frequent inaccuracies, UPI's editor-in-chief, H. L. Stevenson, had his staff prepare a booklet that listed some notable AP errors. He sent it to UPI editors, instructing them to use the materials "discreetly, but use them without hesitation, when the subject of UPI's accuracy comes up. . . ."
- After a San Francisco news conference, a UPI reporter was dictating his story over the only nearby phone. AP's reporter wanted to call in his story. He asked the UPI man to hurry up. The UPI reporter kept talking. The AP man brought out a pair of scissors, cut the phone wire, and walked off.[11]

ASSASSINATION COMPETITORS

In President Kennedy's Dallas motorcade, four reporters and a presidential aide were riding in the radiophone-equipped White House pool car. The aide, Malcolm Kilduff, asked the others what a school book "repository" was. Before anyone could answer, gunshots echoed through the plaza and the President's limousine raced away.

Merriman Smith of UPI was in the front seat of the pool car, sitting between the driver and Kilduff. Smith grabbed the phone from the floor and radioed his Dallas bureau that shots had been fired at the motorcade. From the back seat, Jack Bell of AP demanded to use the phone so he could inform *his* Dallas bureau. But Smith refused to relinquish it. He asked the UPI deskman to read the bulletin back to him. Bell started clawing and punching Smith over the seat. Smith crouched down and crawled under the dashboard, clutching the phone.

Almost five minutes later, as the car pulled into Parkland Hospital, Smith gave Bell the phone. Bell placed his call. Suddenly the phone went dead.

For his assassination coverage, Smith won a Pulitzer Prize.[12]

SELF-PROMOTION

In the '60s the *New York Daily News* sometimes needled other newspapers or promoted itself through casual asides in news columns. On one occasion a *Daily News* article referred to "the *Times*, an English-language morning newspaper." Another time a *Daily News* story had this lead: "A DAILY NEWS reader who works for the Good Humor Ice Cream Co. was sworn as a juror this afternoon in the Dr. Carl Coppolino murder trial here."[13]

WOODWARD AND BERNSTEIN VS. HERSH

In the '70s, relations were cool between the nation's best-known investigative reporters—the *Washington Post* team of Robert Woodward and Carl Bernstein, and *The New York Times*' Seymour Hersh.

In *All the President's Men*, Woodward and Bernstein described an evening with Hersh during their competition for Watergate leads. Hersh was, they wrote, "somewhat pudgy," and he appeared for dinner "in old tennis shoes, a frayed pinstriped shirt that might have been his best in his college freshman year, and rumpled bleached khakis." They quoted Hersh as calling Henry Kissinger a "war criminal" and as referring to a colleague's *Times* story as "lies, lies, lies." Woodward and Bernstein judged him "unlike any reporter" they had known.

In an interview with Leonard Downie, Hersh responded in kind: "Bernstein should talk about how somebody dresses, and do I look pudgy to you? I'm much more of an athlete than either one of them. And that remark about Kissinger being a war criminal—what they didn't say in the book was that we were all sitting around getting high and putting down everybody. I didn't see them put in the book what they were saying about Ben Bradlee that night. Damn cheapshot artists."[14]

HAMILL VS. MURDOCH

In 1977 Pete Hamill of the *New York Daily News* wrote a column criticizing the *New York Post*, and *Post* owner Rupert Murdoch decided to get even. Knowing that Hamill was dating Jacqueline Onassis, Murdoch had a staff member dig up a Hamill column from several years earlier that snidely described Mrs. Onassis. Murdoch republished the most insulting passages in the *Post.*[15]

NO, THANKS

When Don Forst became editor of the *Boston Herald-American,* his counterpart at the *Boston Globe,* Tom Winship, called to invite him to lunch. "I appreciate it," Forst said, "but I never want to have lunch with you. I wake up wanting to sack your village, slaughter your sheep, poison your well, cut down your trees, attack your women. . . . But it's not personal."[16]

WHITE HOUSE COMPETITION

In 1979 Judy Woodruff of NBC learned that President Carter planned to nominate Shirley Hufstedler, a federal judge, to be secretary of education. Woodruff stood in front of the White House and taped her exclusive report for the evening newscast. Lesley Stahl of CBS stood nearby and listened. Before Woodruff's piece aired, Stahl phoned *her* newsroom, and CBS put the news out on radio immediately, undercutting Woodruff's scoop. Stahl later suggested that the incident was Woodruff's fault: "I don't know why she didn't ask me to leave."[17]

NEUHARTH VS. BRADLEE

In 1984 Al Neuharth of *USA Today* and Ben Bradlee of the *Washington Post* got into an acerbic correspondence. The exchange concerned a *Post* business-page report about *USA Today*'s high losses.

In his first letter to Bradlee, Neuharth insisted that the *Post* had gotten the story wrong. He wasn't asking that the story be corrected, Neuharth explained; the *Post*'s correction column "already threatens to become the most rapidly growing section of your newspaper and I do not wish to add to that burden." He offered to arrange for *Post*'s business staff to "sit in on an elementary lesson on Wall Street Analysis 101." The letter was signed: "Affectionately, if not admiringly, Al Neuharth."

Bradlee's response began, "Thank you for your condescending and fundamentally unpleasant letter. . . ." Bradlee wrote that he had examined Neuharth's objections to the *Post* story and found them groundless. The letter, he added, "grates in my craw. When I need help in Wall Street Analysis 101, I can promise you I will turn to someone other than yourself to arrange it." He signed, "Yours in truth, Ben Bradlee."

Neuharth's reply opened, "Aw shucks, I didn't mean to ignite your short fuse!" He added: "In the twilight of your career, my friend, you still have the opportunity to balance your well-deserved reputation for toughness with some late-blooming fairness." He signed: "Love, but no kisses, Al Neuharth."[18]

ROSENTHAL VS. BRADLEE

In early 1986 the *Washington Post* ran a three-part series about A. M. Rosenthal, the executive editor of *The New York Times* who was about to face forced retirement at sixty-five. Rosenthal didn't want to step down, and he didn't like the *Post* calling attention to the matter. He commented that when Ben Bradlee retired from the *Post,* the *Times* would cover it in a single paragraph. Bradlee, who was also sixty-four, heard about the remark, and he mailed Rosenthal a draft of the paragraph: "Benjamin C. Bradlee retired yesterday after 28 years as editor-in-chief of the *Washington Post.* He was 75 years old."[19]

UNVEILED

In 1987 Bob Woodward's forthcoming book about the CIA was kept under tight wraps. Even the name, *Veil,* was kept secret until shortly before publication. But two days before authorized excerpts were to be published in the *Washington Post* and other newspapers, *U.S. News & World Report* revealed many of the book's major disclosures. David Gergen, the magazine's editor and formerly President Reagan's communications director, suggested that scooping the *Post* on its own material was not so difficult: "News organizations aren't very good at managing news." For his part, Woodward echoed

Gergen's ex-boss: "I've had it up to the keister with these leaks."[20]

REMARKS

"Our main concern was not the public's right to know, it wasn't that we ought to tell people about this dreadful war in Vietnam. We had one basic consideration, and that was here was a hell of a news story and we were getting our ass beaten."

—Richard Harwood, a *Washington Post* editor, on the *Post*'s efforts to get a copy of the Pentagon Papers[21]

"We've got a big circulation fight going here."

—Paul Thompson, *San Antonio Express* columnist, explaining the paper's decision to reveal that Mayor Henry Cisneros was having an affair[22]

"Reporters are like crabs in a barrel. When one gets up, others pull him down."

—Jack Anderson, columnist[23]

15

FIRST ROUGH DRAFT OF HISTORY

NEWS TIME

The Declaration of Independence was signed on July 4, 1776, in Philadelphia. Newspapers first reported the event in Philadelphia on July 6, in New York on July 10, in Providence on July 13, and in Boston on July 18.

One hundred eighty-seven years later, word that President Kennedy had been shot reached an estimated 62 percent of the American public within half an hour and 90 percent within an hour.[1]

WHAT IF: THE TEN COMMANDMENTS

Television news people have joked that, given the need to compress information for the evening newscasts, the lead for a story announcing the Ten Commandments would go like this: "Moses came down from Mount Sinai today with the Ten Commandments, the three most important of which are . . ."[2]

STANLEY AND LIVINGSTONE

James Gordon Bennett, Jr., publisher of the *New York Herald,* liked to say, "I *make* news." In 1869 he decided to find David Livingstone, a missionary who had disappeared nearly three years earlier in Africa. Bennett assigned the task to Henry Morton Stanley, a twenty-eight-year-old reporter who had been covering the fighting between American Indians and settlers in the West.

Stanley spent a year getting to Africa, writing articles along the way. In Zanzibar he picked up contradictory rumors—that Livingstone was dead, that he was lost, that he was doing fine. Stanley spent several months raising money and then set out with his two hundred–person entourage.

Eight months later, after getting enmeshed in a tribal war, Stanley reached Lake Tanganyika. Shortly after he had arrived at the small settlement, Stanley was approached by a man who bowed and identified himself as Dr. Livingstone's servant. Stanley followed the servant through a crowd ("a grand triumphal procession," he later wrote) until they came to an elderly man wearing a cap and a red jacket.

"Dr. Livingstone, I presume?" Stanley said.

"Yes."

Stanley's story took nine months to reach New York. Once it got there it entered American folklore. When Livingstone died a few years later, Stanley took over his work exploring Africa. He traced the route of the Congo River, mapped much of the lower continent, and established the Congo Free State.[3]

THE LIZZIE BORDEN SCOOP

In 1892, after Lizzie Borden's arrest for the murder of her parents, the *Boston Globe* purchased what promised to be a historic scoop. E. G. McHenry, a private detective, said he would provide copies of the government's affidavits in the case—affidavits that virtually proved Lizzie Borden's guilt—for a thousand dollars. Henry Trickey, a twenty-four-year-old *Globe* reporter, gave McHenry thirty dollars immediately and, a few weeks later, four hundred dollars more. Satisfied, the detective handed over the files.

The affidavits were all that McHenry had promised. Most provocatively, two witnesses said they had visited the Borden house the night before the murders and overheard Lizzie's father shout that Lizzie must "name the man who got you in trouble or take the door." "LIZZIE BORDEN'S SECRET," the *Globe* called Lizzie's trouble, devoting much of the front page and all of an inside page to the scoop. In the *Globe*'s afternoon edition that day, the headline shifted the focus from Lizzie to the newspaper: "ASTOUNDED / All New England Read the Story / Globes Were Bought by Thousands . . . / Police Think the Scoop is a Corker."

By the next morning, twenty-four hours after initial publication, the scoop had begun to crumble. Several of the witnesses didn't exist, and neither did the street addresses where they supposedly lived. Other witnesses, including a police inspector, denied making the statements attributed to them. The *Globe* reporter nervously pressed detective McHenry. The detective said he had made up names "for obvious reasons," but he insisted that everything else was accurate. The morning *Globe* identified the source and admitted some error: "Detective McHenry Talks / He furnished the Globe with the Borden Story / It has been proved wrong in some particulars." That evening the *Globe* went further in a front-page editorial, admitting that much of the "remarkably ingenious and cunningly contrived story" was false and that by publishing it the newspaper had "innocently added to the terrible burdens on Miss Lizzie Borden. . . . We hereby tender our heartfelt apology for the inhuman reflection on her honor as a woman. . . ." *Globe* editors expected a libel suit, but none came. Eight months later Lizzie Borden was acquitted of all charges.[4]

ASKING FOR ASSASSINATION

On several occasions William Randolph Hearst's *New York Journal* suggested that President McKinley should be killed. One editorial, for instance, declared that "if bad institutions and bad men can be got rid of only by killing, then the killing must be done."

For such remarks the *Journal* was vilified when the President was assassinated in 1901. "The journalism of anarchy," the *Brooklyn Eagle* editorialized, "shares responsibility for the attack on President McKinley." Hearst's enemies spread the false story that McKinley's assassin had been arrested with a copy of the *Journal* in his pocket.

Stung by the criticism, the *Journal* changed the name of its morning edition to the *American.* Bad feelings remained, though, and five years later the McKinley issue helped defeat Hearst in his campaign for governor of New York.[5]

KNOWLEDGEABLE SOURCE

Assigned to investigate the murder of fourteen-year-old Bobby Franks in 1924, *Chicago Daily News* reporters got one of Franks's classmates to steer them to the right sources. Richard Loeb said he had known Franks well. When the reporters asked what Franks had been like, Loeb replied, "Well, if you were going to pick out some kid to kidnap, Bobby was just about the cocky sort of a little chap you'd pick out." A few days later, to the reporters' astonishment, Loeb and his friend Nathan Leopold were arrested for the crime.[6]

GBS VS. AP

The 1925 Nobel Prize for literature produced an uproar when George Bernard Shaw accepted the prize but refused the prize money. James P. Howe, an Associated Press reporter in London, reached Shaw by telephone for an interview. Shaw said he hoped the controversy would prompt a discussion about "the question of giving prizes to writers." When Howe asked if he agreed with Sinclair Lewis that prizes harmed literature, Shaw snapped, "I don't agree with anything!"

The interview, with those and other Shaw observations, was widely published in the United States, and an AP staff member compiled a bulky scrapbook of the clippings. Howe phoned Shaw again and asked the playwright if he would like to look through the scrapbook. Absolutely not, Shaw said. "If I should see that scrapbook, I'd drop dead." Undeterred, Howe said he would leave the book at Shaw's residence. "If you dare do that," Shaw said, "I'll shoot you!"

Howe dropped off the scrapbook anyway. A few days later he got a call from Shaw's secretary asking him to come pick it up. Inside the scrapbook Shaw had written: "The contents of this scrapbook form a masterpiece of modern journalism. This testimonial is to be interpreted in the most unfavorable sense. G. Bernard Shaw."[7]

WHAT IF: THE FIRST CHRISTMAS

In the *New Republic,* Henry Fairlie and Timothy Dickinson suggested how some modern-day journalists might have covered the birth of Jesus:

- Columnist Walter Lippmann: "Even if the method of [God's] intervention had been conventional, it is hard to see how it could have contributed to a peaceful settlement in the Middle East. But to choose a woman and a child as his instruments must seem in the present condition to be the height of imprudence."
- UPI: "Mrs. Jacqueline Kennedy Onassis, accompanied by pianist Peter Duchin, visited the Bethlehem Stable this morning at 10:35, and stayed for 20 minutes. When she left, Mrs. Onassis, who was wearing a chlamys and blue jeans, said: 'I thought the child looked divine.' "
- Columnist Joseph Kraft: "PAPEETE, SAMOA: In the opinion of most of those who are attending the crucial meetings of the Trilateral Commission here, too much attention is being given to the marginal aspects of the new developments in the Middle East.... The rumors that the child king will choose, among his 12 top appointments, a local tax collector, two fishermen and perhaps more, a publican and even a sinner, are not regarded as encouraging here. Of all the new names that have so far been scouted, only one inspires any confidence: that of the financially experienced Judas Iscariot."
- *Washington Post* feature writer Sally Quinn: "Joseph had asked me to meet him at the Stable in the middle of the morning. . . . I looked into his deep blue eyes, the eyes of

a carpenter, and put the question he knew I had come to ask: 'And the child?' 'Don't ask me,' he answered as he gazed into the well by which we were sitting. 'They say that it came from God.' He looked up at me, his eyes now as piercing as the gimlets that are the tools of his trade, and said as he searched my face: 'Perhaps at least you will understand.' I answered that I understood that such things happened in even the best-regulated marriages . . . and he sighed: 'But not like this, Sally, not like this.' He was still clinging to his dreams."

- *Washington Post* investigative reporters: "Joseph Under Investigation for Tax Fraud / 'Wise Men' on Junket With Wives, Secretaries."[8]

INTERVIEWING HITLER

In 1932 radio commentator H. V. Kaltenborn and AP writer Louis P. Lochner were granted a thirty-minute interview with Adolf Hitler, Germany's self-styled Führer (who five months later would be appointed chancellor). Because Hitler often rambled at length, Lochner suggested a plan: They would agree on six questions in advance. Kaltenborn would ask the first one and take notes while Lochner kept track of the time. After five minutes Lochner would interrupt forcefully with the next question. He would then take notes while Kaltenborn watched the time. They would take turns interrupting until the half hour was up. "Our victim may not like this," Lochner said, "but as he probably craves publicity, he won't object." Kaltenborn agreed to give it a try.

Lochner and Kaltenborn arrived at Hitler's Berchtesgaden home just as another reporter was leaving. The other reporter sadly told them his first question had set Hitler off on a monologue and the half hour had ended before the reporter could ask a second question.

Lochner and Kaltenborn sat down with Hitler, and Kaltenborn asked his question. As planned, Lochner interrupted after five minutes. Hitler glowered but listened. The scheme worked: Hitler answered all six questions.[9]

GAUGING HITLER

The influential columnist Dorothy Thompson also visited Hitler in 1932. "When I finally walked into Hitler's salon . . ." she reported, "I was convinced that I was meeting the future dictator of Germany. In something less than fifty seconds I was quite sure I was not. It took me just about that time to measure the startling insignificance of this man who has set the world agog." Hitler was, she found, "the very prototype of the Little Man." A few years later, after Hitler's rise to power, Thompson would grow furious whenever anyone mentioned the article.[10]

THE A-BOMB STORY

In 1940 a *New York Times* reporter, William L. Laurence, wrote a long *Saturday Evening Post* article about an "atomic bomb." Such a bomb was feasible, he reported, and surely the Nazis were working to develop one; why wasn't the United States? The article was published and, to Laurence's disappointment, it seemed to have no impact. Later he learned part of the reason why: The FBI had asked the *Post* to refuse any requests for copies of the issue and to report the names of requesters to the government. Even if few other people saw the article, Manhattan Project officials remembered it, and in 1945 they made Laurence the project's official reporter.[11]

IMPOSSIBILITY

In October 1941 a *Chicago Tribune* editorial reassured readers that Japan "cannot attack us. That is a military impossibility. Even our base at Hawaii is beyond the effective striking power of her fleet."[12]

SPREADING THE NEWS OF WAR

On Sunday afternoon, December 7, 1941, staffers at *Time* in New York sailed paper airplanes from their office windows onto the crowd of passersby below. When unfolded, the papers told that the Japanese had bombed Pearl Harbor.[13]

VISUALS

The infant CBS television network carried President Roosevelt's speech declaring war on Japan. For visuals, the crew placed an American flag in front of the camera, with a fan off-camera to create a breeze.[14]

IWO JIMA

When *Life* received Joe Rosenthal's photo showing troops raising the American flag on Iwo Jima, the photo editor, Daniel Longwell, thought it looked contrived. He asked a *Life* correspondent on Iwo Jima to investigate. The correspondent reported that, as Longwell suspected, the photo had been staged. The marines had raised a small flag for a photographer from *Leatherneck,* the corps magazine. Rosenthal, an AP photographer, had arrived four hours later. At his request the marines had reenacted the event with a larger flag. A staged photo, Longwell concluded, didn't belong in *Life. Time* and other publications used the photo, though, and the public quickly embraced it. "[T]he country believed in that picture," Longwell later said, "and I just had to pipe down." The photo won a Pulitzer Prize, got reproduced on a postage stamp, and became the model for a memorial in Washington.[15]

FIRST IN NAGASAKI

After the United States dropped its atomic bombs and Japan surrendered, General Douglas MacArthur declared one of the A-bombed cities, Nagasaki, off limits to the press. George Weller of the *Chicago Daily News* decided to circumvent MacArthur's order. He hid the "war correspondent" tabs on his uniform and pretended to be a colonel on a secret mission.

In Nagasaki, Weller intimidated the Japanese commander into cooperating. Weller said his mission was to gather facts about Nagasaki (he didn't say for whom). When the commander's translator asked to see his orders, Weller haughtily replied: "If the general doubts our authority, I suggest that he telephone directly to General MacArthur for confirmation. But in making such a call, the general should consider his position." The Japanese general backed down. Weller commandeered two of the general's three cars and set himself up in a villa where, he later wrote, he "lived on lobster, rice and sweet little slices of canned tangerine." Though he was the first reporter in, Weller didn't manage to get the first story out. His dispatches bogged down with censors in Tokyo. After a few days other correspondents arrived in Nagasaki and scooped him.[16]

PHOTOGRAPHER'S ASSIGNMENT

When he learned that crucial work on the atom bomb had taken place nearby, the city editor of the *Nashville Tennessean* told a photographer to go out to the research facility and get two pictures—one of a whole atom, and one after it was split.[17]

WHAT IF: THE EMANCIPATION PROCLAMATION

William Safire of *The New York Times* imagined how twentieth-century columnists might have construed Lincoln's Emancipation Proclamation:

- Rowland Evans and Robert Novak: "At a stormy, secret Cabinet meeting two months before the Emancipation Proclamation, Postmaster General Montgomery Blair—the only man with political savvy still close to the increasingly isolated and morose President—warned Lincoln that the move could spell disaster for candidates in the midterm elections."
- William F. Buckley, Jr.: "The rodomontade accompanying the White House statement—'Emancipation Proclamation' has a mouth-filling quality—obscures one of the recherché ironies of this Administration. Here is a President freeing slaves (on paper, at least) and at the same time imprisoning thousands of his countrymen unlawfully, denying them the basic Anglo-Saxon right to *habeas corpus*.

Can we expect to hear a mighty roar from liberal abolitionists on that issue, sensitive as they are to the cause of human freedom?"

- C. L. Sulzberger: "[T]he emancipation is seen by observers here in Ulan Bator, strategic nerve center of Outer Mongolia, as a diplomatic-military masterstroke."
- Art Buchwald: "Now that emancipation is here, everybody wants to be a slave. My friend, Simon J. Legree, who has just become a management consultant to Little Eva Industries, thinks now that slavery is on the way out, nostalgia for it will grow. 'Chains and flogging turned a lot of people off for awhile,' says Simon. 'But now they're coming to see the advantages: no taxes, no responsibilities, no jury duty.' "[18]

UNIFORMS

In the South, reporters covering the civil rights movement often wore what FBI agents wore: short-sleeved shirts and wash-and-wear pants. Some also stuffed notebooks inside their shirt or jacket pockets to make a gunlike bulge. Rioting mobs sometimes attacked reporters, but they never bothered FBI men.[19]

PACK JOURNALISM

When Tom Pettit of NBC was reporting from Alabama in 1963, he talked by phone with a producer in New York.

"There's a good story in the *New York Times* this morning," the producer said.

"We don't get the *New York Times* down here," Pettit interrupted.

"Well, the night lead of the AP says—"

"We don't have the AP."

"Never mind. The UP's got a pretty good angle on it—"

"We don't have the UP either."

"You don't have the UP?"

"No."

"You don't have the AP?"

"No."

"You don't have the *New York Times?*"

"No."

"Then how do you guys know what's going on down there?"[20]

WHAT IF: MCGOVERN VICTORY

At a party before the 1972 election, three reporters—James Naughton of *The New York Times,* Adam Clymer of the *Baltimore Sun,* and David Murray of the *Chicago Sun-Times*—predicted how several journalists would analyze the election of George McGovern:

- Joseph Alsop, columnist: "The end of Western civilization, as we know it. . . . Now only Nguyen Van Thieu stands as the representative of the Free World."
- Tom Wicker, *New York Times* columnist: "There is gray in Ted Kennedy's hair now, and the sap is freezing in the maples around Hyannis. . . ."
- R. W. Apple, Jr., *New York Times* reporter: "As I predicted two years and three months ago . . ."
- David Broder, *Washington Post* columnist: "The clue of the McGovern victory lies in conversations one housewife had in O'Leary, Ohio . . ."
- Rowland Evans and Robert Novak, columnists: "Despite the revelations of Thomas Eagleton, the American people decided in a secret meeting on Tuesday . . ."[21]

MISSED OPPORTUNITY

During a meeting of Watergate reporters at *The New York Times*' Washington bureau, a photographer named Mike Lien walked in and said he had heard something interesting: A friend in the Secret Service had told him that President Nixon had a taping system that recorded everything in the Oval Office. "Thanks a lot," one of the reporters said. Lien left and the discussion resumed. None of them thought Lien's absurd story could be true. Eight months later White House aide Alexander Butterfield told the Senate Watergate Committee that just such a system existed.[22]

DEEP THROAT

In reporting on Watergate for the *Washington Post,* Bob Woodward relied on a source he called "Deep Throat." Deep Throat was obsessed with secrecy. At first he refused to be quoted; he cooperated on so-called deep background, hence the nickname. According to Woodward and Carl Bernstein's book *All the President's Men,* Deep Throat would meet Woodward late at night in a parking garage. If Woodward wanted a meeting, he would move a planter on his apartment balcony. If Deep Throat wanted a meeting, he would somehow circle a page number in the copy of *The New York Times* delivered to Woodward's apartment.

All the President's Men suggests that Woodward kept the secret of Deep Throat's identity to himself, but Bernstein and *Post* executive editor Ben Bradlee later said they also know. (Bernstein noted in 1986 that he had not shared the secret with his ex-wife, Nora Ephron: "She used to ask me a lot, and I had the good sense not to tell her.") The book describes Deep Throat as holding an "extremely sensitive" executive branch position, and calls him "an incurable gossip" who "could be rowdy, drink too much, overreach." It may be, however, that the hints cannot be relied on. The writer Jim Hougan found that the book's descriptions of the Woodward–Deep Throat signals seem implausible—the flowerpot on Woodward's balcony couldn't have been seen from the street, and unless Deep Throat was a tenant in the same apartment building, he could not have gotten to Woodward's *Times.*

Despite the dubious validity of the available evidence, people have advanced a number of theories about Deep Throat's identity. Candidates from the White House include Kissinger aide Alexander Haig, presidential assistant Fred Fielding, speechwriters Raymond Price and David Gergen, counsel J. Fred Buzhardt, and "Plumber" G. Gordon Liddy. Elsewhere in the executive branch, possibilities include Mark W. Felt, Jr., the deputy associate director of the FBI, and Richard Ober, a CIA official who worked with the White House (though Ben Bradlee has stated that Ober was not Deep Throat).

A favorite candidate outside the government is Bob Bennett, the president of a public relations firm that was a CIA front. A CIA memo that came to light during the Senate Watergate hearings said: "[Bennett] has been feeding stories to Bob Woodward . . . with the understanding there would be no attribution to . . . Bennett. Woodward is suitably grateful for the fine stories and by-lines which he gets and protects Bennett. . . ." Woodward has emphatically denied that Bennett was Deep Throat, and has said that the source was not in the "intelligence community" at all.

A popular theory holds that Deep Throat is not an individual, but a composite. Nixon and many of his former aides endorse that theory, mainly because they believe that no individual could have provided all the information that Woodward and Bernstein attribute to Deep Throat. In addition, as columnist Richard Reeves suggested, Deep Throat's story is worth millions of dollars in book and movie deals; if he exists, why hasn't he cashed in? "He has a career in government," Woodward responded to that line of argument. "He thinks that while he might be a hero to some, he would be a rat or a snitcher in some eyes." Woodward, Bernstein, and Bradlee have all said the composite theory is wrong.

The Deep Throat secret will come out, according to Woodward, if Deep Throat dies or if he releases Woodward from his pledge of secrecy. The latter, Woodward said, might occur. "Some day he'll write a really fascinating book. Carl and I would like to work on it with him."[23]

REMARKS

"Histories are a kind of distilled newspapers."

—Thomas Carlyle[24]

"There is a chilling suspicion that while The Washington Post *as presently constituted would have reported what*

Russell and Palmerston said and did in 1848 and 1859 in Commons, it might not have noted a publication by Marx and a book by Darwin in those years."

—Alfred Friendly, *Washington Post* managing editor, 1964[25]

"So let us drudge on about our inescapably impossible task of providing every week a first rough draft of a history that will never be completed about a world we can never understand."

—Philip L. Graham,
Washington Post publisher[26]

16

THE MEDIA MYSTIQUE

ASSESSING THE PRESS

"The gallery in which the reporters sit has become a fourth estate of the realm."

—Thomas Babington Macaulay[1]

"Whoever can speak, speaking now to the whole nation, becomes a power, a branch of government, with inalienable weight in law-making, in all acts of authority."

—Thomas Carlyle[2]

"If newspapers are useful in overthrowing tyrants, it is only to establish a tyranny of their own."

—James Fenimore Cooper[3]

"We have the newspaper, which does its best to make every square acre of land and sea give an account of itself at your breakfast-table."

—Ralph Waldo Emerson[4]

"Read not the Times. Read the Eternities."

—Henry David Thoreau[5]

"A news-writer is a man without virtue, who writes lies at home for his own profit. To these compositions is required neither genius nor knowledge, neither industry nor sprightliness; but contempt of shame and indifference to truth are absolutely necessary."

—Samuel Johnson[6]

"If I were a father and had a daughter who was seduced, I would not despair over her. But if I had a son who became a journalist and continued to remain one for five years, I would give him up."

—Søren Kierkegaard[7]

"[T]he journalist belongs to a sort of pariah caste."

—Max Weber[8]

"It is permitted to everyone to say what he pleases, but the Press is free to take notice of what he says or not. It can condemn 'truth' to death simply by not undertaking its communication to the world—a terrible censorship of silence, which is all the more potent in that masses of newspaper readers are absolutely unaware that it exists."

—Oswald Spengler[9]

"The press has become the greatest power within Western countries, more powerful than the legislature, the executive, and the judiciary. One would then like to ask: By what law has it been elected and to whom is it responsible?"

—Aleksandr Solzhenitsyn[10]

"In America the President reigns for four years, but Journalism governs for ever and ever."

—Oscar Wilde[11]

THE PRESS AND THE PUBLIC

....

COURTING GIFT

In the early 1700s the price of a newspaper, twopence a copy, was steep. As later gentleman callers would bring flowers or candy, a man of the era would sometimes bring a newspaper as a gift when calling on a woman, so that she could read of the latest Indian raids, escaped slaves, and pirate attacks.[12]

LONELY HEARTS RACKETS

In the 1920s the *New York Graphic* started a "Lonely Hearts" column. The newspaper published letters from people searching for romance and then forwarded replies to the letter-writers. Though the column ultimately became an enormous success, it got off to a rocky start because of two confidence games it helped perpetrate.

In the first scam, a male victim would write to a woman whose letter had been published in the *Graphic.* The woman would reply with an invitation to come to her apartment. There she would challenge him to demonstrate just what kind of lover he was. Moments later the woman's husband would burst in, tear the couple apart, and hurl the man out of the apartment. A few days later the husband's lawyer would notify the visitor that, if he wanted to avoid further problems, he should remit three thousand dollars immediately. The racket netted a small fortune before the police intervened.

Then the *Graphic* published a letter from a young woman who described herself as severely deformed and desperately lonely. She begged men and women to send her letters filled with passion. The plea produced a huge response. A short time later the girl wrote again. The flood of letters, she said, had given her reason to live, but she needed more. In fact, if she didn't receive passionate mail, she would commit suicide. The column editor, Bennie Caroline Hall, decided to try to help the woman. She went to the address given on the letter. There she discovered an undeformed, middle-aged woman, who was plotting to sell the torrid letters back to the writers under threat of blackmail.[13]

DEADLINE

In 1936 the royal physician, acting at the behest of King George's wife and son, injected the king with morphine and cocaine to hasten his death. The purpose, the doctor wrote in his notes, was to get the first news of the king's death into the responsible morning *Times* "rather than the less appropriate evening journals." It worked: The *Times* headline the next morning was "A PEACEFUL ENDING AT MIDNIGHT."[14]

SECRET MESSAGES?

Biographer Kitty Kelley has suggested that Jacqueline Bouvier used a newspaper to send hints to the man she was dating, Senator John F. Kennedy. Bouvier wrote "Inquiring Camera Girl," a person-on-the-street column in the *Washington Times-Herald.* After she started going out with Kennedy, "Camera Girl" inquiries included: "Should a husband wear a wedding ring?" "Should girls live with their families until they get married or see what it's like to live alone?" "What do you think of marriage?"[15]

NEWSCASTERS' PHRASES

Some phrases from television news entered the popular culture of the times:

"Now let's go hopscotching the world for headlines." —John Cameron Swayze's introduction to a series of one-sentence stories on the *Camel News Caravan,* NBC's first television newscast. (Swayze's equally breezy close: "That's the story, folks. Glad we could get together.")

"Good night, Chet." "Good night, David." —David Brinkley's and Chet Huntley's closing lines on NBC's *Huntley-Brinkley Report.* Reuven Frank, who initially produced the program, wrote that exchange in the first night's script. Brinkley didn't like it. Frank said the program had to end with some kind of farewell. "Not this way," said Brinkley, "it makes us sound like fags." Frank told him to come up with something better, but Brinkley never did.

"That's the way it is." —Walter Cronkite's close on the *CBS Evening News.* Many journalists considered the line unwise, on the theory that no newscast could be comprehensive enough to live up to it. "[I]f I were a tyrannical boss," CBS News president Richard Salant once said, "I would forbid Walter to end the *Evening News* that way."[16]

AGNEW AND THE NETWORKS

On November 13, 1969, Vice President Spiro Agnew launched the first of his attacks on the press. Speaking in Des Moines, Iowa, Agnew charged that television news was controlled by "a tiny, enclosed fraternity of privileged men elected by no one." Executives at the three commercial networks subsequently received more than 150,000 telegrams, letters, and phone calls, of which more than two-thirds were pro-Agnew. While the executives fretted about the public hostility, someone at NBC put the matter in perspective: All the negative letters, calls, and telegrams amounted to less than one-fourth of the outraged public response to the network's cancellation of *Star Trek.*[17]

CREDIBILITY CHASM

After Bill Moyers, the television commentator and former White House press secretary, had delivered a college commencement address, a student approached him. "Mr. Moyers," she said, "you've been in both journalism and government. That makes everything you say doubly hard to believe."[18]

WATERGATE: THE MOVIE

The film version of Bob Woodward and Carl Bernstein's best-seller *All the President's Men* achieved notable success on its own, winning the New York Film Critics Circle Award and several Oscars. Films about investigative journalists at work, director Alan J. Pakula said, embodied the sort of "contemporary myths" that could replace Westerns. The myth did seem to strike a chord in some viewers: Applications to journalism schools rose significantly.

Some sidelights of the film's production and aftermath:

- Many *Washington Post* people hated the first draft of William Goldman's script for the film. One editor said, referring to Goldman's best-known previous work, that the draft came across as *Butch Cassidy and the Sundance Kid Bring Down the Government.* Carl Bernstein said it read like "a Henny Youngman script." Bernstein and his then-girlfriend, Nora Ephron, set to work on their own version. Robert Redford, who was helping produce the movie as well as costarring in it, found much of the Bernstein-Ephron version "sophomoric," particularly a new subplot about Bernstein's love life ("Errol Flynn is dead," Redford told Bernstein), but Redford told Goldman to read it anyway and see if anything could be used. Goldman judged that one Bernstein-Ephron scene deserved to be in the film, a moment when Bernstein tricks a secretary in order to get in to see her boss. It was, Goldman later wrote, a "nifty move," but it was also pure fiction—it had never happened. Despite the script's troubled history, Goldman won an Oscar for it.

- *Post* publisher Katharine Graham had signed contracts approving the project, but she began to worry that the movie would hurt the newspaper's image. She ordered her lawyers to try to stop the movie or at least the use of the *Post*'s name in it. The change of heart annoyed Redford. An early version of the script had referred to her as "the unsung heroine" of the story, and Patricia Neal had been considered for the role. Now Redford ordered that the Graham character be eliminated. Only one reference survived: John Mitchell tells Bernstein that, if a particular story is published, "Katie Graham's gonna get her tit caught in a big fat wringer."
- Different editors responded to film immortality in different ways. Ben Bradlee told an interviewer, "I can tell you the name of the executive editor won't be Ben Bradlee." (It was.) In contrast, when Barry Sussman learned that his character was being merged with that of another editor, he bristled: "[I]f they want to accurately represent what things were like at the *Washington Post* and leave me out at the same time, there's something wrong."
- Set designers went to considerable lengths for the sake of authenticity. They tried to duplicate the bricks in the *Post*'s lobby as well as the prints on the office walls. They brought in more than a ton of books to fill shelves. They purchased seventy-two cartons of genuine *Washington Post* trash (at a dollar a box), shipped it to California, and strewed it around newsroom desks on the set. And they purchased *Post*-like newsroom furniture, which Clay Felker subsequently bought for the offices of his magazine *New West.* For their work, the designers won an Oscar.
- In the movie Ben Bradlee (played by Jason Robards, who won the Oscar for best supporting actor) meets with a syndicate salesman who is marketing "yesterday's weather report for people who were drunk and slept all

day." Bradlee tells the salesman: "Jesus, send it out to the *San Francisco Chronicle*—they'll buy anything." *Chronicle* editors remembered the slight. The day after the Janet Cooke hoax was revealed, an editor at the *Chronicle* sent a message to Bradlee: "Congratulations on the Pulitzer. Enclosed find yesterday's weather report."

- In 1986 Carl Bernstein told an interviewer: "[I]t's gotten to the point where sometimes I can't remember what happened in real life, what happens in the book, and what happens in the movie."[19]

CRONKITE FOR PRESIDENT

In 1980 some people urged CBS anchor Walter Cronkite to run for vice president or even president. One colleague remarked: "Why in the world would Cronkite want to be President of the United States and give up all that power?"[20]

NEWS APPETITE

When surveyers asked people what they look forward to each day, "hearing what has happened in the news" ranked fourth, behind "seeing what comes in the mail" and slightly ahead of "going to bed."[21]

PRESS ON PRESS

....

"The age of trashy novels, of more trashy poems, of most trashy quarterly and weekly literature, is rapidly drawing to a close. This is the age of the Daily Press. . . ."

—James Gordon Bennett's *New York Herald,* 1835[22]

"The Nineteenth Century was the era of the novelist. The Twentieth is the era of the journalist."

—James Reston, *New York Times* columnist[23]

"Reporting is not a dignified profession for which men will invest the time and cost of an education, but an underpaid, insecure, anonymous form of drudgery, conducted on catch-as-catch-can principles."

—Walter Lippmann, columnist[24]

"[T]he fact that your voice is amplified to the degree where it reaches from one end of the country to the other does not confer upon you greater wisdom or understanding than you possessed when your voice reached only from one end of the bar to the other."

—Edward R. Murrow, CBS reporter[25]

"Suppose they are not rewarded with much money, or dignity or fame; suppose they are debarred from living the life of a normal man; suppose they wield no power while they last, and cannot last long? What of it? They each yell more, sweat more, hiss more, start more tears and goose flesh in the course of their lives than a dozen normal and ordinary men. They have a helluva good time."

—Gerald W. Johnson, *Baltimore Sun* reporter[26]

"Journalism is the only profession in which you can stay an adolescent all your life."

—Stanley Karnow, columnist[27]

"As I look back over a misspent life, I find myself more and more convinced that I had more fun doing news reporting than in any other enterprise. It really is the life of kings."

—H. L. Mencken[28]

NOTES

INTRODUCTION

1. Willard Grosvenor Bleyer, *Main Currents in the History of American Journalism* (Boston: Houghton Mifflin, 1927), pp. 44–47; Edwin Emery, *The Press and America,* 3d ed. (Englewood Cliffs, NJ: Prentice-Hall, 1972), pp. 26–29; Frank Luther Mott, *American Journalism,* 3d ed. (New York: Macmillan, 1962), pp. 9–11; George Henry Payne, *History of Journalism in the United States* (New York: D. Appleton & Co., 1920), pp. 12–22; Lyman Horace Weeks and Edwin M. Bacon, *An Historical Digest of the Provincial Press,* Massachusetts series, vol. 1 (Boston: Society for Americana, 1911), pp. 24–33. In the quotations, spelling has been modernized and italics have been omitted.

CHAPTER 1: REPORTERS AT WORK

1. "Bennett Covers a Crime of Passion," in Calder M. Pickett, ed., *Voices of the Past* (Columbus, OH: Grid, 1977), pp. 93–94; Thomas C. Leonard, *The Power of the Press* (New York: Oxford, 1986), pp. 146–148; Ishbel Ross, *Ladies of the Press* (New York: Harper & Bros., 1936), p. 15;

Simon Michael Bessie, *Jazz Journalism* (New York: Dutton, 1938), p. 49. Emphasis omitted from one quotation.

2. W. A. Swanberg, *Pulitzer* (New York: Scribner's, 1967), pp. 13–17, 20; David Davidson, "What Made the 'World' Great?" *American Heritage* (October–November 1982): 64.

3. Mignon Rittenhouse, *The Amazing Nellie Bly* (New York: Dutton, 1936), pp. 141–215; Swanberg, *Pulitzer,* pp. 157–158; Kay Mills, *A Place in the News* (New York: Dodd, Mead, 1988), pp. 24–25; "Nellie Bly Goes Around the World," in Pickett, ed., *Voices of the Past,* p. 181.

4. Oliver Pilat, *Pegler* (Boston: Beacon, 1963), p. 46.

5. Gary Cummings, "The Last 'Front Page,'" *Columbia Journalism Review* (November–December 1974): 47; Doug Fetherling, *The Five Lives of Ben Hecht* (Toronto: Lester & Orpen, 1977), pp. 69–79; Donald Paneth, *The Encyclopedia of American Journalism* (New York: Facts on File, 1983), pp. 220–221.

6. John Hohenberg, ed., *The Pulitzer Prize Story* (New York: Columbia University Press, 1959), pp. 264–268; Pickett, ed., *Voices of the Past,* pp. 268–269.

7. Jimmy Jemail, "Jemail Inquires of Jemail, Gets Human Interest as Usual," in George Britt, ed., *Shoeleather and Printers' Ink* (New York: Times Books, 1974), p. 297.

8. Edwin Emery, *The Press and America,* 3d ed. (Englewood Cliffs, NJ: Prentice-Hall, 1972), pp. 552, 559–560; Bessie, *Jazz Journalism,* pp. 116–117.

9. Charles Fisher, *The Columnists* (New York: Howell, Soskin, 1944), p. 131.

10. John Tebbel and Sarah Miles Watts, *The Press and the Presidency* (New York: Oxford, 1985), p. 462.

11. James W. Carey, "The Dark Continent of American Journalism," in Robert Karl Manoff and Michael Schudson, eds., *Reading the News* (New York: Pantheon, 1986), p. 147.

12. Elie Abel, *Leaking* (New York: Priority Press, 1987), p. 29.

13. John Chancellor and Walter R. Mears, *The News Business* (New York: Mentor, 1984), p. 222.

14. James Deakin, *Straight Stuff* (New York: Morrow, 1984), p. 26 (White House doctor); Robert Pierpoint, *At the White House* (New York: Putnam's, 1981), p. 31 (same); Cliff Jahr, "Dan Rather: Soft Side of a Tough Anchorman," *Ladies Home Journal* (July 1980): 138 (Rather); "Playboy Interview: Dan Rather," *Playboy* (January 1984): 270 (same); Dr. Hunter S. Thompson, *Fear and Loathing on the Campaign Trail '72* (New York: Popular Library, 1973), p. 425 (McGovern plane); Timothy

Crouse, *The Boys on the Bus* (New York: Ballantine, 1974), p. 372 (same); Michael A. Ledeen, "Scoop and Dagger," *Harper's* (January 1979): 94 (Oster); Pierpoint, *At the White House,* p. 31 (network); Diana McLellan, *Ear on Washington* (New York: Arbor House, 1982), p. 237 (*Times* draft); Jody Powell, *The Other Side of the Story* (New York: Quill, 1984), pp. 147–148 (*Times* staff); Eleanor Randolph, "Post's Woodward Cites Rumors of Drug Use at Paper," *Washington Post,* 8 June 1984, p. B2 (*Post* staff); David Hill, "Totenberg Nails Judge," *Washington Journalism Review* (January–February 1988): 9 (Totenberg); "People Watch," *USA Today,* 17 November 1987, p. 4A (informal survey); Nick Ravo, "Rolling Stone Turns a Prosperous 20," *New York Times,* 23 August 1987 *(Rolling Stone);* Michael Hoyt and Mary Ellen Schoonmaker, "Cracking Down on Drugs," *Columbia Journalism Review* (May–June 1986): 37 *(Journal, Herald).*

15. "A Concise Bartlett's for Journalists," *Columbia Journalism Review* (Winter 1966): 66.

16. James M. Langley, "Editor Composed Own Death Notice," *Concord Daily Monitor,* 24 June 1968, p. 1.

17. "Playboy Interview: Carl Bernstein," *Playboy* (September 1986): 50.

18. William L. Rivers, *The Other Government* (New York: Universe, 1982), pp. 214–215.

19. Ralph Renick, "The Cumulative Impact of News Consultants After Ten Years in the Field," in Marvin Barrett, ed., *Broadcast Journalism* (New York: Everest House, 1982), pp. 198–199.

20. Nicholas Tomalin, "Stop the Press, I Want to Get On," in *Nicholas Tomalin Reporting* (London: André Deutsch Ltd., 1975), pp. 77–78.

21. Quoted in Jerry Shriver, "Thompson, the Terror of Power Town," *USA Today,* 19 July 1988, p. 2D.

CHAPTER 2: TELEVISION NEWS

1. Harry F. Waters, "TV of Tomorrow," *Newsweek,* 3 July 1978, p. 73.

2. Mike Wallace and Gary Paul Gates, *Close Encounters* (New York: Berkley, 1985), p. 91.

3. Brian Donlon, "The Star Journalists," *USA Today,* 9 May 1988, p. 3D (Hartman, Hartley); Peter McCabe, *Bad News at Black Rock* (New York: Arbor House, 1987), p. 31 (Van Dyke); Barbara Matusow, *The Evening Stars* (Boston: Houghton Mifflin, 1983), p. 69 (Stewart); Robert Metz, *The Today Show* (Chicago: Playboy Press, 1977), p. 91 (Henderson, Palmer); ibid., pp. 176–180 (O'Sullivan); Candice Bergen, interview on *Late Night*

With David Letterman, NBC, 23 November 1988 (Bergen); Matusow, *Evening Stars,* p. 216 (Alda); ibid., pp. 50–51 (Edwards); Wallace and Gates, *Close Encounters,* pp. 8–10 (Wallace).

4. Metz, *Today Show,* p. 49.

5. Ibid., p. 69.

6. William Rivers, *The Adversaries* (Boston: Beacon, 1970), p. 258.

7. Bruce McCabe, "A Hollywood Version of TV News and the Industry's Reaction to It," *Boston Globe,* 3 January 1988, p. B3.

8. Michael J. Arlen, *Living-Room War* (New York: Penguin, 1982; orig. publ. 1969), pp. 200–201.

9. Marvin Barrett, ed., *The Politics of Broadcasting* (New York: Crowell, 1973), p. 36 (KGO cowboys); "Darts and Laurels," *Columbia Journalism Review* (January–February 1984): 20–21 (KGO Santa Claus); Barrett, ed., *Politics of Broadcasting,* p. 36 (KRON); Edwin Diamond, *Good News, Bad News* (Cambridge: MIT Press, 1980), p. 110 (WBZ).

10. Edward W. Barrett, "Hire One, Help Two," *Columbia Journalism Review* (November–December 1973): 19.

11. Ben H. Bagdikian, "Fire, Sex, and Freaks," in Robert Atwan, Barry Orton, and William Vesterman, *American Mass Media* (New York: Random House, 1978), p. 272.

12. Barrett, ed., *Politics of Broadcasting,* p. 7; Edwin Diamond, *The Tin Kazoo* (Cambridge: MIT Press, 1975), pp. 66–67.

13. Mary Ellen Schoonmaker, "TV News and the Face-Lift Factor," *Columbia Journalism Review* (March–April 1987): 50.

14. Alan Pell Crawford, "The Fall and Rise of Nicholas von Hoffman," *City Paper,* 6 May 1988.

15. Gary Paul Gates, *Air Time* (New York: Harper & Row, 1978), p. 127.

16. Quoted in Jessica Savitch, *Anchorwoman* (New York: Berkley, 1983), p. 26.

17. Quoted in Judy Woodruff with Kathleen Maxa, *"This is Judy Woodruff at the White House"* (Reading, MA: Addison-Wesley, 1982), p. 187.

18. Quoted in Christine Craft, *An Anchorwoman's Story* (Santa Barbara, CA: Capra Rhodora, 1986), p. 7.

19. Quoted in Peter Boyer, "Broadcast Blues," *Vanity Fair* (January 1988): 64 (Rather); Barbara Matusow, "The Incredible Shrinking Anchor," *Washingtonian* (June 1987): 102 (Rather salary); Donald McDonald, "The Media's Conflicts of Interest," *Center Magazine* (November–December 1976): 23 (Salant); Marvin Barrett and Zachary Sklar, *The Eye of the Storm* (New York: Lippincott & Crowell, 1980), p. 54 (Cronkite); ibid. (Seib); Matusow, *Evening Stars,* p. 176 *(Daily News);* Judith Hennessee, "The Press's Very Own Barbara Walters Show," *Columbia Journalism Review* (July–August 1976): 24 (Smith).

20. Mary Battiata, "Lesley Stahl," *Washington Journalism Review* (October 1982): 45; Savitch, *Anchorwoman,* p. 186.

21. Ron Powers, *The Newscasters* (New York: St. Martin's, 1978), pp. 35–36.

22. Karl Vick, "The Sweater Weather Girl," *Washington Journalism Review* (December 1985): 11.

23. Quoted in Monica Collins, "At the Convention, Everything But News," *USA Today,* 22 July 1988, p. 3D.

24. Bill Leonard, *In the Storm of the Eye* (New York: Putnam's, 1987), p. 225.

25. Wallace and Gates, *Close Encounters,* pp. 436–443; Nancy Skelton, "Bank Catches Interviewer Mike Wallace Off Guard," *Los Angeles Times,* 10 January 1982, pp. 1, 3, 24.

26. "Playboy Interview: Dan Rather," *Playboy* (January 1984): 274; "Rather Not," *Time,* 3 October 1983, p. 77; Tom Goldstein, *The News at Any Cost* (New York: Simon & Schuster, 1985), pp. 253–254.

27. C. Fraser Smith, "Reporting Grief," *Washington Journalism Review* (March 1984): 22.

28. Martin Schram, *The Great American Video Game* (New York: Morrow, 1987), pp. 23–26; Lesley Stahl, interviewed on "Prime-Time President," PBS, 3 October 1988.

29. Richard Zoglin, " 'I Was Trained to Ask Questions,' " *Time,* 8 February 1988, pp. 24–26; Harry F. Waters, "Dan Rather Draws a Blank," *Newsweek,* 28 September 1987, pp. 47–48; Boyer, "Broadcast Blues," p. 113; Edwin Diamond, "Rather Strange," *New York,* 28 September 1987, pp. 28, 30; Brian Donlon, "Will CBS News Explain the 6-Minute Gap?" *USA Today,* 14 September 1987, p. 1D; Brian Donlon, "The Agony and the Anchorman," *USA Today,* 15 September 1987, p. 1D; Matt Roush, "Rather Tells Critics About His 'Bad Day,' " *USA Today,* 18 January 1988, p. 3D.

30. John Horn, "Anchor Ducks Earthquake," *Washington Journalism Review* (December 1987): 10.

31. Barrett, ed., *Politics of Broadcasting,* p. 10; Michael Wheeler, *Lies, Damn Lies, and Statistics* (New York: Dell, 1977), p. 237.

32. Charles Fountain, "The Great Ratings Flap," *Columbia Journalism Review* (November–December 1987): 46–50; Bill Girdner, " 'Sweeps' Time is Hype Time for TV Stations," *Boston Globe,* 21 June 1987, p. 12; "L.A. Court Denies CapCities Injunction Against Nielsen Co.," *Variety,* 17 June 1987, pp. 65, 85.

33. Phillip Weiss and Laurence Zuckerman, "The Shadow of a Medium," *Columbia Journalism Review* (March–April 1987): 35.

34. Robert Sam Anson, "Behind the Lines in the Network News War," *Playboy* (September 1982): 170.

35. Quoted in ibid., p. 134.

36. Edward R. Murrow, "Murrow's Indictment of Broadcasting," *Columbia Journalism Review* (Summer 1965): 32.

37. Robert MacNeil, *The Right Place at the Right Time* (Boston: Little, Brown, 1982), p. 306.

38. Quoted in Stephan Lesher, *Media Unbound* (Boston: Houghton Mifflin, 1982), p. 108.

CHAPTER 3: COLUMNS, COMICS, AND REVIEWS

1. Charles Fisher, *The Columnists* (New York: Howell, Soskin, 1944), p. 21.

2. Ibid., p. 32.

3. Gay Talese, *The Kingdom and the Power* (Garden City, NY: Doubleday Anchor, 1978; orig. publ. 1969), p. 204.

4. Howard Bray, *The Pillars of the Post* (New York: Norton, 1980), p. 52.

5. Don Hewitt, *Minute by Minute . . .* (New York: Random House, 1985), p. 85.

6. Robert G. Sherrill, "Drew Pearson: An Interview," *Nation,* 7 July 1969, p. 16; Dom Bonafede, "Jack Muckraker Anderson," *Washington Journalism Review* (April 1980): 46; Milt Machlin, *The Gossip Wars* (New York: Tower, 1981), p. 228.

7. Neil A. Grauer, *Wits and Sages* (Baltimore: Johns Hopkins University Press, 1984), pp. 23–24.

8. Christopher Hitchens, "Blabscam," *Harper's* (March 1987): 76.

9. Gail Sheehy, "Is George Bush Too Nice to Be President?" *Vanity Fair* (February 1987): 119; Hugh Sidey, "Taking Confidences to the Grave," *Time,* 18 April 1988, p. 26.

10. Quoted in Grauer, *Wits and Sages,* p. 5.

11. Quoted in Henry Kissinger, *White House Years* (Boston: Little, Brown, 1979), pp. 18–19.

12. Walter Lippmann, "Sketches in the Sand," in Calder M. Pickett, ed., *Voices of the Past* (Columbus, OH: Grid, 1977), p. 259.

13. Quoted in Martin Walker, *Powers of the Press* (New York: Adama, 1983), p. 225.

14. Sidney Skolsky, *Don't Get Me Wrong—I Love Hollywood* (New York: Putnam's, 1975), pp. 41–44; Machlin, *Gossip Wars,* pp. 150–152.

15. Machlin, *Gossip Wars,* pp. 47–48; Michael David Harris, *Always on Sunday* (New York: Meredith Press, 1968), p. 47.

16. "Passing Comment," *Columbia Journalism Review* (Fall 1968): 2; "Unfinished Business," *Columbia Journalism Review* (Spring 1969): 47.

17. Quoted in Grauer, *Wits and Sages,* p. 12.

18. Richard Kluger, *The Paper* (New York: Knopf, 1986), p. 671.

19. Dennis Holder, "Joe Bob Driven Out of Dallas," *Washington Journalism Review* (June 1985): 18–19.

20. W. A. Swanberg, *Pulitzer* (New York: Scribner's, 1967), pp. 206–207; Clark Kinnaird, "Cavalcade of the Funnies," in David Manning White and Robert H. Abel, eds., *The Funnies* (New York: Macmillan, 1963), p. 91; Randall P. Harrison, *The Cartoon* (Beverly Hills, CA: Sage, 1981), pp. 86–87; Edwin Emery, *The Press and America,* 3d ed. (Englewood Cliffs, NJ: Prentice-Hall, 1972), p. 357.

21. Simon Michael Bessie, *Jazz Journalism* (New York: Dutton, 1938), p. 57; Kinnaird, "Cavalcade of the Funnies," in White and Abel, eds., *Funnies,* p. 91.

22. Harrison, *Cartoon,* p. 87; Harry Hershfield, "In Pre-Abe-Kabibble Days, Life was a Lusty Song," in George Britt, ed., *Shoeleather and Printers' Ink* (New York: Times Books, 1974), p. 255.

23. Martin Sheridan, *Comics and Their Creators* (n.p.: Hale, Cushman & Flint, 1942), p. 243; David Manning White and Robert H. Abel, "Comic Strips and American Culture," in White and Abel, eds., *Funnies,* p. 6; Kinnaird, "Cavalcade of the Funnies," in White and Abel, eds., *Funnies,* p. 93.

24. Sheridan, *Comics and Their Creators,* p. 132.

25. Robert H. Abel, "The Art of Personal Journalism," in White and Abel, eds., *Funnies,* p. 122.

26. John L. Hulteng and Roy Paul Nelson, *The Fourth Estate,* 2d ed. (New York: Harper & Row, 1983), p. 296; Art Seidenbaum, "Suddenly, Al Capp Guns for the Liberals," *West Magazine (Los Angeles Times),* 5 March 1967, pp. 20–21.

27. Curtis Prendergast with Geoffrey Colvin, *The World of Time Inc.,* vol. 3 (1960–1980) (New York: Atheneum, 1986), p. 528.

28. Alan Prendergast, "Of Penguins and Pulitzers," *Washington Journalism Review* (October 1987): 20; Neil A. Grauer, "The Great Bloom County Feud," *Columbia Journalism Review* (October 1987): 52.

29. Robert C. Maynard, "A Comic Strip Isn't a Court," in Laura Longley Babb, ed., *Of the Press, By the Press, For the Press (And Others, Too)* (Washington, DC: Washington Post Co., 1974), pp. 200–201; Hulteng and Nelson, *Fourth Estate,* p. 295; "Savage Pen," *Time,* 12 November 1984, p. 89; Jonathan Alter, "Doonesbury Contra Sinatra," *Newsweek,* 24 June 1985, p. 82; Garry Trudeau, "The 'Doonesbury' You Probably Didn't See," *Ms.* (November 1985): 101; Grauer, *Wits and Sages,* p. 88; "Paper Clips

Strip," *USA Today,* 14 December 1988, p. 2B; Lee Salem, editorial director, Universal Press Syndicate, telephone interview, 20 December 1988.

30. Abel, "Art of Personal Journalism," in White and Abel, eds., *Funnies,* pp. 114–119 ("Little Orphan Annie"); White and Abel, "Comic Strips and American Culture," in White and Abel, eds., *Funnies,* p. 30 ("Pogo"); Hulteng and Nelson, *Fourth Estate,* p. 295 ("Beetle Bailey"); Harrison, *Cartoon,* p. 42 (same); Charles Stein, "Beetle, Unbowed," *Columbia Journalism Review* (July–August 1982): 16 (same); Mike Booth, " 'Beetle' Gets Bounced," *Washington Journalism Review* (September 1984): 11–12 (same); "Breathedless," *Boston Globe,* 7 November 1987, p. 2 ("Bloom County"); Joan Vennochi, " 'Bloom County' Brouhaha," *Boston Globe,* 30 December 1988, p. 37 (same); Matt Roush, "Aaach! 'Cathy' Stirs Up a Controversy," *USA Today,* 11 November 1988, p. 3D ("Cathy"); "Darts and Laurels: Campaign '88," *Columbia Journalism Review* (January–February 1989): 21 (same); Salem, telephone interview (same); ibid. ("Calvin and Hobbes"); Alfred Appel, Jr., introduction to Vladimir Nabokov, *The Annotated Lolita* (New York: McGraw-Hill, 1970), p. xxv ("Dick Tracy"); Sheridan, *Comics and Their Creators,* p. 20 *(Deseret News);* "The Lower Case," *Columbia Journalism Review* (September–October 1975): 73 ("Steve Canyon").

31. Syd Hoff, *Editorial and Political Cartooning* (New York: Stravon, 1976), pp. 75–78; Meyer Berger, *The Story of The New York Times, 1851–1951* (New York: Simon & Schuster, 1951), p. 52.

32. David Davidson, "What Made the 'World' Great?" *American Heritage* (October–November 1982): 70; Swanberg, *Pulitzer,* p. 132.

33. Jerry Adler, "The Finer Art of Politics," *Newsweek,* 13 October 1980, p. 78; Lee Judge and Richard Samuel West, "Why Political Cartoonists Sell Out," *Washington Monthly* (September 1988): 41.

34. Johanna Glover, "How's That Again, Yuri?" *Columbia Journalism Review* (September–October 1983): 9; David Shaw, *Press Watch* (New York: Macmillan, 1984), p. 252.

35. "Information Please," *Washingtonian* (November 1985): 29.

36. Quoted in Adler, "Finer Art of Politics," p. 74.

37. Quoted in Hoff, *Editorial and Political Cartooning,* p. 15.

38. L. U. Reavis, *A Representative Life of Horace Greeley* (New York: G. W. Carleton & Co., 1872), pp. 529–537; Ishbel Ross, *Ladies of the Press* (New York: Harper & Bros., 1936), pp. 400–403; Kay Mills, *A Place in the News* (New York: Dodd, Mead, 1988), pp. 21–23.

39. Melvin M. Belli with Robert Blair Kaiser, *My Life on Trial* (New York: Morrow, 1976), p. 296 n.

40. Tom Goldstein, *The News at Any Cost* (New York: Simon & Schuster, 1985), pp. 139–140; Shaw, *Press Watch,* pp. 148–149; Norman

E. Isaacs, *Untended Gates* (New York: Columbia University Press, 1986), p. 33.

41. Harris, *Always on Sunday,* p. 48.

42. Jerry Stagg, *The Brothers Shubert* (New York: Random House, 1968), pp. 115–116.

43. Ibid., pp. 115, 137–139; Berger, *Story of The New York Times,* pp. 215–216; Machlin, *Gossip Wars,* pp. 22–23, 110.

44. Felix Kessler, "Clive Barnes: Man on the Aisle," in A. Kent MacDougall, ed., *The Press* (Princeton, NJ: Dow, Jones, 1972), p. 99.

45. "Bad Review for a Critic," *New York Times,* 18 August 1987, p. 34; Michele Bennett, "Drivel and Drool," *Spy* (November 1987): 79.

46. Shaw, *Press Watch,* p. 264.

47. "Darts and Laurels," *Columbia Journalism Review* (July–August 1988): 18.

48. Alan Richman, "Gastronomic Grudge Match," *People,* 7 December 1987, p. 68.

49. Quoted in Arthur Herzog, *The B.S. Factor* (New York: Penguin, 1974), p. 70.

50. Quoted in Michele Halberstadt, "Redford: A Conversation," *Premiere* (March 1988): 41.

51. Quoted in John Simon, "Bringing Up Mother," *New York,* 30 May 1988, p. 88.

52. Ibid.

CHAPTER 4: THE NEWS PACKAGE

1. Quoted in Donald Paneth, *The Encyclopedia of American Journalism* (New York: Facts on File, 1983), p. 513 (Bogart); Martin Mayer, *Making News* (Garden City, NY: Doubleday, 1987), p. 17 (Lippmann); Leo C. Rosten, *The Washington Correspondents* (New York: Harcourt, Brace, 1937), p. 113 (Rosten); John Chancellor and Walter R. Mears, *The News Business* (New York: Mentor, 1984), p. 36 (Johnson); Douglass Cater, "Remarks," in George F. Will, ed., *Press, Politics, and Popular Government* (Washington, DC: American Enterprise Institute, 1972), p. 33 (Cater); Edith Efron, *The News Twisters* (n.p.: Manor, 1972), p. 6 (Brinkley); Robert E. Park, "The Natural History of the Newspaper," in Everette E. Dennis, Arnold H. Ismach, and Donald M. Gillmor, *Enduring Issues in Mass Communications* (St. Paul, MN: West, 1978), p. 136 (Dana, McEwen); Evelyn Waugh, *Scoop* (Boston: Little, Brown, 1977; orig. publ. 1937), p. 91 (Corker); Hillier Krieghbaum, *Pressures on the Press* (New York: Apollo, 1973), p. 105 (Walker); Nicholas Tomalin, "Stop the Press, I Want to Get On," in *Nicholas Tomalin Reporting* (London: André

Deutsch Ltd., 1975), p. 77 (Tomalin); Mayer, *Making News,* p. 9 (Northcliffe).

2. Frank Luther Mott, *American Journalism,* 3d ed. (New York: Macmillan, 1962), p. 13.

3. Charles M. Thomas, "The Publication of Newspapers During the American Revolution," *Journalism Quarterly* 9 (1932): 362; John Hohenberg, *Free Press/Free People* (New York: Columbia University Press, 1971), pp. 58–59.

4. Louis M. Lyons, *Newspaper Story* (Cambridge: Harvard University Press, 1971), p. 251.

5. Stephen Bates, ed., *The Media and the Congress* (Columbus, OH: Publishing Horizons, 1987), p. 50.

6. Rosten, *Washington Correspondents,* pp. 79–80 (Senate reporters); Robert Cirino, *Don't Blame the People* (New York: Vintage, 1972), p. 78 (Richards radio stations); "Conflicts of Interest, Pressures Still Distort Some Papers' Coverage," *Wall Street Journal,* 25 July 1967, p. 18 *(Inquirer);* Matthew Cooper, "Hot Chain Nixes Wingo," *Washington Monthly* (September 1987): 17 (same); Edward Jay Epstein, *News from Nowhere* (New York: Vintage, 1974), p. 192 (NBC); Jonathan Alter, "When Sources Get Immunity," *Newsweek,* 19 January 1987, p. 54 (AP); Mark Hertsgaard, *On Bended Knee* (New York: Farrar Straus Giroux, 1988), pp. 314–315 (same).

7. Jill Nelson, "Integration When? A Tale of Three Cities," *Columbia Journalism Review* (January–February 1987): 42; Geoffrey Stokes, "The 'News': New York's Racist Newspaper?" *Village Voice,* 28 April 1987, p. 23.

8. Lyons, *Newspaper Story,* p. 114 *(Globe);* "Capital Comment," *Washingtonian* (November 1982): 11 *(Post);* "Darts and Laurels," *Columbia Journalism Review* (July–August 1973): 7 (*Times* and paternity suit); Norman E. Isaacs, *Untended Gates* (New York: Columbia University Press, 1986), p. 128 (*Times* and News Council); Edwin Diamond, "The *Times* of Frankel," *New York,* 10 August 1987, p. 31 (*Times* and candidates); Mayer, *Making News,* p. 223 (OSHA).

9. Maxine Cheshire with John Greenya, *Maxine Cheshire, Reporter* (Boston: Houghton Mifflin, 1978), p. 148.

10. Doris A. Graber, *Mass Media and American Politics* (Washington, DC: Congressional Quarterly Press, 1980), p. 69, table 3-3 (study); Mort Rosenblum, *Coups and Earthquakes* (New York: Harper & Row, 1979), p. 124 (Rosenblum); Stanley Walker, *City Editor* (New York: Frederick A. Stokes Co., 1934), p. 87 *(Denver Post).*

11. Peter Prichard, *The Making of McPaper* (Kansas City, MO: Andrews, McMeel & Parker, 1987), pp. 4–6.

12. Henry David Thoreau, *Walden* (New York: New American Library, 1960), p. 68.

13. Quoted in Cater, "Remarks," in Will, ed., *Press, Politics, and Popular Government,* p. 35.

14. Quoted in Krieghbaum, *Pressures on the Press,* p. 112.

15. Walter Lippmann, *Liberty and the News* (New York: Harcourt, Brace & Howe, 1920), pp. 47–48.

16. Quoted in Laurence J. Peter, *Peter's Quotations* (New York: Bantam, 1979), p. 329.

17. Elmer Davis, *History of the New York Times, 1851–1921* (New York: Greenwood, 1969; orig. publ. 1921), p. 21.

18. Delt Edwards, "How He Became a Newspaperman—Advice of Greeley, Dana, Bennett," in George Britt, ed., *Shoeleather and Printers' Ink* (New York: Times Books, 1974), p. 262.

19. Paneth, *Encyclopedia of American Journalism,* p. 364.

20. Ransdell Pierson, "Uptight on Gay News," *Columbia Journalism Review* (March–April 1982): 29.

21. H. L. Mencken, *The American Language,* 4th ed. (New York: Knopf, 1937), p. 561 (Winchell); Milt Machlin, *The Gossip Wars* (New York: Tower, 1981), pp. 64–65 (same); Michael Gross, "Inside Gossip," *New York,* 9 May 1988, p. 45 (Cassini); David Manning White and Robert H. Abel, "Comic Strips and American Culture," in David Manning White and Robert H. Abel, eds., *The Funnies* (New York: Macmillan, 1963), pp. 18–19 (comics); Clark Kinnaird, "Cavalcade of the Funnies," in White and Able, eds., *Funnies,* p. 94 (same); Mencken, *American Language,* p. 184 (same); H. L. Mencken, *The American Language,* supplement I (New York: Knopf, 1948), p. 333 (same); Simon Michael Bessie, *Jazz Journalism* (New York: Dutton, 1938), p. 151 (same); Barbara Schaaf, "Finley Peter Dunne," *Harvard Magazine* (March–April 1988): 38 (Dunne); Walker, *City Editor,* p. 292 (O'Malley); William Safire, "Coiners' Corner," *New York Times Magazine,* 17 July 1988, p. 8 (politics); William Safire, *Safire's Political Dictionary* (New York: Ballantine, 1980), pp. 127–128 (same).

22. Lloyd Wendt, *Chicago Tribune* (Chicago: Rand McNally, 1979), p. 568; "To Phyllis Who Might Spell It Phreight," in Calder M. Pickett, ed., *Voices of the Past* (Columbus, OH: Grid, 1977), pp. 362–363.

23. "All Things Considered," National Public Radio, 12 January 1988.

24. "The Lower Case," *Columbia Journalism Review* (Fall 1968): 66.

25. "Overheard," *Newsweek,* 30 June 1986, p. 13.

26. Quoted in James Aronson, *Deadline for the Media* (Indianapolis: Bobbs-Merrill, 1972), pp. 183–184.

27. A. J. Liebling, *The Press* (New York: Ballantine, 1975; orig. publ.

1961), p. 92; Daniel Schorr, *Clearing the Air* (Boston: Houghton Mifflin, 1977), p. 11; Alexander Cockburn, "How to Earn Your Trenchcoat," in Richard Pollak, ed., *Stop the Presses, I Want to Get Off!* (New York: Delta, 1976), p. 25.

28. "Bulletin from the Cliche Front," *Columbia Journalism Review* (July–August 1980): 10.

29. "Modern Journalese," *Washingtonian* (November 1985): 25.

30. Turner Catledge, *My Life and The Times* (New York: Harper & Row, 1971), p. 196; Gay Talese, *The Kingdom and the Power* (Garden City, NY: Doubleday Anchor, 1978; orig. publ. 1969), p. 272.

31. Quoted in Frank Luther Mott, *The News in America* (Cambridge: Harvard University Press, 1962), p. 162.

32. Robert MacNeil, *The Right Place at the Right Time* (Boston: Little, Brown, 1982), p. 10.

33. Quoted in James David Barber, "Characters in the Campaign: The Literary Problem," in James David Barber, ed., *Race for the Presidency* (Englewood Cliffs, NJ: Prentice-Hall paperback, 1978), p. 130.

34. Quoted in Paneth, *Encyclopedia of American Journalism,* p. 332 *(Pennsylvania Journal);* Davis, *History of the New York Times,* ill. following p. 114 *(New York Times);* W. A. Swanberg, *Citizen Hearst* (New York: Bantam, 1971; orig. publ. 1961), p. 173 *(New York Journal);* "Wall Street Lays an Egg," in Pickett, ed., *Voices of the Past,* p. 284 *(Variety);* Edwin Diamond, "Chicago Press: Rebellion and Retrenchment," *Columbia Journalism Review* (Fall 1968): 13 *(Chicago Daily News);* Martin Schram, *Running for President 1976* (New York: Stein & Day, 1977), p. 204 *(New York Daily News).*

35. "The Lower Case," *Columbia Journalism Review,* (May-June 1980): 105.

36. Quoted in Mordechai Richler, "Necklines Rise as Nazis Invade Poland," *GQ* (December 1987): 185.

37. "Spy's World of Tomorrow—Today," *Spy* (October 1987): 30 *(Post);* "3 Best Words: Win Free Sex!" *Newsweek,* 7 November 1988, p. 75 *(Star).*

38. Martin Walker, *Powers of the Press* (New York: Adama, 1983), p. 246 *(Washington Post);* John B. Donnelly, "As Bronx as Bronx Itself—As O'Flaherty as O'Flaherty," in Britt, ed., *Shoeleather and Printers' Ink,* p. 126 *(Bronx Home News);* A. Kent MacDougall, "New York Daily News," in A. Kent MacDougall, ed., *The Press* (Princeton, NJ: Dow, Jones, 1972), p. 8 *(New York Daily News);* Lyons, *Newspaper Story,* p. 334 *(Boston Globe); El Paso Times,* 9 October 1963, p. 1; "Names and Faces," *Boston Globe,* 26 February 1989, p. 81 *(Leader Herald-News Gazette); New York Post,* 15 April 1983, p. 1; Linda Ellerbee, *"And So It Goes"* (New York:

Berkley, 1987), p. 133 *(NBC Overnight);* Ron Powers, *The Newscasters* (New York: St. Martin's, 1978), p. 206 (KGO).

39. Vincent Musetto, "Tots Nix Blazing Coeds!" *People,* 1 June 1987.

40. Herman Mankiewicz and Orson Welles, screenplay to *Citizen Kane,* in *The Citizen Kane Book* (New York: Bantam, 1971), p. 163.

41. Mott, *American Journalism,* pp. 10–11; Edwin Emery, *The Press and America,* 3d ed. (Englewood Cliffs, NJ: Prentice-Hall, 1972), p. 27.

42. David Fridtjof Halaas, *Boom Town Newspapers* (Albuquerque: University of New Mexico Press, 1981), p. 7; Phillip Knightley, *The First Casualty* (New York: Harvest, 1976), p. 25.

43. John Hohenberg, *Foreign Correspondence* (New York: Columbia University Press, 1964), p. 255.

44. Davis, *History of the New York Times,* pp. 200, 211–212.

45. Quoted in Mott, *American Journalism,* p. 8 *(Present State);* Paneth, *Encyclopedia of American Journalism,* p. 114 *(New York Sun);* Wendt, *Chicago Tribune,* p. 637 *(Chicago Tribune);* Bessie, *Jazz Journalism,* p. 147 *(New York Journal);* Clifton Fadiman, ed., *American Treasury 1455–1955* (New York: Harper & Bros., 1955), p. 285 *(Christian Science Monitor);* Paneth, *Encyclopedia of American Journalism,* p. 25 *(Danbury News);* Mott, *American Journalism,* p. 569 *(Denver Post);* Edward W. Barrett, "Newspapers as Time-fillers," *Columbia Journalism Review* (Winter 1966–1967): 38 *(World Journal Tribune);* Fadiman, *American Treasury,* p. 285 *(San Francisco Chronicle);* "A Concise Bartlett's for Journalists," *Columbia Journalism Review* (Fall 1963): 42 *(Bettendorf News);* John Morton, "Quality is Job One," *Washington Journalism Review* (December 1987): 52 *(Marble Hill Era);* Tom Wicker, *On Press* (New York: Viking, 1978), p. 30 *(Jacksonville Daily News).*

46. Lyons, *Newspaper Story,* pp. 197–198.

47. Douglas Steinbauer, "Faking It With Pictures," *American Heritage* (October–November 1982): 52–57; Frank Mallen, *Sauce for the Gander* (White Plains, NY: Baldwin, 1954), p. 105; Bessie, *Jazz Journalism,* pp. 184, 196–198; Emery, *Press and America,* p. 559.

48. Barbara Matusow, *The Evening Stars* (Boston: Houghton Mifflin, 1983), p. 64.

49. Thomas Kiernan, *Citizen Murdoch* (New York: Dodd, Mead, 1986), pp. 199–200.

50. Mott, *American Journalism,* p. 232.

51. Glyndon G. Van Deusen, *Horace Greeley* (Philadelphia: University of Pennsylvania Press, 1953), pp. 21, 51; Don C. Seitz, *Horace Greeley* (Indianapolis: Bobbs-Merrill, 1926), p. 70; L. U. Reavis, *A Representative Life of Horace Greeley* (New York: G. W. Carleton & Co., 1872), p. 66; "On 'Satanic' Newspapers," in Pickett, ed., *Voices of the Past,* pp. 95–96;

Mott, *American Journalism,* pp. 270–271; Davis, *History of the New York Times,* p. 10. Capitalization and spelling in the quotations have been modernized.

52. Davis, *History of the New York Times,* p. 224.

53. Fadiman, ed., *American Treasury,* p. 281.

54. Quoted in Lee Brown, *The Reluctant Reformation* (New York: David McKay Co., 1974), pp. 104–118; Walker, *City Editor,* pp. 174, 176 (emphasis omitted).

55. Catledge, *My Life,* p. 246; A. Kent MacDougall, "Chicago Tribune," in MacDougall, ed., *Press,* p. 28.

56. Kenneth Stewart and John Tebbel, *Makers of Modern Journalism* (New York: Prentice-Hall, 1952), p. 373.

57. Talese, *Kingdom and the Power,* pp. 232–233.

58. Kiernan, *Citizen Murdoch,* pp. 224–225.

59. David Shaw, *Journalism Today* (New York: Harper & Row paperback, 1977), pp. 210–211.

60. Lee H. Smith, "Is Anything Unprintable?" *Columbia Journalism Review* (Spring 1968): 19–23 *('Tis Pity She's a Whore);* "The Lower Case," *Columbia Journalism Review,* (July-August 1975): 65 *(Happy Hooker);* "Defending Southern Womanhood," *Columbia Journalism Review* (January–February 1976): 34 *(Mandingo);* Tom Goldstein, *A Two-Faced Press?* (New York: Priority, 1986), pp. 40–41 *(Sexual Perversity in Chicago);* "Part of the Title Gets Cut," *USA Today,* 2 November 1987, p. 5D *(Sammie and Rosie Get Laid);* " 'Full Metal' Front," *Los Angeles Times,* 14 June 1987, Calendar section, p. 27 *(Full Metal Jacket).*

61. "Bowdlerizing Butz's Blunder," *Columbia Journalism Review* (November–December 1976): 9; "Blinking at Butz," *Columbia Journalism Review* (January–February 1977): 58; Priscilla S. Meyer, "Hello, Rolling Stone? What Did Butz Say?" *Wall Street Journal,* 7 October 1976; Shaw, *Journalism Today,* pp. 205, 211; Mitchell Stephens and Eliot Frankel, "All the Obscenity That's Fit to Print," *Washington Journalism Review* (April 1981): 16, 19.

62. Stephens and Frankel, "All the Obscenity That's Fit to Print," pp. 16, 19; Jack W. Germond and Jules Witcover, *Wake Us When It's Over* (New York: Macmillan, 1985), p. 523 n.

63. Quoted in Mott, *American Journalism,* p. 233.

64. Quoted in Walker, *City Editor,* p. 175.

65. Quoted in Keen Rafferty, "A Collection of Famous Quotations on Journalism," *Journalism Quarterly* 25 (December 1948): 596.

66. Quoted in Davis, *History of the New York Times,* p. 199.

67. Quoted in Prichard, *Making of McPaper,* p. 300.

CHAPTER 5: LAWMAKERS AND OFFICIALS

1. Stanley Nider Katz, introduction to James Alexander, *A Brief Narrative of the Case and Trial of John Peter Zenger* (Cambridge: Harvard University Press, 1972), p. 9.

2. Elmer Davis, *History of the New York Times, 1851–1921* (New York: Greenwood, 1969; orig. publ. 1921), pp. 86–116; Meyer Berger, *The Story of The New York Times, 1851–1951* (New York: Simon & Schuster, 1951), pp. 35–51; Thomas C. Leonard, *The Power of the Press* (New York: Oxford, 1986), pp. 116–123; Edwin Emery, *The Press and America,* 3d ed. (Englewood Cliffs, NJ: Prentice-Hall, 1972), p. 265.

3. John Wilds, *Afternoon Story* (Baton Rouge: Louisiana State University Press, 1976), p. 236.

4. Louis M. Lyons, *Newspaper Story* (Cambridge: Harvard University Press, 1971), p. 261.

5. Robert Pack, "The Press as Enemy, the Press as Friend," *Washingtonian* (March 1982): 107–108; Edwin R. Bayley, *Joe McCarthy and the Press* (Madison: University of Wisconsin Press, 1981), p. 166; Oliver Pilat, *Pegler* (Boston: Beacon, 1963), p. 239.

6. Dan Rather with Mickey Herskowitz, *The Camera Never Blinks* (New York: Ballantine, 1978), pp. 162–164; Norman King, *Dan Rather* (New York: Leisure, 1981), pp. 54–55.

7. "Hushed Money," *Columbia Journalism Review* (January–February 1988): 54.

8. Janet Cooke and Benjamin Weiser, "Anatomy of a Washington Rumor," *Washington Post,* 22 March 1981, pp. A1, A14; Sandra McElwaine, "This Is Your Wife," *Lear's* (November–December 1988): 135; interview with Peter Teeley, former press secretary to Vice President Bush, 21 February 1989; confidential interview.

9. Eleanor Randolph, "The Secret Pleasures of the White House Press," *Washington Monthly* (March 1978): 30 (Daley); Howie Carr, "Boomerang," *Boston* (December 1987): 114 (Regan); Nancy Lewis, "Rowan Calls City's Case 'Malicious,'" *Washington Post,* 7 October 1988, p. 1 (Rowan); Nancy Lewis, "Reagan Calls to Congratulate Rowan 'on Winning the Case,'" *Washington Post,* 8 October 1988, p. 1 (same); Susan Winchurch, "Mayor Barry Said To Offer Rowan Deal," *Legal Times,* 8 August 1988, p. 7 (same); Jeffrey Schmalz, "The Mystery of Mario Cuomo," *New York Times Magazine,* 15 May 1988, p. 40 (Cuomo); Peter Goudinoff and Sheila Tobias, "Arizona Airhead," *New Republic,* 26 October 1987, p. 16 (Mecham); William J. Small, *Political Power and the Press* (New York: Norton, 1972), p. 173 (briefing paper); Phil Gailey,

"Photographers Finding Reagan Picture Perfect," *New York Times,* 4 November 1981, p. A20 (Congress).

10. Richard Valeriani, *Travels With Henry* (Boston: Houghton Mifflin, 1979), pp. 353–356; James Deakin, *Straight Stuff* (New York: Morrow, 1984), pp. 69–70; John Hohenberg, *A Crisis for the American Press* (New York: Columbia University Press, 1978), pp. 163–164; David Shaw, *Press Watch* (New York: Macmillan, 1984), p. 79.

11. Martin Linsky, *Impact* (New York: Norton, 1986), appendix C, p. 238.

12. Quoted in Tom Goldstein, *The News at Any Cost* (New York: Simon & Schuster, 1985), p. 241 (Cuomo); William Safire, "Is Ronald Reagan Confusing His Wishes with Reality?" *Boston Herald,* 9 November 1982, p. 25 (Reagan).

13. Phillip Knightley, *The First Casualty* (New York: Harvest, 1976), p. 130 (Pegler); William Rivers, *The Adversaries* (Boston: Beacon, 1970), p. 28 (Hoover); Lyons, *Newspaper Story,* pp. 226, 292–294 (Lyons); Doris Kearns Goodwin, *The Fitzgeralds and the Kennedys* (New York: Simon & Schuster, 1987), pp. 614–616 (same); J. Anthony Lukas, *Common Ground* (New York: Knopf, 1985), p. 485 (same); Pierre Salinger, *With Kennedy* (New York: Avon, 1967), p. 399 (Halberstam); Daniel Schorr, *Clearing the Air* (Boston: Houghton Mifflin, 1977), p. 6 (Schorr); Osborn Elliott, *The World of Oz* (New York: Viking, 1980), p. 154 (Flynn); Robert MacNeil, *The Right Place at the Right Time* (Boston: Little, Brown, 1982), p. 283 (Lisagor); Sam Donaldson, "On the Dukakis Campaign Trail," *Gannett Center Journal* (Fall 1988): 97–98 (Donaldson).

14. The Rev. John C. Danforth, sermon delivered at Princeton University Chapel, 16 October 1983, p. 3 (provided by Senator Danforth's office).

15. Matt Roush, "The Big News, Iran," *USA Today,* 20 October 1987, p. 3D.

16. Quoted in Valeriani, *Travels With Henry,* p. 347.

17. Quoted in Hohenberg, *Crisis for the American Press,* p. 125.

18. Nearly identical versions of the admonition are quoted in Robert H. Fleming, "Looking Down on News Men—And Why," *Nieman Reports* (March 1963): 13 (Sullivan); Stewart Alsop, *The Center* (London: Hodder & Stoughton, 1968), p. 10 (Kent); and Harold Brayman, *The President Speaks Off-the-Record* (Princeton, NJ: Dow, Jones Books, 1976), p. 667 (Twain).

19. Joseph and Stewart Alsop, *The Reporter's Trade* (New York: Reynal & Co., 1958), p. 18.

20. Quoted in David Halberstam, *The Powers That Be* (New York: Knopf, 1979), p. 221.

21. Quoted in Sam Acheson, *35,000 Days in Texas* (Westport, CT: Greenwood, 1973; orig. publ. 1938), pp. 37–38.

22. Quoted in Robert Gottlieb and Irene Wolt, *Thinking Big* (New York: Putnam's, 1977), p. 79.

23. Quoted in Laurence J. Peter, *Peter's Quotations* (New York: Bantam, 1979), p. 328.

24. Quoted in Woody Klein, *Lindsay's Promise* (New York: Macmillan, 1970), p. 62.

25. Interviewed on *The Conservatives,* PBS, 1987.

26. Quoted in Tom Wicker, *On Press* (New York: Viking, 1978), p. 51.

27. Quoted in Doris A. Graber, *Mass Media and American Politics* (Washington, DC: Congressional Quarterly Press, 1980), p. 193.

28. Deakin, *Straight Stuff,* p. 23.

CHAPTER 6: THE WHITE HOUSE

1. M. L. Stein, *When Presidents Meet the Press* (New York: Messner, 1969), p. 26 (exclusive); James Deakin, *Straight Stuff* (New York: Morrow, 1984), p. 60 (groups); Stein, *When Presidents,* p. 43 (press releases); Deakin, *Straight Stuff,* p. 60 (pressroom); Stein, *When Presidents,* p. 60 (off the record); Newton N. Minow, John Bartlow Martin, and Lee M. Mitchell, *Presidential Television* (New York: Basic, 1973), p. 26 (radio); John Tebbel and Sarah Miles Watts, *The Press and the Presidency* (New York: Oxford, 1985), p. 439 (lengthy background); Erik Barnouw, *Tube of Plenty* (New York: Oxford, 1975), p. 89 (television appearance); Tebbel and Watts, *Press and the Presidency,* p. 441 (ovation); Charlene J. Brown, Trevor R. Brown, and William L. Rivers, *The Media and the People* (New York: Holt, Rinehart & Winston, 1978), p. 318 (prepared statement); Deakin, *Straight Stuff,* p. 65 (TV film, TV live).

2. Stein, *When Presidents,* p. 90 (FDR); James E. Pollard, *The Presidents and the Press* (New York: Octagon, 1973; orig. publ. 1947), p. 784 (same); Michael Baruch Grossman and Martha Joynt Kumar, *Portraying the President* (Baltimore: Johns Hopkins University Press, 1981), p. 67 (Eisenhower); Pierre Salinger, *With Kennedy* (New York: Avon, 1967), p. 187 (JFK); Deakin, *Straight Stuff,* pp. 223–225 (LBJ); Stein, *When Presidents,* p. 164 (same); Timothy Crouse, *The Boys on the Bus* (New York: Ballantine, 1972), p. 232 (Horner); Salinger, *With Kennedy,* p. 187 (Folliard); Edward P. Morgan, *The Presidency and the Press Conference* (Washington, DC: American Enterprise Institute, 1971), p. 38 (Mollenhoff); Eleanor Clift, "All the President's Nods," *Harper's* (September 1986): 55 (Beckwith).

3. Pollard, *Presidents and the Press,* pp. 383–384; Bernard A. Weisberger, *Reporters for the Union* (Boston: Little, Brown, 1953), pp. 136–138; Tebbel and Watts, *Press and the Presidency,* pp. 182–183.

4. Stephen W. Sears, "The First News Blackout," *American Heritage* (June–July 1985): 26.

5. Ken Hoyt and Frances Spatz Leighton, *Drunk Before Noon* (Englewood Cliffs, NJ: Prentice-Hall, 1979), p. 115.

6. Stein, *When Presidents,* p. 56.

7. William C. Spragens, *From Spokesman to Press Secretary* (Lanham, MD: University Press of America, 1980), p. 84.

8. Arthur Krock, *Memoirs* (New York: Funk & Wagnalls, 1968), p. 129.

9. Helen Thomas, *Dateline: White House* (New York: Macmillan, 1975), p. 281.

10. James B. Reston, "The Press, the President, and Foreign Policy," *Foreign Affairs* (July 1966): 563; William J. Small, *Political Power and the Press* (New York: Norton, 1972), p. 61; Graham J. White, *FDR and the Press* (Chicago: University of Chicago Press, 1979), pp. 44–45.

11. Kay Mills, *A Place in the News* (New York: Dodd, Mead, 1988), p. 36; Kay Mills, "Women Shaping the News," *Washington Journalism Review* (January–February 1988): 40.

12. Martin Mayer, *Making News* (Garden City, NY: Doubleday, 1987), p. 110 (Trout); William L. Rivers, *The Opinionmakers* (Boston: Beacon, 1967), p. 137 (photographers); Robert T. Elson, *The World of Time Inc.,* vol. 2 (1941–1960) (New York: Atheneum, 1973), p. 92 (Luce).

13. Tebbel and Watts, *Press and the Presidency,* pp. 460–461.

14. Stanford N. Sesser, "Washington Post," in A. Kent MacDougall, ed., *The Press* (Princeton, NJ: Dow, Jones, 1972), p. 14.

15. Deakin, *Straight Stuff,* p. 27.

16. Neil A. Grauer, *Wits and Sages* (Baltimore: Johns Hopkins University Press, 1984), p. 45.

17. "TV News Conferences: A Footnote," *Columbia Journalism Review* (Fall 1961): 44.

18. Stewart Alsop, " 'Breach of Security,' " *Newsweek,* 28 June 1971, p. 96 *(Saturday Evening Post);* Garry Wills, *The Kennedy Imprisonment* (New York: Pocket, 1983), p. 277 (same); Arthur M. Schlesinger, Jr., *A Thousand Days* (New York: Fawcett, 1965), pp. 763–765 (same); Kenneth P. O'Donnell and David F. Powers with Joe McCarthy, *"Johnny, We Hardly Knew Ye"* (Boston: Little, Brown, 1972), p. 323 (same); Benjamin C. Bradlee, *Conversations with Kennedy* (New York: Norton, 1975), pp. 115–117 *(Newsweek);* David Sanford, "The Wizard of *Newsweek,*" *Harper's* (August 1980): 74 (same).

19. Tom Wicker, *On Press* (New York: Viking, 1978), p. 110.

20. Bradlee, *Conversations with Kennedy,* p. 50.

21. Louis M. Lyons, *Newspaper Story* (Cambridge: Harvard University Press, 1971), pp. 343–344; J. Anthony Lukas, *Common Ground* (New York: Knopf, 1985), p. 489; Robert Healy, telephone interview, 20 December 1988.

22. Harold Brayman, *The President Speaks Off-the-Record* (Princeton, NJ: Dow, Jones Books, 1976), p. 645.

23. Ibid., pp. 651–652, 658.

24. Erik Barnouw, *Tube of Plenty* (New York: Oxford, 1977), p. 331.

25. Theodore H. White, *The Making of the President 1964* (New York: Atheneum, 1965), p. 283; Thomas, *Dateline: White House,* p. 65.

26. Robert Pierpoint, *At the White House* (New York: Putnam's, 1981), pp. 130–136.

27. Grossman and Kumar, *Portraying the President,* p. 216.

28. Pierpoint, *At the White House,* p. 74; Rowland Evans and Robert Novak, *Lyndon B. Johnson* (New York: New American Library, 1968), p. 529 (Cutler); Doris Kearns, *Lyndon Johnson and the American Dream* (New York: Harper & Row, 1976), p. 249 (Food for Peace); Wicker, *On Press,* p. 126 (California trip); David Halberstam, *The Powers That Be* (New York: Knopf, 1979), p. 543 (Hoover).

29. Gary Paul Gates, *Air Time* (New York: Harper & Row, 1978), pp. 123, 295.

30. Quoted in Kearns, *Lyndon Johnson,* pp. 127–128.

31. Thomas, *Dateline: White House,* p. 75.

32. Quoted in Richard Nixon, *RN* (New York: Grosset & Dunlap, 1978), p. 245 ("last press conference"); Pierpoint, *At the White House,* p. 111 ("not going to pay"); William Safire, *Before the Fall* (New York: Ballantine, 1977), p. 440 ("enemy"); ibid., p. 461 ("contempt"); John Ehrlichman, *Witness to Power* (New York: Pocket, 1982), p. 260 ("kicking"); Joseph C. Spear, *Presidents and the Press* (Cambridge: MIT Press, 1984), p. 200 ("outrageous"); ibid., pp. 200–201 ("those he respects"); Tebbel and Watts, *Press and the Presidency,* p. 500 ("no enemies").

33. Spear, *Presidents and the Press,* p. 42.

34. Crouse, *Boys on the Bus,* p. 233.

35. Howard Bray, *The Pillars of the Post* (New York: Norton, 1980), p. 92.

36. Ehrlichman, *Witness to Power,* pp. 253–255.

37. Donald Paneth, *The Encyclopedia of American Journalism* (New York: Facts on File, 1983), p. 511.

38. Jeb Stuart Magruder, *An American Life* (New York: Pocket, 1975), pp. 111–112.

39. Robert Sam Anson, *Exile* (New York: Touchstone, 1985), p. 21.

40. Ron Nessen, "Running the World is Funnier Than You Think," *Playboy* (July 1977): 193.

41. Anthony Marro, "When the Government Tells Lies," *Columbia Journalism Review* (March–April 1985): 30.

42. Harrison E. Salisbury, *Without Fear or Favor* (New York: Times Books, 1980), pp. 536–539; Clifton Daniel, *Lords, Ladies and Gentlemen* (New York: Arbor House, 1984), pp. 121–122; Wicker, *On Press,* pp. 188–196; Daniel Schorr, *Clearing the Air* (Boston: Houghton Mifflin, 1977), pp. 144–146.

43. Sam Donaldson, *Hold On, Mr. President!* (New York: Random House, 1987), p. 15.

44. Spear, *Presidents and the Press,* p. 7.

45. Phil Gailey, "The Trail of the Rumor on Blair House 'Bug,' " *New York Times,* 18 November 1981, p. A24; Stephan Lesher, *Media Unbound* (Boston: Houghton Mifflin, 1982), pp. 50–52; "F.Y.I.," *Washington Post,* 14 October 1981; Timothy Noah, "The *Post* Takes It On the Ear," *Washington Journalism Review* (December 1981): 36–37; David S. Broder, *Behind the Front Page* (New York: Simon & Schuster, 1987), pp. 314–316; Paul Taylor, "Dear Jimmy: We're Sorry—The Post," *Boston Globe,* 23 October 1981, p. 1.

46. "Capital Comment," *Washingtonian* (September 1983): 19.

47. "Speakes Says He Fooled Press," *New York Times,* 3 December 1983, p. 9; Larry Speakes with Robert Pack, *Speaking Out* (New York: Scribner's, 1988), pp. 256–257; William A. Henry III, "Journalism Under Fire," *Time,* 12 December 1983, p. 86.

48. Mark Hertsgaard, *On Bended Knee* (New York: Farrar Straus Giroux, 1988), pp. 141–143 (1982 incident); Mark Hertsgaard, "The White House Press Takes a Stand," *Columbia Journalism Review* (January–February 1986): pp. 9–10 (1985 incident); David Hoffman, "Angered Photographers Stage a Boycott at White House," *Washington Post,* 26 July 1983, p. A11 (1983 incident).

49. Tebell and Watts, *Press and the Presidency,* p. 552.

50. Lou Cannon, "The President and the Press," *Boston Globe,* 28 November 1983.

51. Quoted in Edwin Emery, *The Press and America,* 3d ed. (Englewood Cliffs, NJ: Prentice-Hall, 1972), p. 131 (Jefferson); Spear, *Presidents and the Press,* p. 36 (Cleveland); Arthur and Lila Weinberg, eds., *The Muckrakers* (New York: Putnam's, 1964), pp. 58–59 (Roosevelt); Stein, *When Presidents,* p. 56 (Wilson); Max M. Kampelman, "When Press Bites Man," *Columbia Journalism Review* (Spring 1968): 43 (Truman); transcript of news conference, 18 January 1961, in *Public Papers of the Presidents: Dwight D. Eisenhower, 1960–1961* (Washington, DC: Govern-

ment Printing Office, 1961), p. 1042 (Eisenhower); Richard J. Whalen, *Catch the Falling Flag* (Boston: Houghton Mifflin, 1972), p. 100 (LBJ); Broder, *Behind the Front Page,* p. 165 (Nixon); "Larry King's People," *USA Today,* 22 June 1987, p. 2D (Carter); "An Expletive from Reagan," *New York Times,* 1 March 1986, p. 7 (Reagan).

CHAPTER 7: POLITICAL CAMPAIGNS

1. Wm. David Sloan, "The Editorial That Swung an Election," *Masthead* (Spring 1982): 17–19; David Davidson, "What Made the 'World' Great?" *American Heritage* (October–November 1982): 67.

2. Oliver Pilat, *Pegler* (Boston: Beacon, 1963), pp. 55–57; Lloyd Wendt, *Chicago Tribune* (Chicago: Rand McNally, 1979), p. 388.

3. James Aronson, *The Press and the Cold War* (Boston: Beacon, 1970), pp. 48–49; Harold Brayman, *The President Speaks Off-the-Record* (Princeton, NJ: Dow, Jones Books, 1976), p. 15.

4. Don Hewitt, *Minute by Minute . . .* (New York: Random House, 1985), p. 154.

5. Maxine Cheshire with John Greenya, *Maxine Cheshire, Reporter* (Boston: Houghton Mifflin, 1978), p. 95.

6. Charles Mohr, "Whistle Stop Woes," in Ruth Adler, ed., *The Working Press* (New York: Bantam, 1970), p. 22.

7. Erik Barnouw, *Tube of Plenty* (New York: Oxford, 1977), p. 366; "Prime-Time President," PBS, 3 October 1988.

8. Dan Rather with Mickey Herskowitz, *The Camera Never Blinks* (New York: Ballantine, 1978), pp. 346–348; Mike Wallace and Gary Paul Gates, *Close Encounters* (New York: Berkley, 1985), pp. 118–120; Gary Paul Gates, *Air Time* (New York: Harper & Row, 1978), p. 200; Edwin Diamond, "Chicago Press: Rebellion and Retrenchment," *Columbia Journalism Review* (Fall 1968): 10.

9. Ernest R. May and Janet Fraser, eds., *Campaign '72* (Cambridge: Harvard University Press, 1973), p. 258.

10. Jules Witcover, *Marathon* (New York: Viking, 1977), pp. 407–408; James Deakin, *Straight Stuff* (New York: Morrow, 1984), pp. 139–140.

11. Eleanor Randolph, "The 'Whip-His-Ass' Story, or, The Gang That Couldn't Leak Straight," *Washington Monthly* (September 1979): 50–51.

12. Joel Swerdlow, "The Decline of the Boys on the Bus," *Washington Journalism Review* (January–February 1981): 19.

13. Diana McLellan, *Ear on Washington* (New York: Arbor House, 1982), p. 122.

14. Stephan Lesher, *Media Unbound* (Boston: Houghton Mifflin, 1982), p. 93.

15. Les Payne, "Black Reporters, White Press—and the Jackson Campaign," *Columbia Journalism Review* (July–August 1984): 36.

16. Laurence Zuckerman, "Full Disclosure, Semi-Outrage," *Time,* 22 June 1987; Eleanor Randolph, "Times Editor Says Candidate Queries Went 'A Bit Too Far,'" *Boston Globe,* 20 June 1987, p. 42; Edwin Diamond, "The Times of Frankel," *New York,* 10 August 1987, p. 30; Michael Wines, "In Bed with the Press," *Washington Journalism Review* (September 1987): 17; "Newsman Criticizes the 'Blood Hunt,'" *Boston Globe,* 19 July 1987, p. 13; "Backing Off," *USA Today,* 22 June 1987, p. 4A.

17. "The Lower Case," *Columbia Journalism Review* (July–August 1987): 73 (editorial); "Verbatim: Questioning the Press," *New York Times,* 19 July 1987, p. 26 (Nixon); Tim Allis, "Chatter," *People,* 1 June 1987, p. 112 (shoes); "Key Players in Hart Scandal: What's Happened to Them Since," *USA Today,* 8 September 1987, p. 8A (same); "Miami is Miffed at Johnson," *USA Today,* 12 October 1987, p. 2D (Johnson).

18. Pamela Lansden, "Take One," *People,* 25 May 1987, p. 29.

19. Richard Stengel, "Bushwhacked!" *Time,* 8 February 1988, pp. 16–20; Richard Zoglin, "'I Was Trained to Ask Questions,'" *Time,* 8 February 1988, pp. 24–26; Jonathan Alter, "The Great TV Shout-Out," *Newsweek,* 8 February 1988, pp. 20–23; Walter V. Robinson, "Rather Defends Role; Gains Seen for Bush," *Boston Globe,* 27 January 1988, pp. 1, 14; Walter V. Robinson, "Bush Rages After Rather," *Boston Globe,* 27 January 1988, p. 14; "Text of Remarks by Rather on Bush Interview," *Boston Globe,* 27 January 1988, p. 14; E. J. Dionne, Jr., "Bush Camp Feels Galvanized After Showdown With Rather," *New York Times,* 27 January 1988, pp. A1, A16; "Who Was Unfair on the Air?" *New York Times,* 27 January 1988, p. A26; David Colton and Matt Roush, "On-Air Bash: Who Got Mugged?" *USA Today,* 26 January 1988, pp. 1A, 2A; Paul Leavitt, "Bush Beats Rather, Not Dole," *USA Today,* 27 January 1988, p. 1A; Monica Collins, "Newsman Dan in the News Again," *USA Today,* 27 January 1988, p. D1.

20. Quoted in Thomas C. Leonard, *The Power of the Press* (New York: Oxford, 1986), p. 88.

21. "Transcript of Hart Statement Withdrawing His Candidacy," *New York Times,* 9 May 1987, p. 9.

22. Quoted in "Talking Points," *USA Today,* 1 April 1988, p. 4A.

CHAPTER 8: FOREIGN ASSIGNMENTS AND WARS

1. Charles M. Thomas, "The Publication of Newspapers During the American Revolution," *Journalism Quarterly* 9 (1932): 368–372.

2. Stephen W. Sears, "The First News Blackout," *American Heritage* (June–July 1985): 31; Bernard A. Weisberger, *Reporters for the Union*

(Boston: Little, Brown, 1953), p. 289; Phillip Knightley, *The First Casualty* (New York: Harvest, 1976), pp. 27–28; Joseph J. Mathews, *Reporting the Wars* (Minneapolis: University of Minnesota Press, 1957), p. 84.

3. Knightley, *First Casualty,* p. 23.

4. Joseph H. Ewing, "The New Sherman Letters," *American Heritage* (July–August 1987): 30; Weisberger, *Reporters for the Union,* p. 108.

5. James R. Mock, "Censorship in American History," in Robert E. Summers, ed., *Wartime Censorship of Press and Radio* (New York: H. W. Wilson, 1942), pp. 54–55; Edwin Emery, *The Press and America,* 3d ed. (Englewood Cliffs, NJ: Prentice-Hall, 1972), pp. 243–244; Nat Hentoff, *The First Freedom* (New York: Delacorte, 1980), p. 94; Weisberger, *Reporters for the Union,* pp. 79–80.

6. Sears, "First News Blackout," p. 30; Weisberger, *Reporters for the Union,* pp. 292–293.

7. William A. Henry III, "Journalism Under Fire," *Time,* 12 December 1983, p. 93; Sears, "First News Blackout," p. 25.

8. W. A. Swanberg, *Citizen Hearst* (New York: Bantam, 1971; orig. publ. 1961), p. 127; Emery, *Press and America,* p. 365; George Seldes, *Freedom of the Press* (Indianapolis: Bobbs-Merrill, 1935), p. 217.

9. Frank Luther Mott, *American Journalism,* 3d ed. (New York: Macmillan, 1962), p. 535; Frank Luther Mott, *The News in America* (Cambridge: Harvard University Press, 1962), p. 47.

10. Walter Lippmann and Charles Merz, "A Test of the News," *New Republic,* 4 August 1920.

11. Knightley, *First Casualty,* p. 124; Oliver Pilat, *Pegler* (Boston: Beacon, 1963), p. 75.

12. Milt Machlin, *The Gossip Wars* (New York: Tower, 1981), p. 90.

13. "Race Riot Ban," in Summers, ed., *Wartime Censorship,* pp. 194–195 (riots); "Florida Censorship," in ibid., pp. 168–169 (ship); "The Case of the L.A. Times," in ibid., pp. 184–185 (Lombard); "Snowfall Censored," in ibid., pp. 196–197 (weather).

14. "The Japanese Press in America," in Summers, ed., *Wartime Censorship,* p. 211.

15. John Chancellor, "From Normany to Grenada," *American Heritage* (June–July 1985): 32.

16. Judith Adler Hennessee, "Annals of Checking," in Richard Pollak, ed., *Stop the Presses, I Want to Get Off!* (New York: Delta, 1976), p. 312 (fires); Knightley, *First Casualty,* p. 297 (same); Turner Catledge, *My Life and The Times* (New York: Harper & Row, 1971), pp. 174–176 (atomic bomb); John Hohenberg, *Foreign Correspondence* (New York: Columbia University Press, 1964), p. 397 (Eisenhower).

17. William L. Rivers, *The Opinionmakers* (Boston: Beacon, 1967), p. 186.

18. Hohenberg, *Foreign Correspondence,* p. 391.

19. Robert MacNeil, *The Right Place at the Right Time* (Boston: Little, Brown, 1982), pp. 55–56.

20. Peter Braestrup, *Big Story* (New York: Anchor, 1978) (abridged ed.), p. 1.

21. Howard Bray, *The Pillars of the Post* (New York: Norton, 1980), p. 55.

22. Mort Rosenblum, *Coups and Earthquakes* (New York: Harper & Row, 1979), p. 131; "The Second Coming," *Newsweek,* 18 June 1973, p. 59.

23. Marvin Barrett and Zachary Sklar, *The Eye of the Storm* (New York: Lippincott & Crowell, 1980), pp. 79–85; Don Hewitt, *Minute by Minute . . .* (New York: Random House, 1985), pp. 216–217; MacNeil, *Right Place at the Right Time,* pp. 317–323; Lester A. Sobel, ed., *Media Controversies* (New York: Facts on File, 1981), pp. 90–91; Charles Paul Freund, "Iran: How Do You Speak to a Terrorist?" *Washington Journalism Review* (January–February 1980): 17.

24. Nicholas Daniloff, letter to the editor, *New Republic,* 19 January 1987.

25. Knightley, *First Casualty,* p. 131 (Williams); Hohenberg, *Foreign Correspondence,* pp. 309–310 (United Press); Gay Talese, *The Kingdom and the Power* (Garden City, NY: Doubleday Anchor, 1978; orig. publ. 1969), pp. 18–19 (Reston); John Chancellor and Walter R. Mears, *The News Business* (New York: Mentor, 1984), pp. 176–177 (AP).

26. Quoted in Knightley, *First Casualty,* p. 307.

27. Ruth Adler, ed., *The Working Press* (New York: Bantam, 1970), p. 81.

28. Byron Price, "Censorship and the Press," in Summers, ed., *Wartime Censorship,* p. 32.

29. Quoted in James Aronson, *The Press and the Cold War* (Boston: Beacon, 1970), pp. 244–245.

CHAPTER 9: PRIVACY, SECRECY, AND LAW

1. "Benjamin Harris's Brief Experiment," in Calder M. Pickett, ed., *Voices of the Past* (Columbus, OH: Grid, 1977), pp. 20–21; John Tebbel, *The Media in America* (New York: Crowell, 1974), p. 14; Edwin Emery, *The Press and America,* 3d ed. (Englewood Cliffs, NJ: Prentice-Hall, 1972), pp. 28–29. Spelling and capitalization have been modernized.

2. " 'This Is Vicious,' " *Time,* 22 February 1960, p. 59.

3. Deni Elliott and Marty Linsky, "The Oliver Sipple Story," *Bulletin of the American Society of Newspaper Editors* (September 1982): 3–7; Tom Wicker, *On Press* (New York: Viking, 1978), p. 245; Marshall Berges, *The Life and Times of Los Angeles* (New York: Atheneum, 1984), p. 203; "Hero Who Foiled Attack on Ford," *Chicago Tribune,* 6 February 1989, p. C7; Dan Morain, "Sorrow Trailed a Veteran Who Saved a President and then was Cast in an Unwanted Spotlight," *Los Angeles Times,* 13 February 1989, p. V1; Dan Morain, " 'Forever Grateful' to Ex-Marine, Ford Says," *Los Angeles Times,* 8 March 1989, p. V2; *Sipple v. Chronicle Publishing Co.,* 154 Cal.App.3d 1040, 201 Cal.Rptr. 665 (1st Dist. 1984).

4. Philip Meyer, *Editors, Publishers and Newspaper Ethics* (Washington, DC: American Society of Newspaper Editors, 1983), pp. 72–73.

5. Nora Ephron, *Scribble Scribble* (New York: Knopf, 1978), pp. 121–127 (Riegle); Alex Taylor III, "Mudslinging in Michigan," *Columbia Journalism Review* (January–February 1977): 43 (same); Colleen O'Connor, "Again, Sex and Politics," *Newsweek,* 15 June 1987, p. 33 (Celeste); Michael Wines, "In Bed with the Press," *Washington Journalism Review* (September 1987): 19 (same); "Robertson: I Sowed Wild Oats," *Boston Herald,* 9 October 1987, p. 19 (Robertson); Edwin Diamond, "Gotcha!" *New York,* 26 October 1987, p. 50 (Jackson); Eleanor Randolph, "Bush Rumor Created Dilemma for Media," *Washington Post,* 22 October 1988 (Bush).

6. Marc A. Franklin, *Mass Media Law* (Mineola, NY: Foundation, 1982), p. 415; Kitty Kelley, *Jackie Oh!* (Seacaucus, NJ: Lyle Stuart, 1978), pp. 304–305.

7. Maxine Cheshire with John Greenya, *Maxine Cheshire, Reporter* (Boston: Houghton Mifflin, 1978), pp. 45–48; Robert Pierpoint, *At the White House* (New York: Putnam's, 1981), pp. 193–194; Kelley, *Jackie Oh!* p. 119; R. W. Apple, Jr., "Changing Morality: Press and Politics," *New York Times,* 6 May 1987, p. B8.

8. "FBI Spread Stories to Tarnish Reputation," *USA Today,* 2 June 1987, p. 9A (King); Laura Foreman, "My Side of the Story," *Washington Monthly* (May 1978): 52 (Rizzo); Rudy Maxa, "Gossip Is to News What Yeast Is to Bread," *Washington Journalism Review* (April–May 1979): 24–25 (Mills, Long, Williams); Pierpoint, *At the White House,* p. 195 (LBJ); Maxa, "Gossip Is to News," pp. 24–25 (Hays); Ted Gup, "Identifying Homosexuals," *Washington Journalism Review* (October 1988): 30 (Reagan advisers); Curtis Wilkie, "Too Hot to Handle," *Washington Journalism Review* (March 1984): 38–39, 58 (Allain); Charles Shepard, *Charlotte Observer* reporter, interviewed on "Weekend Edition," National Public Radio, 2 May 1987 (Hahn); Marguerite Johnston, "David X," *Washington Journalism Review* (May 1984): 9–10 (bubble).

9. E. J. Kahn, Jr., "Profiles ('60 Minutes'—Part II)," *New Yorker,* 26 July 1982, p. 45.

10. Quoted in Anthony Summers, *Goddess* (New York: Macmillan, 1985), p. 316.

11. Quoted in Louis Romano, "The Power of the Press?" *Washington Post,* 16 November 1981, p. B1.

12. Quoted in Richard Lee, "Carl Bernstein: Life After Watergate," *Washingtonian* (July 1981): 82.

13. Caitlin Thomas, "Not Quite Posthumous Letter to My Daughter," *Harper's* (August 1962): 29.

14. Quoted in "Bond Rips Media on Issue of Privacy," *Boston Globe,* 14 June 1987, p. 11.

15. Quoted in Wines, "In Bed with the Press," p. 17.

16. Quoted in Larry Speakes with Robert Pack, *Speaking Out* (New York: Scribner's, 1988), p. 230.

17. Max Farrand, *The Framing of the Constitution of the United States* (New Haven: Yale University Press, 1978; orig. publ. 1913), pp. 58, 65, 195.

18. Lloyd Wendt, *Chicago Tribune* (Chicago: Rand McNally, 1979), pp. 628–636; Phillip Knightley, *The First Casualty* (New York: Harvest, 1976), pp. 283–284; John Hohenberg, *Foreign Correspondence* (New York: Columbia University Press, 1964), p. 351.

19. Sanford J. Ungar, "The Voice of Middle America," in Richard Pollak, ed., *Stop the Presses, I Want to Get Off!* (New York: Delta, 1976), pp. 207–208.

20. Gay Talese, *The Kingdom and the Power* (Garden City, NY: Doubleday Anchor, 1978; orig. publ. 1969), p. 497 (U-2); Harrison E. Salisbury, *Without Fear or Favor* (New York: Times Books, 1980), p. 512 (same); Pierre Salinger, *With Kennedy* (New York: Avon, 1967), pp. 186–187 (fliers); Peter Wyden, *Bay of Pigs* (New York: Simon & Schuster, 1979), pp. 142–143, 153–155 (Bay of Pigs); James Aronson, *The Press and the Cold War* (Boston: Beacon, 1973), pp. 153–169 (same); Salinger, *With Kennedy,* pp. 194, 208–209 (same); John M. Crewdson, "The CIA's 3-Decade Effort To Mold the World's Views," *New York Times,* 25 December 1977, p. 12 (same); Aronson, *Press and the Cold War,* pp. 170–179 (Cuban missile crisis); Kenneth P. O'Donnell and David F. Powers with Joe McCarthy, *"Johnny, We Hardly Knew Ye"* (Boston: Little, Brown, 1972), pp. 320–326 (same).

21. John F. Kennedy, "The President and the Press: Restraints of National Security," *Vital Speeches* 27 (1961): 450; Arthur Krock, *Memoirs* (New York: Funk & Wagnalls, 1968), p. 375; O'Donnell and Powers with McCarthy, *"Johnny,"* p. 277; Salinger, *With Kennedy,* pp. 208–209;

Turner Catledge, *My Life and The Times* (New York: Harper & Row, 1971), p. 264; Aronson, *Press and the Cold War,* p. 166; Bernard Roshco, *Newsmaking* (Chicago: University of Chicago Press, 1975), p. 146 n.

22. Quoted in Michael Baruch Grossman and Martha Joynt Kumar, *Portraying the President* (Baltimore: Johns Hopkins University Press, 1981), p. 303 (Nixon); Stewart Alsop, " 'Breach of Security,' " *Newsweek,* 28 June 1974, p. 96 *(Times).*

23. Jules Witcover, "Two Weeks that Shook the Press," *Columbia Journalism Review* (September–October 1971): 15; Alexander M. Bickel, *The Morality of Consent* (New Haven: Yale University Press, 1975), p. 61; Sanford J. Ungar, *The Papers and The Papers* (New York: Dutton, 1975), p. 304; Erwin N. Griswold, "Teaching Alone Is Not Enough," *Journal of Legal Education* 25 (1973): 258.

24. Salisbury, *Without Fear or Favor,* pp. 540–555; Wicker, *On Press,* pp. 213–223; Clifton Daniel, *Lords, Ladies and Gentlemen* (New York: Arbor House, 1984), pp. 219–223; John Hohenberg, *A Crisis for the American Press* (New York: Columbia University Press, 1978), pp. 151–152.

25. Benjamin C. Bradlee, speech at dedication ceremonies of Joan Shorenstein Barone Center on the Press, Politics, and Public Policy, John F. Kennedy School of Government, Harvard, 27 September 1986; Benjamin C. Bradlee, "The Post and Pelton: How the Press Looks at National Security," *Washington Post,* 8 June 1986, pp. F1, F4; Benjamin C. Bradlee, "The Pelton Case, the Press and National Security," *Boston Globe,* 22 June 1986; Jay Peterzell, "Can the CIA Spook the Press?" *Columbia Journalism Review* (September–October 1986): 29–34; "The Casey Offensive," *Columbia Journalism Review* (July–August 1986): 18–19; Mark Hertsgaard, *On Bended Knee* (New York: Farrar Straus Giroux, 1988), p. 226.

26. Elmer Roessner, "What Could Anxious Brass Do About It?" in George Britt, ed., *Shoeleather and Printers' Ink* (New York: Times Books, 1974), pp. 240–241.

27. Quoted in Joseph J. Mathews, *Reporting the Wars* (Minneapolis: University of Minnesota Press, 1957), p. 199.

28. Quoted in James C. Thomson, Jr., "Government and Press," *New York Times Magazine,* 25 November 1973, p. 113.

29. Quoted in "News vs. Security," *Columbia Journalism Review* (Fall 1961): 46.

30. Quoted in Martin Mayer, *Making News* (Garden City, NY: Doubleday, 1987), p. 8.

31. Thomas C. Leonard, *The Power of the Press* (New York: Oxford, 1986), pp. 137–138.

32. Clarence S. Brigham, *Journals and Journeymen* (Philadelphia: University of Pennsylvania Press, 1950), p. 69. Emphasis omitted; spelling and capitalization modernized.

33. Thomas R. Lounsbury, *James Fenimore Cooper* (Detroit: Gale Research, 1968; orig. publ. 1882), pp. 183, 197; L. U. Reavis, *A Representative Life of Horace Greeley* (New York: G. W. Carleton & Co., 1872), p. 79; Horace Greeley, *Recollections of a Busy Life* (New York: J. B. Ford & Co., 1868), pp. 263–264; Donald Paneth, *The Encyclopedia of American Journalism* (New York: Facts on File, 1983), p. 101.

34. Michael Gartner, "Fair Comment," *American Heritage* (October–November 1982): 29–30.

35. J. Anthony Lukas, "High Rolling in Las Vegas," in Pollak, ed., *Stop the Presses,* pp. 220–221.

36. Salisbury, *Without Fear or Favor,* pp. 383–384.

37. Barbara Matusow, *The Evening Stars* (Boston: Houghton Mifflin, 1983), p. 90 (Huntley); "Libel: What's in a Name?" *Time,* 11 December 1964, p. 62 (Pearson); John B. Judis, *William F. Buckley, Jr.* (New York: Simon & Schuster, 1988), pp. 293–294 (Buckley); Salisbury, *Without Fear or Favor,* pp. 450, 561 (Sulzberger); Oliver Pilat, *Pegler* (Boston: Beacon Press, 1963), pp. 164–165, 203, 214–218 (Reynolds); Louis Nizer, *My Life in Court* (New York: Pyramid, 1963), pp. 19–20 (same).

38. Dan Oberdorfer, "Is 'Burning a Source' a Breach of Contract?" *National Law Journal,* 1 August 1988, p. 8; "Newspapers Lose," *National Law Journal,* 8 August 1988, p. 6; Albert Scardino, "Newspaper in New Case Over Naming Source," *New York Times,* 24 July 1988, p. 14; Eleanor Randolph, "Confidentiality Trouble for Minneapolis Newspaper," *Washington Post,* 23 July 1988, p. A7; John H. Kennedy, "Tables Turned on the Press for Baring a Source's Identity," *Boston Globe,* 7 August 1988, p. A18; "MacNeil-Lehrer Newshour," 26 July 1988; Andrew Dunn, attorney with Faegre & Benson, Minneapolis, representing Cowles Media Co., telephone interviews, 20 December 1988, 8 May 1989.

39. James E. Pollard, *The Presidents and the Press* (New York: Octagon, 1973; orig. publ. 1947), pp. 585–589; Hohenberg, *Foreign Correspondence,* pp. 110–111.

40. Catledge, *My Life,* pp. 291–292.

41. Marvin Barrett, ed., *Survey of Broadcast Journalism 1970–1971* (New York: Grosset & Dunlap, 1971), pp. 32–49; Lester A. Sobel, ed., *Media Controversies* (New York: Facts on File, 1981), pp. 31–44; Bill Leonard, *In the Storm of the Eye* (New York: Putnam's, 1987), pp. 162–166.

42. Harold Brayman, *The President Speaks Off-the-Record* (Princeton, NJ: Dow, Jones Books, 1976), pp. 776–777.

43. Daniel Schorr, *Clearing the Air* (Boston: Houghton Mifflin, 1977), pp. 71–73, 81–84; Joseph C. Spear, *Presidents and the Press* (Cambridge: MIT Press, 1984), pp. 148–149.

44. William L. Rivers, *The Other Government* (New York: Universe, 1982), p. 203.

45. "Panama Holds Up Release of Magazine," *USA Today,* 27 July 1988, p. 6A.

46. Quoted in Frank Thayer, *Legal Control of the Press,* 2d ed. (Brooklyn, NY: Foundation Press, 1950), pp. 41–42.

47. Quoted in Keen Rafferty, "A Collection of Famous Quotations on Journalism," *Journalism Quarterly* 25 (1948): 593.

48. Quoted in ibid., p. 592.

CHAPTER 10: ETHICS

1. "Hot on the Line," *Time,* 29 July 1966, pp. 56–57; "Killing the Front Page," *Newsweek,* 18 August 1969, p. 91; Timothy Ingram, "Investigative Reporting: Is It Getting Too Sexy?" *Washington Monthly* (April 1975): 56; William L. Rivers, *The Other Government* (New York: Universe, 1982), p. 130; Ann Zimmerman, "By Any Other Name . . ." *Washington Journalism Review* (November–December 1979): 34.

2. Carl Bernstein and Bob Woodward, *All the President's Men* (New York: Warner, 1975), pp. 36, 41, 55–56, 62, 125, 180, 213–214, 218, 235, 250.

3. Kay Mills, *A Place in the News* (New York: Dodd, Mead, 1988), p. 24 (Bly); Frank Mallen, *Sauce for the Gander* (White Plains, NY: Baldwin, 1954), p. 66 *(Titanic);* Pierre Salinger, *With Kennedy* (New York: Avon, 1967), pp. 34, 101 (Salinger); James Deakin, *Straight Stuff* (New York: Morrow, 1984), p. 171 (same); Gloria Steinem, *Outrageous Acts and Everyday Rebellions* (New York: Holt, Rinehart & Winston, 1983), pp. 16, 29–69 (bunny); J. Anthony Lukas, *Common Ground* (New York: Knopf, 1985), p. 504 (South Boston); Tom Goldstein, *The News at Any Cost* (New York: Simon & Schuster, 1985), pp. 130–132 (Mirage); David Shaw, *Press Watch* (New York: Macmillan, 1984), pp. 138–139 (same); Zimmerman, "By Any Other Name," p. 32 (campaign contributions); Shaw, *Press Watch,* pp. 138–139 (garment factory); Goldstein, *News at Any Cost,* pp. 128–129 (morgue).

4. Silas Bent, "Journalism and Morality," *Atlantic Monthly* (June 1926): 761.

5. Quoted in Goldstein, *News at Any Cost,* pp. 116–117.

6. Wendell Rawls, Jr., "Interviewing: The Crafty Art," *Columbia Journalism Review* (November–December 1982): 47.

7. Quoted in Robert Pack, "Inside the *Post," Washingtonian* (December 1982): 199.

8. "The Speech of Miss Polly Baker," in Benjamin Franklin, *Writings* (New York: Library of America, 1987), pp. 305–308; Max Hall, *Benjamin Franklin and Polly Baker* (Chapel Hill: University of North Carolina Press, 1960); Jeffery A. Smith, *Printers and Press Freedom* (New York: Oxford, 1988), pp. 116–117; Claude-Ann Lopez and Eugenia W. Herbert, *The Private Franklin* (New York: Norton, 1975), pp. 34–35. Spelling, capitalization, and punctuation have been modernized.

9. "The Great Moon Hoax," in Calder M. Pickett, ed., *Voices of the Past* (Columbus, OH: Grid, 1977), pp. 88–89; Curtis D. MacDougall, *Hoaxes* (New York: Macmillan, 1940), p. 230.

10. "An Ocean Voyage by Balloon," in Pickett, ed., *Voices of the Past,* pp. 89–90.

11. Paul Lancaster, "Faking It," *American Heritage* (October–November 1982): 55–56.

12. H. L. Mencken, *The Bathtub Hoax and Other Blasts and Bravos from the Chicago Tribune* (New York: Knopf, 1958), pp. 4–19.

13. Raymond Sokolov, *Wayward Reporter* (San Francisco: Donald S. Ellis, 1980), pp. 61–62.

14. "Television: The Most Intimate Medium," *Time,* 14 October 1966, p. 63.

15. "Staying Alive If . . ." *Newsweek,* 25 July 1960, p. 96; " 'Survival' and a Spat," *Newsweek,* 1 August 1960, p. 51; "Last Man on Earth," *Time,* 1 August 1960, p. 53; William L. Rivers and David M. Rubin, *A Region's Press* (Berkeley, CA: Institute of Governmental Studies, 1971), p. 31.

16. "Is Fact Necessary?" *Columbia Journalism Review* (Winter 1966): 29–34; "William and the Wolfe," *Newsweek,* 19 April 1965, pp. 62, 64; "Big Bad Wolfe?" *Newsweek,* 31 January 1966, p. 60; Richard Kluger, *The Paper* (New York: Knopf, 1986), pp. 706–708.

17. Bill Green, "Janet's World," *Washington Post,* 19 April 1981; Tom Kelly, *The Imperial Post* (New York: Morrow, 1983), pp. 255–269; Goldstein, *News at Any Cost,* pp. 215–219; "Janet Cooke," *Washingtonian* (June 1981): 101–104; National News Council, " 'Post' Thought Too Little About Jimmy," *Columbia Journalism Review* (September–October 1981): 81–83; "Exploring 'Jimmy's World,' " *Columbia Journalism Review* (July–August 1981): 28–36; Norman E. Isaacs, *Untended Gates* (New York: Columbia University Press, 1986), pp. 63–81; Stephan Lesher, *Media Unbound* (Boston: Houghton Mifflin, 1982), pp. 22–26; "Washington Post Blames Its Untrue Story on 'Complete Systems Failure' by Editors," *Wall Street Journal,* 20 April 1981, p. 4; Howard Bray, *The Pillars of the Post* (New York: Norton, 1980), p. 247; Barbara Matusow, "Wood-

ward Strikes Again," *Washingtonian* (September 1987): 236; "Capital Comment," *Washingtonian* (January 1982): 15; "Information Please," *Washingtonian* (June 1982): 27.

18. Virginius Dabney, *Pistols and Pointed Pens* (Chapel Hill, NC: Algonquin, 1987), p. xix (Callender); John Tebbel and Sarah Miles Watts, *The Press and the Presidency* (New York: Oxford, 1985), p. 37 (same); James E. Pollard, *The Presidents and the Press* (New York: Octagon, 1973; orig. publ. 1947), pp. 71–72 (same); Fawn M. Brodie, *Thomas Jefferson* (New York: Norton, 1974), pp. 349–351 (same); Lancaster, "Faking It," p. 51 (Dreiser); MacDougall, *Hoaxes,* pp. 8–9 (Ferguson); Oliver Pilat, *Pegler* (Boston: Beacon, 1963), p. 98 (Pegler); Goldstein, *News at Any Cost,* pp. 205, 221 (Reid); W. Stewart Pinkerton, Jr., " 'New Journalism': Believe It or Not," in A. Kent MacDougall, ed., *The Press* (Princeton, NJ: Dow, Jones, 1972), pp. 161–162 (Freeman); David Denby, "Presence of Malice," *New York,* 30 March 1987, p. 90 (same); "FYI: Fun and Games?" in Laura Longley Babb, ed., *Of the Press, By the Press, For the Press (And Others, Too)* (Washington, DC: Washington Post Co., 1974), pp. 82–83 (Buckley); Neil A. Grauer, *Wits and Sages* (Baltimore: Johns Hopkins University Press, 1984), pp. 153–154 (same); Isaacs, *Untended Gates,* pp. 61–62 (Jones); Goldstein, *News at Any Cost,* p. 218 (same); Lesher, *Media Unbound,* p. 40 (Daly); Ron Powers, "Post-objectivity," *Columbia Journalism Review* (July–August 1981): 31 (same); Goldstein, *News at Any Cost,* p. 218 (same); Isaacs, *Untended Gates,* p. 60 (same); " 'Voice' Article Called Unfair and Reckless," National News Council Report, *Columbia Journalism Review* (September–October 1981): pp. 85–86 (Carpenter); Patrick Brogan, *Spiked* (New York: Priority, 1985), pp. 67–68 (same); Lesher, *Media Unbound,* p. 41 (same).

19. Douglass Cater, *The Fourth Branch of Government* (New York: Vintage, 1965), p. 51 (Speaker); John Hohenberg, *Foreign Correspondence* (New York: Columbia University Press, 1964), p. 197 (Peary); ibid., p. 273 (Lindbergh); Curtis Prendergast with Geoffrey Colvin, *The World of Time Inc.,* vol. 3 (1960–1980) (New York: Atheneum, 1986), p. 59 (*Mercury*); ibid., pp. 123–125, 131 (Zapruder); ibid., p. 132 (Oswald); Brogan, *Spiked,* pp. 63–64 (murderer); "A Viet Nam Register," *Columbia Journalism Review* (Winter 1967–1968): 11–12 (Vietnam prisoners); Don Hewitt, *Minute by Minute . . .* (New York: Random House, 1985), p. 97 (Haldeman, Liddy); ibid., pp. 104–107 (Hoffa); E. J. Kahn, Jr., "Profiles ('60 Minutes'—Part II)," *New Yorker,* 26 July 1982, p. 39 (same).

20. Milt Machlin, *The Gossip Wars* (New York: Tower, 1981), pp. 16–17.

21. Charles Peters, "Why the White House Press Didn't Get the Watergate Story," *Washington Monthly* (July–August 1973): 9.

22. Curtis Wilkie, "Carter's Memoirs: The Other Version," *Boston Globe,* 17 October 1982, p. A1 (Carter); "Presidents Who Speak Their Minds," *Brockton* (MA) *Enterprise,* 18 October 1982 (same); "Two Leaks, But by Whom?" *Newsweek,* 27 July 1987, p. 16 (North); "Ollie's Follies, Continued," *USA Today,* 21 July 1987, p. 4A (same); "Media Notes," *USA Today,* 23 July 1987, p. 2B (same); Monica Langley and Lee Levine, "Broken Promises," *Columbia Journalism Review* (July–August 1988): 21–24 (Casey).

23. Richard L. Rubin, *Press, Party, and Presidency* (New York: Norton, 1981), pp. 38–39 (Jackson administration); Lancaster, "Faking It," p. 53 (1872 reporters); Bill Hosokawa, *Thunder in the Rockies* (New York: Morrow, 1976), pp. 138–147 *(Denver Post);* Edwin Emery, *The Press and America,* 3d ed. (Englewood Cliffs, NJ: Prentice-Hall, 1972), p. 436 (same); A. A. Dornfeld, *Behind the Front Page* (Chicago: Academy Chicago, 1983), pp. 140–141 (Lingle); John Tebbel, *An American Dynasty* (Garden City, NY: Doubleday, 1947), p. 145 (same); Mallen, *Sauce for the Gander,* p. 83 (Valentino funeral); Lukas, *Common Ground,* pp. 484–485 (Kennedy); John Hohenberg, ed., *The Pulitzer Prize Story* (New York: Columbia University Press, 1959), p. 60 (Illinois government); Isaacs, *Untended Gates,* p. 34 (Karafin); "The Karafin Case," *Columbia Journalism Review* (Spring 1967): 3 (same); "Harry the Muckraker," *Time,* 21 April 1967, pp. 84–85 (same); R. Foster Winans, "The Crash of a Wall Street Reporter," *Esquire* (September 1986): 233–241 (Winans); Isaacs, *Untended Gates,* p. 34 (same).

24. Harrison E. Salisbury, *Without Fear or Favor* (New York: Times Books, 1980), pp. 453–454 (British); Donald Paneth, *The Encyclopedia of American Journalism* (New York: Facts on File, 1983), p. 56 (Burdett); Sanford J. Ungar, "Among the Piranhas: A Journalist and the F.B.I.," *Columbia Journalism Review* (September–October 1976): 19–23 (Srouji).

25. Woody Klein, *Lindsay's Promise* (New York: Macmillan, 1970), pp. 10–11, 15–16 (Klein); James H. Dygert, *The Investigative Journalist* (Englewood Cliffs, NJ: Prentice-Hall, 1976), p. 176 (Freidin and Goldberg); J. Anthony Lukas, *Nightmare* (New York: Viking, 1976), p. 161 (same); Joseph C. Spear, *Presidents and the Press* (Cambridge: MIT Press, 1984), p. 183 (same); Stuart H. Loory, "The CIA's Use of the Press: A 'Mighty Wurlitzer,' " *Columbia Journalism Review* (September–October 1974): 9 (same); "Scattered Returns," *Columbia Journalism Review* (November–December 1973): 5 (same); Goldstein, *News at Any Cost,* pp. 78–81 (Will); Grauer, *Wits and Sages,* pp. 247–248 (same).

26. Harold Brayman, *The President Speaks Off-the-Record* (Princeton, NJ: Dow, Jones Books, 1976), pp. 133–135 (Essary); Eleanor Randolph, "ABC's Walters Relayed Note for Iran Middleman," *Washington Post,*

17 March 1987, p. A11 (Walters); Gerald M. Boyd, "Barbara Walters Gave Reagan Papers on Iran," *New York Times,* 17 March 1987, p. A9 (same).

27. Laura Foreman, "My Side of the Story," *Washington Monthly* (May 1978): 49–54; Tony Schwartz, "A Philadelphia Story," *Newsweek,* 14 November 1977, p. 48; "Perching on the Edge of the Bed," *Columbia Journalism Review* (November–December 1977): 18; Eleanor Randolph, "Conflict of Interest: A Growing Problem for Couples," *Esquire* (February 1978): 124.

28. Quoted in Isaacs, *Untended Gates,* p. 25.

29. Quoted in *Oxford Dictionary of Quotations,* 3d ed. (New York: Oxford, 1979), p. 576.

30. Quoted in Randolph, "Conflict of Interest," p. 128.

31. Quoted in Ben H. Bagdikian, *The Media Monopoly* (Boston: Beacon, 1983), pp. 48–49.

CHAPTER 11: THE PRESS AS A BUSINESS

1. Benjamin Franklin, *Writings* (New York: Library of America, 1987), p. 1323; Isaiah Thomas, *The History of Printing in America,* 2d ed. (New York: Weathervane, 1970; orig. publ. 1874), pp. 105–106. Spelling and capitalization have been modernized.

2. Arthur M. Schlesinger, *Prelude to Independence* (Boston: Northeastern University Press, 1980; orig. publ. 1957), pp. 53–54.

3. Edwin Emery, *The Press and America,* 3d ed. (Englewood Cliffs, NJ: Prentice-Hall, 1972), pp. 450–453.

4. William J. Lanouette, "Newspapers Fear the Public Will 'Let Their Fingers Do the Walking' on TV," *National Journal,* 6 June 1981, p. 1017; Wallace Turner, "Publishers Foresee Struggle With Bell Over Electronic News," *New York Times,* 29 April 1982, p. A26; Michael Kinsley, "The Latest Moos," *New Republic,* 16 September 1981, pp. 20–21.

5. A. J. Liebling, *The Press* (New York: Ballantine, 1975; orig. publ. 1961), p. 32.

6. Quoted in Thomas Kiernan, *Citizen Murdoch* (New York: Dodd, Mead, 1986), p. 219.

7. Louis M. Lyons, *Newspaper Story* (Cambridge: Harvard University Press, 1971), p. 135.

8. George Seldes, *Freedom of the Press* (Indianapolis: Bobbs-Merrill, 1935), pp. 62–64; Lyons, *Newspaper Story,* pp. 158–159.

9. Elmer Davis, *History of the New York Times, 1851–1921* (New York: Greenwood, 1969; orig. publ. 1921), pp. 222–223, 317–318.

10. Seldes, *Freedom of the Press,* p. 43; O. Henry, "An Unfinished

Story," in *The Complete Works of O. Henry* (New York: Doubleday, Page/Funk & Wagnalls, 1926), pp. 58–60.

11. Leon Svirsky, ed., *Your Newspaper* (New York: Macmillan, 1947), p. 29; Donald Paneth, *The Encyclopedia of American Journalism* (New York: Facts on File, 1983), p. 381; Kenneth Stewart and John Tebbel, *Makers of Modern Journalism* (New York: Prentice-Hall, 1952), pp. 270–271; Lewis Donohew, "PM: An Anniversary Assessment," *Columbia Journalism Review* (Summer 1965): 33–36; Frank Luther Mott, *American Journalism,* 3d ed. (New York: Macmillan, 1962), p. 688; Frank Luther Mott, *The News in America* (Cambridge: Harvard University Press, 1962), p. 11.

12. Erik Barnouw, *Tube of Plenty* (New York: Oxford, 1977), p. 170.

13. "Conflicts of Interest, Pressures Still Distort Some Papers' Coverage," *Wall Street Journal,* 25 July 1967, p. 16 *(Bee);* Arthur E. Rowse, "Easters and Nor'easters," *Columbia Journalism Review* (Spring 1967): 31 (Boston papers).

14. Robert Gottlieb and Irene Wolt, *Thinking Big* (New York: Putnam's, 1977), p. 107 *(Municipal News);* Gene R. Beley, "This Ad Was Unacceptable," *Columbia Journalism Review* (Winter 1966–1967): 48–49 (*Los Angeles Times* and Galar); Tom Goldstein, *A Two-Faced Press?* (New York: Priority, 1986), p. 38 (*Los Angeles Times* and smog); Robert Cirino, *Don't Blame the People* (New York: Vintage, 1971), p. 302 (*New York Times* and Vietnam); Jim Cox, "Charlie Ad Not Fit for 'Times,' " *USA Today,* 30 July 1987, p. 1B (*New York Times* and Charlie); Goldstein, *Two-Faced Press?* p. 38 *(Boston Globe);* Stewart and Tebbel, *Makers of Modern Journalism,* p. 364 *(Christian Science Monitor);* Goldstein, *Two-Faced Press?* p. 39 *(Deseret News).*

15. Francis Pollock, "The Florists' Crusade," *Columbia Journalism Review* (March–April 1976): 15–16.

16. Fred W. Friendly, *Due to Circumstances Beyond Our Control . . .* (New York: Vintage, 1968), pp. 234–235; "Passing Comment," *Columbia Journalism Review* (Winter 1966–1967): pp. 3–4.

17. Ben H. Bagdikian, "The Best News Money Can Buy," *Human Behavior* (October 1978): 64; William L. Rivers, Wilbur Schramm, and Clifford G. Christians, *Responsibility in Mass Communication,* 3d ed. (New York: Harper Colophon, 1980), pp. 210, 215; David Shaw, *Journalism Today* (New York: Harper & Row, 1977), pp. 215–216.

18. Norman E. Isaacs, *Untended Gates* (New York: Columbia University Press, 1986), p. 202; Kiernan, *Citizen Murdoch,* p. 252.

19. Quoted in Fred W. Friendly, *The Good Guys, the Bad Guys and the First Amendment* (New York: Vintage, 1977), p. 102.

20. Quoted in Larry Van Dyne, "The Bottom Line on Katharine Graham," *Washingtonian* (December 1985): 128.

21. Quoted in Cirino, *Don't Blame the People,* p. 91.

22. Quoted in Clifton Fadiman, ed., *American Treasury 1455–1955* (New York: Harper & Bros., 1955), p. 280.

CHAPTER 12: OBSTACLES TO TRUTH

1. Harold Brayman, *The President Speaks Off-the-Record* (Princeton, NJ: Dow, Jones Books, 1976), p. 290 n.

2. Leon Svirsky, ed., *Your Newspaper* (New York: Macmillan, 1947), p. 134.

3. Louis M. Lyons, *Newspaper Story* (Cambridge: Harvard University Press, 1971), p. 295; Paul Lancaster, "Faking It," *American Heritage* (October–November 1982): 52.

4. A. Kent MacDougall, "Obituaries: Telling It Like It Was," in A. Kent MacDougall, ed., *The Press* (Princeton, NJ: Dow, Jones Books, 1972), p. 123.

5. "Litmus Test," *Columbia Journalism Review* (Fall 1967): 29, 38.

6. Rick Ackerman, "Temp Typ Sks Job in Journ," *Columbia Journalism Review* (May–June 1981): 50.

7. Quoted in Norman E. Isaacs, *Untended Gates* (New York: Columbia University Press, 1986), p. 59 *(Post);* Martin F. Nolan, "The Goods on Gossip," *Washington Journalism Review* (May 1983): 60 ("Ear"); "Play It Again, Dave," *Columbia Journalism Review* (September–October 1982): 9 *(People);* "Best Correction," *Parade,* 3 January 1988, p. 10 *(American-Statesman);* "Corrections," *New York Times,* 15 November 1988, p. A3 *(Times);* "The Lower Case," *Columbia Journalism Review* (September–October 1987) *(Virginian-Pilot).*

8. Quoted in Frank Luther Mott, *The News in America* (Cambridge: Harvard University Press, 1962), p. 85.

9. Quoted in W. A. Swanberg, *Pulitzer* (New York: Scribner's, 1967), p. 127.

10. Quoted in Clifton Fadiman, ed., *American Treasury 1455–1955* (New York: Harper & Bros., 1955), p. 279.

11. Quoted in Pamela Ridder, "There are TK Fact-Checkers in the U.S.," *Columbia Journalism Review* (November–December 1980): 59.

12. Robert Metz, *The Today Show* (Chicago: Playboy Press, 1977), p. 193.

13. Robert Harris, *Selling Hitler* (New York: Pantheon, 1986); "Uncovering the Hitler Hoax," *Newsweek,* 16 May 1983, pp. 56–62; "Hitler's

Forged Diaries," *Time,* 16 May 1983, pp. 36–47; "Burdens of Bad Judgment," *Time,* 23 May 1983, pp. 50–52; C. T. Hanson, "Megatrendy," *Columbia Journalism Review* (July–August 1983): 20 n.; Jonathan Friendly, "Newsweek's New Line-Up," *Washington Journalism Review* (March 1984): 50.

14. Annetta Miller, "Putting Faith in Trends," *Newsweek,* 15 June 1987, p. 46.

15. Laurie Winer, "Gotcha!" *Columbia Journalism Review* (September–October 1986): 4, 6; Jay Sharbutt, "Alan Abel: The Antics of a Hoaxer Running Loose," *Los Angeles Times,* 5 September 1988, p. VI-6; Martin Mayer, *Making News* (Garden City, NY: Doubleday, 1987), p. 19; "Alan Abel, Satirist Created Campaign to Clothe Animals," *New York Times,* 2 January 1980, p. B15.

16. Daniel P. Moynihan, response to letters, *Commentary* (July 1971): 28.

17. Crocker Coulson, "Pulling Punches," *New Republic,* 25 May 1987, pp. 10–12.

18. Deborah Davis, *Katharine the Great,* 1st ed. (New York: Harcourt Brace Jovanovich, 1979), 2d ed. (Bethesda, MD: National Press, 1987); Ray White, "Ben Bradlee Irked By Errors In Graham Book," *Washington Journalism Review* (January–February 1980): 22; Geoffrey Stokes, "Press Clips," *Village Voice,* 16 June 1987, p. 8; "Media Notes," *USA Today,* 9 June 1987; "Katharine Graham Book Being Reissued," *Boston Globe,* 10 May 1987, p. 10.

19. Terry Carter, "Legal Wrangles Don't Stop Publication of Bingham Book," *National Law Journal,* 21 December 1987, p. 8; Mark Feeney, "The Tale of a House Divided," *Boston Globe,* 13 March 1988, p. 97; David Leon Chandler with Mary Voelz Chandler, *The Binghams of Louisville* (New York: Crown, 1987), pp. vi–viii.

20. " 'Under Cover' Subject of Threatened Libel Suits," *Publishers Weekly,* 14 August 1943, pp. 488–490 (Carlson); "Charges Attempt to Suppress Book," *New York Times,* 6 August 1943, p. 13 (same); Kenneth Stewart and John Tebbel, *Makers of Modern Journalism* (New York: Prentice-Hall, 1952), p. 335 (same); Edith Efron, *How CBS Tried to Kill a Book* (Los Angeles: Nash, 1972), pp. ix–xlii (Efron); Fred Barnes, "Westy's Revenge," *New Republic,* 6 April 1987, p. 25 (same, Kowet); Don Kowet, *A Matter of Honor* (New York: Macmillan, 1984), p. 12 (Kowet); Renata Adler, *Reckless Disregard* (New York: Knopf, 1986), pp. 230–231 (Adler); Barbara Kantrowitz, "Time and CBS: Still Arguing Their Cases," *Newsweek,* 10 November 1986, p. 77 (same); Barnes, "Westy's Revenge," p. 25 (same).

21. Quoted in Richard M. Schmidt, Jr., "Tracing Libel to Its Source," *Washington Journalism Review* (January–February 1988): 58.

22. Quoted in "Capital Comment," *Washingtonian* (April 1982): 11.

23. Quoted in Tom Kelly, "Tom Shales," *Washington Journalism Review* (December 1987): 35.

24. Quoted in Tom Goldstein, *The News at Any Cost* (New York: Simon & Schuster, 1985), p. 243.

25. Ben H. Bagdikian, *The Media Monopoly* (Boston: Beacon, 1983), p. xiii (Goethe); Keen Rafferty, "A Collection of Famous Quotations on Journalism," *Journalism Quarterly* 25 (1948): 593 (Jefferson); Henry Grunwald, "Don't Love the Press, But Understand It," *Time,* 8 July 1974, p. 74 n. (Cabet); A. J. Liebling, *The Press* (New York: Ballantine, 1975; orig. publ. 1961), p. 22 n. (Camus); Upton Sinclair, *The Brass Check* (Pasadena, CA: privately published, 1920), p. 404 (Sinclair); Dana L. Thomas, *The Media Moguls* (New York: Putnam's, 1981), p. 14 (Liebling).

CHAPTER 13: NEWSROOM RELATIONS

1. John Hohenberg, *Foreign Correspondence* (New York: Columbia University Press, 1964), p. 89; Calder M. Pickett, ed., *Voices of the Past* (Columbus, OH: Grid, 1977), p. 165; Kenneth Stewart and John Tebbel, *Makers of Modern Journalism* (New York: Prentice-Hall, 1952), p. 56.

2. Morton Borden, "Some Notes on Horace Greeley, Charles Dana and Karl Marx," *Journalism Quarterly* 34 (1957): 457–465; Isaiah Berlin, *Karl Marx,* 3d ed. (New York: Oxford, 1963), p. 229; John F. Kennedy, "The President and the Press: Restraints of National Security," *Vital Speeches* 27 (1961): 450.

3. W. A. Swanberg, *Pulitzer* (New York: Scribner's, 1967), p. 293; David Davidson, "What Made the 'World' Great?" *American Heritage* (October–November 1982): 67.

4. Stewart and Tebbel, *Makers of Modern Journalism,* pp. 219–220; John Tebbel, *An American Dynasty* (Garden City, NY: Doubleday, 1947), p. 7.

5. Stanley Walker, *City Editor* (New York: Frederick A. Stokes Co., 1934), pp. vii, 4–7; Murray Davis, "Two Men Not Enough for Fooling Chapin," in George Britt, ed., *Shoeleather and Printers' Ink* (New York: Times Books, 1974), p. 98; Swanberg, *Pulitzer,* p. 329.

6. Ralph G. Martin, *Cissy* (New York: Simon & Schuster, 1979), pp. 430–431; Bob Thomas, *Winchell* (Garden City, NY: Doubleday, 1971), pp.

170–171; Walter Winchell, *Winchell Exclusive* (Englewood Cliffs, NJ: Prentice-Hall, 1975), pp. 130–132.

7. Richard Kluger, *The Paper* (New York: Knopf, 1986), p. 404.

8. Turner Catledge, *My Life and The Times* (New York: Harper & Row, 1971), pp. 233–235; James Aronson, "The Fifth Remembered," *Nation,* 27 December 1986–3 January 1987, pp. 732–733.

9. Robert Metz, *The Today Show* (Chicago: Playboy Press, 1977), pp. 77–78.

10. Thomas Whiteside, "Corridor of Mirrors," *Columbia Journalism Review* (Winter 1968–1969): 40.

11. Tom Kelly, *The Imperial Post* (New York: Morrow, 1983), pp. 105–106.

12. Quoted in Mary Costello, "Blacks in the News Media," *Editorial Research Reports* 2 (7) (1972): 627.

13. Quoted in Howard Bray, *The Pillars of the Post* (New York: Norton, 1980), p. 174.

14. National Advisory Commission on Civil Disorders, *Report* (Washington, DC: Government Printing Office, 1968), p. 213.

15. Quoted in "A Concise Bartlett's for Journalists," *Columbia Journalism Review* (Summer 1967): 62.

16. "Playboy Interview: Carl Bernstein," *Playboy* (September 1986): 58.

17. Dana L. Thomas, *The Media Moguls* (New York: Putnam's, 1981), p. 105.

18. Laurence Stern, "The Daniel Schorr Affair," *Columbia Journalism Review* (June 1976): 20–25; Daniel Schorr, " 'The Daniel Schorr Affair': A Reply," *Columbia Journalism Review* (July–August 1976): 48–49; Nora Ephron, *Scribble Scribble* (New York: Knopf, 1978), pp. 93–99; Gary Paul Gates, *Air Time* (New York: Harper & Row, 1978), pp. 390–396; Daniel Schorr, *Clearing the Air* (Boston: Houghton Mifflin, 1977), pp. 195–207; Edmund B. Lambeth, *Committed Journalism* (Bloomington: Indiana University Press, 1986), pp. 111–115; John Hohenberg, *A Crisis for the American Press* (New York: Columbia University Press, 1978), p. 175.

19. James Deakin, *Straight Stuff* (New York: Morrow, 1984), pp. 143–144.

20. David Shaw, *Press Watch* (New York: Macmillan, 1984), p. 63.

21. Tom Shales, Tom Zito, and Jeannette Smyth, "When Worlds Collide: Lights! Cameras! Egos!" *Washington Post,* 11 April 1975, p. B6.

22. Peter Prichard, *The Making of McPaper* (Kansas City, MO: Andrews, McMeel & Parker, 1987), pp. 285–289.

23. Jonathan Alter, "A New Regime at the Times," *Newsweek,* 20 October 1986, p. 68.

24. Gates, *Air Time,* p. 372 (CBS special unit); Charles Pooter, "Hey, Hey, Goodbye," *Spy* (September 1988): 132 (CBS phones); Joseph Nocera, "Making It at the *Washington Post," Washington Monthly* (January 1979): 16 (*Post* memo); Rozanne Weissman, " 'Creative Tension' at *Post* Made the Gossip Column Choke," *Washington Journalism Review* (October 1977): 12 (*Post* edict); Eleanor Randolph, "The Troubled Times: Gray Lady in Limbo," *Washington Post,* 7 January 1986, p. C4 *(Times).*

25. Quoted in Harrison E. Salisbury, *Without Fear or Favor* (New York: Times Books, 1980), p. 66.

26. Quoted in "Abe Rosenthal, Letting Go," *Washington Post,* 8 January 1986, p. C3.

27. Quoted in J. Anthony Lukas, "Taking Our Cue from Joe," in Richard Pollak, ed., *Stop the Presses, I Want to Get Off!* (New York: Delta, 1976), p. 235.

28. Quoted in Edwin Emery, *The Press and America,* 3d ed. (Englewood Cliffs, NJ: Prentice-Hall, 1972), p. 386.

CHAPTER 14: COMPETITORS

1. John Hohenberg, *Foreign Correspondence* (New York: Columbia University Press, 1964), pp. 27–28; Frank Luther Mott, *American Journalism,* 3d ed. (New York: Macmillan, 1962), pp. 246–247.

2. Elmer Davis, *History of the New York Times, 1851–1921* (New York: Greenwood, 1969; orig. publ. 1921), pp. 34–36.

3. Quoted in Meyer Berger, *The Story of The New York Times, 1851–1951* (New York: Simon & Schuster, 1951), p. 38 *(New York Sun);* Bernard A. Weisberger, *Reporters for the Union* (Boston: Little, Brown, 1953), p. 16 *(New York Times);* ibid. *(New York Tribune);* David Fridtjof Halaas, *Boom Town Newspapers* (Albuquerque: University of New Mexico Press, 1981), p. 71 *(Rocky Mountain News).*

4. Davis, *History of the New York Times,* p. 64.

5. Donald Paneth, *The Encyclopedia of American Journalism* (New York: Facts on File, 1983), p. 465 *(Chicago Daily News* and *Post & Mail);* Ed Randall, "Traps for the Unwary Betray Straying Steps," in George Britt, ed., *Shoeleather and Printers' Ink* (New York: Times Books, 1974), pp. 234–235 *(New York Evening Mail* and *Daily News);* W. A. Swanberg, *Citizen Hearst* (New York: Bantam, 1971; orig. publ. 1961), pp. 176–177 *(New York Journal* and *World);* W. A. Swanberg, *Pulitzer* (New York: Scribner's, 1967), pp. 251–252 (same).

6. Gary Cummings, "The Last 'Front Page,' " *Columbia Journalism*

Review (November–December 1974): 47; Lloyd Wendt, *Chicago Tribune* (Chicago: Rand McNally, 1979), p. 462.

7. Fred W. Friendly, *Due to Circumstances Beyond Our Control . . .* (New York: Vintage, 1968), p. 182.

8. Robert T. Elson, *The World of Time Inc.*, vol. 1 (1923–1941) (New York: Atheneum, 1968), pp. 264–268.

9. Osborn Elliott, *The World of Oz* (New York: Viking, 1980), pp. 71–72.

10. Don Hewitt, *Minute by Minute . . .* (New York: Random House, 1985), p. 151; Gary Paul Gates, *Air Time* (New York: Harper & Row, 1978), pp. 67–68.

11. David Shaw, *Press Watch* (New York: Macmillan, 1984), p. 189 (Pulitzers); James J. Cramer, "UPI Takes Off the Gloves," *Columbia Journalism Review* (March–April 1980): 7 (booklet); Norman E. Isaacs, *Untended Gates* (New York: Columbia University Press, 1986), p. 50 (telephone).

12. "The Reporters' Story," *Columbia Journalism Review* (Winter 1964): 6–7; John Chancellor and Walter R. Mears, *The News Business* (New York: Mentor, 1984), pp. 173–175.

13. "A Concise Bartlett's for Journalists," *Columbia Journalism Review* (Fall 1961): 60; Thomas F. Mitchell, "The News Holds Court," *Columbia Journalism Review* (Winter 1966–1967): 19.

14. Carl Bernstein and Bob Woodward, *All the President's Men* (New York: Warner, 1975), pp. 311–312; Leonard Downie, Jr., *The New Muckrakers* (New York: New American Library, 1978), p. 92.

15. Thomas Kiernan, *Citizen Murdoch* (New York: Dodd, Mead, 1986), p. 222.

16. Don Forst, telephone interview, 12 January 1988.

17. Judy Woodruff with Kathleen Maxa, *"This is Judy Woodruff at the White House"* (Reading, MA: Addison-Wesley, 1982), pp. 32–33; Mary Battiata, "Lesley Stahl," *Washington Journalism Review* (October 1982): 43–44.

18. Quoted in Peter Prichard, *The Making of McPaper* (Kansas City, MO: Andrews, McMeel & Parker, 1987), pp. 278–283.

19. "Post Watch," *Washingtonian* (March 1986): 11.

20. "Print Rival Scoops Post at Its Own Game," *Boston Globe,* 27 September 1987, p. 29.

21. Quoted in Howard Bray, *The Pillars of the Post* (New York: Norton, 1980), p. 116.

22. Quoted in Daniel Pedersen, " 'I Am Not Perfect,' " *Newsweek,* 24 October 1988, p. 25.

23. Quoted in Dom Bonafede, "Jack Muckraker Anderson," *Washington Journalism Review* (April 1980): 46.

CHAPTER 15: FIRST ROUGH DRAFT OF HISTORY

1. Clarence S. Brigham, *Journals and Journeymen* (Philadelphia: University of Pennsylvania Press, 1950), pp. 58–59 (Declaration of Independence); Ben H. Bagdikian, *The Information Machines* (New York: Harper & Row, 1971), p. 39 (Kennedy).

2. Gary Paul Gates, *Air Time* (New York: Harper & Row, 1978), p. 304.

3. John Hohenberg, *Foreign Correspondence* (New York: Columbia University Press, 1964), pp. 86–92; "A Reporter Finds David Livingstone," in Calder M. Pickett, ed., *Voices of the Past* (Columbus, OH: Grid, 1977), pp. 165–167; Donald Paneth, *The Encyclopedia of American Journalism* (New York: Facts on File, 1983), p. 31.

4. Louis M. Lyons, *Newspaper Story* (Cambridge: Harvard University Press, 1971), pp. 86–97; Edward D. Radin, *Lizzie Borden* (New York: Simon & Schuster, 1961), pp. 99–101.

5. Edwin Emery, *The Press and America,* 3d ed. (Englewood Cliffs, NJ: Prentice-Hall, 1972), pp. 389–390; W. A. Swanberg, *Citizen Hearst* (New York: Bantam, 1971; orig. publ. 1961), pp. 214, 230–232; "Yellow Journalism and Anarchy," in Pickett, ed., *Voices of the Past,* p. 191.

6. Maureen McKernan, *The Amazing Crime and Trial of Leopold and Loeb* (Chicago: Plymouth Court, 1924), pp. 14–15; John Hohenberg, ed., *The Pulitzer Prize Story* (New York: Columbia University Press, 1959), p. 15.

7. James P. Howe, " 'If You Dare Do That, I'll Shoot You!' " in David Brown and W. Richard Bruner, eds., *How I Got That Story* (New York: E. P. Dutton, 1967), pp. 29–34.

8. Henry Fairlie and Timothy Dickinson, "How the Glad Tidings Were Transmitted By Our Elders and Betters," *New Republic,* 25 December 1976, pp. 15–19.

9. Louis P. Lochner, "Hitler, the Torrential Talker, or Cutting In to Get an Answer," in George Britt, ed., *Shoeleather and Printers' Ink* (New York: Times Books, 1974), pp. 185–187; H. V. Kaltenborn, *Fifty Fabulous Years* (New York: Putnam's, 1950), pp. 186–189.

10. Charles Fisher, *The Columnists* (New York: Howell, Soskin, 1944), pp. 30–31.

11. William L. Laurence, "The Greatest Story," in Brown and Bruner, eds., *How I Got That Story,* pp. 199–200; Hohenberg, *Foreign Correspondence,* pp. 373–376.

12. Paneth, *Encyclopedia of American Journalism,* p. 79.

13. Theodore H. White, *In Search of History* (New York: Warner, 1979), p. 130.

14. Gates, *Air Time,* p. 52.

15. Robert T. Elson, *The World of Time Inc.*, vol. 2 (1941–1960) (New York: Atheneum, 1973), p. 56; Phillip Knightley, *The First Casualty* (New York: Harvest, 1976), p. 295 n.; "Veteran of Iwo Jima Recalls the 'Genuine' Flag-Raising," *Springfield* (MA) *Republican*, 29 May 1988.

16. George Weller, "Back in Nagasaki," in Brown and Bruner, eds., *How I Got That Story*, pp. 209–227.

17. Martin Mayer, *Making News* (Garden City, NY: Doubleday, 1987), p. 10.

18. William Safire, "On Emancipation," *New York Times*, 11 February 1974, p. 35.

19. Ruth Adler, ed., *The Working Press* (New York: Bantam, 1970), p. 213; Howard Bray, *The Pillars of the Post* (New York: Norton, 1980), p. 171; David Shaw, *Press Watch* (New York: Macmillan, 1984), p. 145.

20. Robert MacNeil, *The People Machine* (New York: Harper & Row, 1968), p. 30.

21. Timothy Crouse, *The Boys on the Bus* (New York: Ballantine, 1974), p. 378.

22. Harrison E. Salisbury, *Without Fear or Favor* (New York: Times Books, 1980), pp. 433–434.

23. " 'Deep Throat': Narrowing the Field," *Time*, 3 May 1976, pp. 17–18; "Woodward on the Record—Sort Of," *Time*, 3 May 1976, p. 17; "The Honorable Tradition of Deep Throat Reporting," *Macleans*, 9 June 1980, p. 17; "Playboy Interview: Carl Bernstein," *Playboy* (September 1986): 59; "Playboy Interview: Bob Woodward," *Playboy* (February 1989): 60; "Rudy Maxa's Diary," *Washingtonian* (July 1986): 19; Carl Bernstein and Bob Woodward, *All the President's Men* (New York: Warner, 1975), pp. 73–75, 137, 262, 297; Jim Hougan, *Secret Agenda* (New York: Random House, 1984), pp. 264–301; H. R. Haldeman with Joseph DiMona, *The Ends of Power* (New York: Times Books, 1978), pp. 136–137; Raymond Price, *With Nixon* (New York: Viking, 1977), p. 225; Herbert G. Klein, *Making It Perfectly Clear* (Garden City, NY: Doubleday, 1980), p. 430; J. Anthony Lukas, *Nightmare* (New York: Viking, 1976), p. 273; Leonard Downie, Jr., *The New Muckrakers* (New York: New American Library, 1978), p. 47; Barry Sussman, *The Great Cover-Up* (New York: Crowell, 1974), pp. 110–111; Deborah Davis, *Katharine the Great* (New York: Harcourt Brace Jovanovich, 1979), pp. 266–273; Edward Jay Epstein, *Between Fact and Fiction* (New York: Vintage, 1975), pp. 30–31; John Chancellor and Walter R. Mears, *The News Business* (New York: Mentor, 1984), p. 150; Howard Kohn, "The Hughes-Nixon-Lansky Connection: The Secret Alliances of the CIA from World War II to Watergate," *Rolling Stone*, 20 May 1976, pp. 86–88; Ray White, "Ben Bradlee Irked By

Errors In Graham Book," *Washington Journalism Review* (January–February 1980): 22; Dick Kirschten, "In Reagan's White House, It's Gergen Who's Taken Control of Communications," *National Journal,* 25 July 1981, p. 1330; "Haig's Departure Should Plug a Lot of Leaks He Engineered," *Washingtonian* (August 1982): 13; "The Sage of Saddle River," *Newsweek,* 19 May 1986, p. 34.

24. Quoted in Frank Luther Mott, *The News in America* (Cambridge: Harvard University Press, 1962), p. 38.

25. Quoted in "A Concise Bartlett's for Journalists," *Columbia Journalism Review* (Winter 1964): 57.

26. Quoted in "Philip L. Graham, 1915–1963," *Newsweek,* 12 August 1963, p. 13.

CHAPTER 16: THE MEDIA MYSTIQUE

1. Quoted in Frank Luther Mott, *The News in America* (Cambridge: Harvard University Press, 1962), p. 6.

2. Thomas Carlyle, *On Heroes, Hero-Worship, and the Heroic in History* (London: Chapman & Hall, 1897), p. 164.

3. Quoted in Laurence J. Peter, *Peter's Quotations* (New York: Bantam, 1979), p. 327.

4. Quoted in Ben H. Bagdikian, *The Information Machines* (New York: Harper & Row, 1971), p. xiii.

5. Quoted in Clifton Fadiman, ed., *American Treasury 1455–1955* (New York: Harper & Bros., 1955), p. 278.

6. Quoted in Keen Rafferty, "A Collection of Famous Quotations on Journalism," *Journalism Quarterly* 25 (1948): 594.

7. Quoted in Tom Goldstein, *The News at Any Cost* (New York: Simon & Schuster, 1985), p. 155.

8. Quoted in Stephen Hess, *The Washington Reporters* (Washington, DC: Brookings, 1981), p. 116.

9. Quoted in Eugene McCarthy, "Sins of Omission," *Harper's* (June 1977): 90.

10. Quoted in William L. Rivers, Wilbur Schramm, and Clifford G. Christians, *Responsibility in Mass Communications,* 3d ed. (New York: Harper & Row, 1980), p. 1.

11. Quoted in Rafferty, "Collection of Famous Quotations on Journalism," p. 598.

12. Frank Luther Mott, *American Journalism,* 3d ed. (New York: Macmillan, 1962), p. 12.

13. Frank Mallen, *Sauce for the Gander* (White Plains, NY: Baldwin, 1954), pp. 20–21, 24.

14. "Managing the News," *Newsweek,* 8 December 1986, p. 60; "A Royal Mercy Killing," *Time,* 8 December 1986, p. 55.

15. John Sansing and Drew Mayer, "Have You Ever Seen the Easter Bunny?" *Washingtonian* (September 1981): 157.

16. Erik Barnouw, *Tube of Plenty* (New York: Oxford, 1977), pp. 102–103 (Swayze); William Whitworth, "Profiles—An Accident of Casting," *New Yorker,* 3 August 1968, p. 53 (Huntley and Brinkley); Gary Paul Gates, *Air Time* (New York: Harper & Row, 1978), p. 205 (Cronkite).

17. Marvin Barrett, ed., *Survey of Broadcast Journalism 1969–1970* (New York: Grosset & Dunlap, 1970), pp. 31–32.

18. Quoted in Marvin Barrett, ed., *The Politics of Broadcasting* (New York: Crowell, 1973), p. 46.

19. Leonard Downie, Jr., *The New Muckrakers* (New York: New American Library, 1978), p. 6 (Pakula); ibid., p. 51 (script troubles); William Goldman, *Adventures in the Screen Trade* (New York: Warner, 1984), pp. 220–223 (same); Tom Shales, Tom Zito, and Jeannette Smyth, "When Worlds Collide: Lights! Cameras! Egos!" *Washington Post,* 11 April 1975, p. B6 (same); "Dossier: Woodward and Bernstein," *Esquire* (December 1983): 506 (same); Deborah Davis, *Katharine the Great* (New York: Harcourt Brace Jovanovich, 1979), p. 10 (Graham); Shales, Zito, and Smyth, "When Worlds Collide," p. B6 (same); Julia Cameron, "A Portrait of the Investigative Reporter as a Young, Rich, Sexy, Glamorous Star," *Washingtonian* (May 1974): 90 (editors); Shales, Zito, and Smyth, "When Worlds Collide," p. B6 (same); ibid. (set); Harry Clein, "Progress Report: *All the President's Men,*" *American Film* (October 1975): 25 (same); Howard Bray, *The Pillars of the Post* (New York: Norton, 1980), p. 215 n. (same); "Janet Cooke," *Washingtonian* (June 1981): 104 (San Francisco); "Playboy Interview: Carl Bernstein," *Playboy* (September 1986): 50 (reality).

20. Judy Woodruff with Kathleen Maxa, *"This is Judy Woodruff at the White House"* (Reading, MA: Addison-Wesley, 1982), p. 203.

21. Television Information Office, "America's Watching" (New York, 1987).

22. Quoted in "The Mighty Mission of a Newspaper," in Calder M. Pickett, ed., *Voices of the Past* (Columbus, OH: Grid, 1977), p. 91.

23. Quoted in William L. Rivers, *The Opinionmakers* (Boston: Beacon, 1967), p. 75.

24. Quoted in Donald Grant, "Staff Writer," in *Newsmen's Holiday* (Cambridge: Harvard University Press, 1942), p. 72.

25. Edward R. Murrow, "Murrow's Indictment of Broadcasting," *Columbia Journalism Review* (Summer 1965): 27.

26. Quoted in Leo C. Rosten, *The Washington Correspondents* (New York: Harcourt, Brace, 1937), p. 243.

27. Quoted in Hess, *Washington Reporters,* p. 128.

28. Quoted in John Chancellor and Walter R. Mears, *The News Business* (New York: Mentor, 1984), p. 19.

INDEX